GREEK MYTHOLOGY

GREEK MYTHOLOGY

GREEK MYTHOLOGY

PAUL HAMLYN · LONDON

colour plates

First edition 1964

Second impression 1964

Third impression 1965

GREEK MYTHOLOGY

Félix Guirands's text translated by Delano Ames from Mythologie Générale Larousse
first published by Augé, Gillon, Hollier-Larousse, Moreau et Cie

PAUL HAMLYN LIMITED

Westbook House · Fulham Broadway · London

© Paul Hamlyn Limited 1963

Printed in Czechoslovakia by Polygrafia, Prague

T 1480

contents

Acknowledgments

Illustrations have been drawn from the following sources:

Colour plates

Berghaus Verlag, 37
Hirmer Verlag, 17, 35
Photographie Giraudon, 75, 117
Scala Istituto Fotografico, 18, 78, 118, 135
Uni-Dia-Verlag, 56
V.E.B. Verlag der Kunst, 97
Zentrale Farbbild Agentur (Seiler), 57b, 77, 95, 136

Black and white illustrations

Alinari—Mansell, 28, 29b, 39c, 45a, 46, 60a, 63, 67a, 104b, 106a, 107, 109, 112, 113b, 122, 126c, 139a, 147,
Alinari—Viollet, 24b, 50, 99b, 105, 111a, 130b
Anderson—Mansell, 13b, 26b, 27a, 29a, 32a, 33a, 39a, 39b, 40, 43b, 49a, 49b, 64, 65, 66a, 70c, 88b 121a, 121c, 129b, 130a, 141b, 143, 150
Anderson—Viollet, 19b, 73a, 138b, 146a
Archiv für Kunst und Geschichte, 43a, 71, 104a, 119
Berlin Museum, 23, 31b, 100
Boissonas, 8
British Museum, 30, 41b, 44, 47, 51b, 52a, 53a, 54b, 70a, 74, 87, 88a, 89b, 93, 94b, 99a, 101, 102, 108, 111b, 121b, 128a, 129a, 132, 133, 137b, 140, 141a, 144
Brogi—Mansell, 12, 54a, 114b, 138a
Bruckmann, 15b, 31a, 33b, 51a, 52b, 53b, 59, 69, 80, 83, 86a, 114a, 123, 126a, 127a
Camera Press—Swaan, 10a
Deutsche Fotothek Dresden, 19a, 48a, 49c, 62, 79, 92a, 110
Giraudon, 24a, 81b, 94a, 145a
Giraudon—Mansell, 13a, 25
Kaufmann, 60b
Mansell, 9, 11b, 16, 20, 21, 22, 26a, 41a, 42, 45b, 61, 66b, 82a, 86b, 90b, 92b, 103, 106b, 120, 124, 127b, 128b, 139b, 142, 145b,
Radio Times Hulton Picture Library, 14, 15a, 82b, 84, 85, 89a, 125b, 126b, 131, 134, 148-9
Ilse Schneider—Lengyel, 68a, 72
Roger—Viollet, 10b, 34, 68b, 125a
V.E.B. Verlag der Kunst, 48b, 113a

Numbers refer to pages, and letters to position on the page from top to bottom, and left to right.

introduction

Mythology in all advanced civilisations contains many elements, and none is more diverse than that of the Greeks. The figures that people Greek mythology fall into three groups. The first is that of the gods of Olympus, many of whom owe some attributes to the primitive fertility gods which they supplanted. The ideals that the gods embodied developed and changed with the growing sophistication of Greek civilisation. Yet the gods retained many characteristics which today we might consider all too human, unworthy of a god: notably, they were often lustful or vengeful. But the Greek concept of 'religion' was very different from our own, and the way in which the gods are shown to take an active part in the affairs of mortal beings, to love them on occasion and even (as Aphrodite) to be wounded by them, implies no disrespect. Gods and mortals had many characteristics in common, but the differences between them were if anything accentuated by the belief that the origins of the two races were connected.

The second category of Greek myths seeks to explain natural phenomena such as the sun, the moon, the winds, sea storms, the seasons, fertility, and so forth. These myths are generally straightforward, details of the stories being often directly related to the natural phenomena concerned.

The third category of myth centres on the heroes. These were mortals, but they often had at least one immortal ancestor; they often excited the enmity of both gods and humans, and though they could be killed they were sometimes, like Hercules, admitted to Olympus on their death.

Greek mythology has been a source of inspiration to artists and writers for centuries, especially during the Renaissance and in our own century. The present volume, which draws upon the best scholarly sources, is a reliable guide to this unending source of artistic inspiration and the stories for themselves never fail to make stimulating and enjoyable reading.

From the third century B.C. the Greek and Roman gods were equated and the Greek gods were given new names which usage has made familiar. It may, therefore, be useful to give a list of such names in both their Greek and Latin forms.

Cronus	*Saturn*	Eros	*Cupid*
Gaea	*Tellus*	Charites	*Gratiae (Graces)*
Zeus	*Jupiter*	Poseidon	*Neptune*
Hera	*Juno*	Hestia	*Vesta*
Athene	*Minerva*	Demeter	*Ceres*
Artemis	*Diana*	Dionysus	*Bacchus*
Apollo	*Apollo*	Asclepius	*Aesculapius*
Selene	*Luna*	Moerae	*Parcae (Fates)*
Hermes	*Mercury*	Hades	*Pluto*
Ares	*Mars*	Persephone	*Proserpina*
Hephaestus	*Vulcan*	Erinnyes	*Furiae (Furies)*
Aphrodite	*Venus*	Heracles	*Hercules*

Prehellenic mythology

It is now known that well before the peoples whom we know as the Greeks had emerged from primitive barbarism there existed in the basin of the Aegean Sea a Mediterranean civilisation which had its centre in Crete. Aegean civilisation, which had already made tentative beginnings in the third millennium, reached its apogee towards the sixteenth century B.C. when it spread to continental Greece, starting in Argolis (Mycenae). This Cretan civilisation, called Minoan after King Minos its traditional founder, lost most of its influence about 1400 B.C. with the destruction by invaders or perhaps by earthquake or volcanic eruptions of the Palace of Cnossus. The Mycenean civilisation collapsed in turn with the Dorian invasions of 1200 B.C. It was destroyed in the twelfth century by the invasions of the Dorians, a people coming from the north of Greece.

The first form Aegean religion took was fetishism —the worship of sacred stones, of pillars, of weapons (particularly the double-axe), of trees and animals.

Later, when an anthropomorphic conception of divinity had arisen, the Cretan pantheon was formed and myths were created. We find survivals of such myths in a great many Greek legends; for instance, the birth of Zeus in Crete, Europa and the bull, Cretans brought by Apollo to Delphi to be priests of his cult, the Minotaur, etc. When they moved to continental Greece, however, the Aegean divinities took on a Hellenic aspect beneath which their original physiognomy disappeared. Thus what we know about the Aegean pantheon is reduced to very little.

The Aegean Pantheon

The Great Goddess.   The chief deity of the Aegeans was—like that of many Asiatic cults — feminine. She was the *Great Goddess*, the *Universal Mother*, in whom were united all the attributes and functions of divinity. Above all she symbolised fertility, and her influence extended over plants and animals as well as humans. All the universe was her domain. As celestial goddess she regulated the course of the heavenly bodies and controlled the alternating seasons. On earth she caused the products of the soil to flourish, gave men riches, protected them in battle and at sea guided them on their adventurous voyages. She killed or tamed fierce beasts; and finally she also reigned over the Underworld.

The Great Goddess is represented, depending on the epoch, either crouching or standing. Sometimes she is nude, sometimes dressed like a Cretan woman. In the latter case she wears a flounced skirt and her

Opposite, the peaks of Olympus. The throne of Zeus and the seats of the gods.

bosom is either entirely bare or covered with a corsage which leaves her breasts exposed. Her head-dress varies: the hair may be free, knotted with a simple fillet; it may be covered either by a sort of turban decorated with flowers or aigrettes, or by a conical tiara in the Oriental manner, or, again, by a very tall tiara in the shape of a topless cone.

Although the type is always the same and only the attributes and details of dress vary, it is questionable if a single divinity is concerned; on the contrary, these various representations may well depict distinct goddesses, each having her own character.

What was the name of the mother-goddess of the Aegeans? Here again in the absence of documentation we are left to conjecture. It seems that she was worshipped in Crete under the name *Rhea*. At least this was the name later associated with the ancient Cretan divinity in the cult of Zeus. Zeus was said to be her son—a tradition which Hesiod was to revive in his *Theogony*.

Two other names of Cretan goddesses have been preserved: *Dictynna* and *Britomartis*. In legends the Greeks applied the two names to the same divinity.

The Snake Goddess. Her dress leaves her breast exposed, she holds a snake in each hand and her headdress is surmounted by a bird. Statuette in faïence from Cnossus. Heraclion Museum.

Delphi, one of the foremost centres of divination in ancient Greece and renowned particularly for its association with the cult of Apollo.

Dictynna, whom the Greeks called the 'goddess of the nets', was perhaps the goddess of Mount Dicte, a mountain in Crete which was later said to be the birthplace of Zeus. She would, then, be the mother-goddess.

Britomartis means 'the sweet virgin', a denomination which could not very well be applied to the Great Mother of the universe.

According to the Greek legend, Britomartis was a young virgin huntress who pursued wild beasts in the forests of Crete. She was said to be the daughter of Zeus. Minos saw her and was captivated by her beauty. He offered her his love, but was refused. He

Head of a bull, symbolising the bull-god. From Cnossus. Olympia Museum.

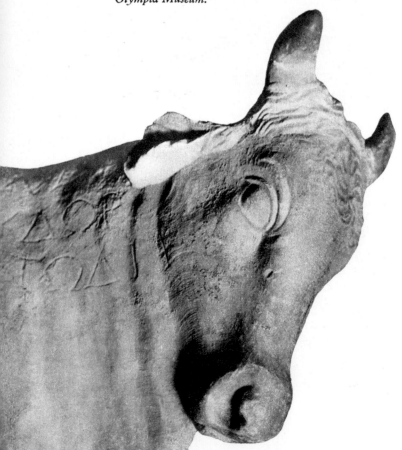

then attempted violence but Britomartis fled and, after a race which lasted no less than nine months, in order finally to escape Minos she flung herself off a high rock into the sea. She fell into the nets of a fisherman and for that reason received the name Dictynna. As a reward for her chastity, Artemis raised her to the rank of the immortals and thenceforth she appeared during the night to navigators. The Greeks made the assimilation even closer and called Dictynna-Britomartis the Cretan Artemis.

The God.   The Aegeans associated a god with the Great Goddess. It seems that, at least originally, in imitation of the cults of Western Asie, this god was thought of as subordinate to the goddess; but though we are informed of the relationship between Tammuz and Ishtar, between Attis and Cybele, and between Adonis and Astarte, no indication has yet come to light about the relationship between the Aegean god and goddess.

A celestial divinity, like the goddess with whom he was associated, the Aegean god bore the epithet *Asterius* (the 'starry'). He is found again under the name Asterion, king of Crete, who married Europa after her adventure with Zeus. Afterwards he was assimilated with Zeus himself, whose legend was thus enriched with Cretan contributions.

The peculiarity of the Cretan god was the mingling of animal and human features which composed his nature. The bull, as in many Asiatic religions, had been adopted since the earliest ages as the Aegean symbol of strength and creative energy. It later became the emblem of the Great God, and as such played an important part in Cretan legends. It even became incorporated in the divine nature: the Minotaur is analogous to the bull-god of the Elamites and to the Enki of the Sumerians, who was also 'the savage bull of the sky and the earth'.

The bull-god was not the only aspect under which the Cretan god appeared. Besides the *Minotaur* there was also *Minos*. Therefore the god was also conceived in human form, and it was thus that he sometimes appeared to his worshippers in all his terrifying majesty.

But whether we are concerned with Minos or the

Above, Minoan goddess rising amidst plants from the ground. The goddess holds flowers in her hand. Impression from a seal.
Below, goddess and her attendant, from a Minoan seal.

A female idol, probably a mother-goddess. She is depicted with the bull's horns of consecration and birds on her head. Clay figure of the later Minoan period, about 1400 B.C.

Minotaur we know them only through the modifications they underwent when Hellenised. We therefore mention them here only in passing and reserve a later occasion to discuss them at greater length, when we meet them again in the heroic legends of classical Greece.

The mythology of classical Greece

Greek Theogonies. The Greek pantheon was established as early as the Homeric epoch. The many divinities of which it was composed generally appear in the *Iliad* and the *Odyssey* with their characteristic physiognomy, their traditional attributes and their own time-honoured legends. But the poet tells us nothing of their origin or their past. At the most he mentions that Zeus is the son of Cronus and says incidentally that Oceanus and his spouse Tethys were the creators of gods and living beings.

It was only later that the Greeks felt the need to provide their gods with a genealogy and a history. Hesiod's poem, the *Theogony*, written in about the eighth century B.C., is the oldest Greek attempt at mythological classification. While recounting the origin of the gods, recalling their chief adventures and establishing their relationships, he also claims to explain the formation of the universe. The poem is thus as much a cosmogony as a theogony. A reflection

of popular beliefs, the *Theogony* of Hesiod had a kind of official recognition in Greece.

From the sixth century B.C., until the beginning of the Christian era, however, other theogonies were elaborated under the influence of Orphic doctrines; and these theogonies departed widely from the traditions of Hesiod. But the Orphic theogonies, known only to the initiated, were never popular. In addition they were too intermingled with foreign contributions, notably Asiatic, to be specifically Greek in character. We shall therefore merely give a summary of their principal features, having first given Hesiod's version of the origins of the world.

The formation of the world and the birth of the gods

Chaos and Gaea. In the beginning, Hesiod says, there was Chaos, vast and dark space. Then appeared Gaea, the deep-breasted earth, and finally Eros, 'the love which softens hearts', whose fructifying influence would thenceforth preside over the formation of beings and things.

From Chaos were born Erebus and Night who, uniting, gave birth in their turn to Ether and Hemera, the day.

For her part Gaea first bore Uranus, the sky crowned with stars, 'whom she made her equal in grandeur, so that he entirely covered her'. Then she created the high mountains and Pontus, 'the sterile sea,' with its harmonious waves.

Uranus and Gaea—The Uranus group. The universe had been formed. It remained to be peopled. Gaea united with her son Uranus and produced the first race—the Titans. There were twelve of them, six male and six female: Oceanus, Coeus, Hyperion, Crius, Iapetus, Cronus; Theia, Rhea, Mnemosyne, Phoebe, Tethys and Themis.

Uranus and Gaea then gave birth to the Cyclopes: Brontes, Steropes and Arges, 'who resembled the other gods but had only one eye in the middle of their forehead'. Finally they bore three monsters: Cottus, Briareus and Gyges. 'From their shoulders sprang a hundred invincible arms and above these powerful limbs rose fifty heads attached to their backs.' For this reason they were called the Hecatoncheires or the Centimanes.

Uranus could only regard his offspring with horror, and as soon as they were born he shut them up in the depths of the earth. Gaea at first mourned, but afterwards grew angry and meditated terrible vengeance against her husband. From her bosom she drew forth gleaming steel, fashioned a sharp sickle or *harpe* and explained to her children the plan she had made. All of them hesitated, struck with horror. Only the astute Cronus, her last-born, volunteered to support his mother. When evening fell Uranus, accompanied by Night, came as usual to rejoin his wife. While he unsuspectingly slept, Cronus, who with his mother's aid lay in hiding, armed himself with the sickle, atrociously mutilated his father and cast the bleeding genitals into the sea. From the terrible wound black blood dropped and the drops, seeping into the earth, gave birth to the redoubtable Furies, to monstrous giants and to the ash-tree nymphs, the Meliae. As for the debris which floated on the surface of the waves, it broke into a white foam from which was born a young goddess, Aphrodite, 'who was first carried towards the divine Cythera and thence as far as Cyprus surrounded with waves'.

The Character of the First Gods. Such are the first divine figures and the first drama they underwent. Some of the actors are, however, rather ill-defined.

Hesiod's 'Chaos', a name which comes from a Greek root meaning 'to gape', simply designates open space. Only later, because of a false derivation from a word meaning 'to pour', was Chaos considered to mean the confused and unorganised mass of the elements scattered through space.

The same may be said of Hesiod's Eros, who has nothing in common with the Eros whom we shall meet in later legends. Here Eros has only a metaphysical significance: he represents the force of attraction which causes beings to come together.

Uranus, son and husband of Gaea, is the starlit sky. It may be pointed out that he received no cult in Greece. This conception of the sky and the earth as two primordial divinities, is common to all Indo-European peoples.

Gaea. The only divinity with well-defined features is Gaea, the earth. According to Hesiod it seems likely that Gaea, from whom all things issued, had been the great deity of the primitive Greeks. Like the Aegeans and like the peoples of Asia, the Greeks must doubtless have originally worshipped the Earth in whom they beheld the mother-goddess. This is again confirmed by the Homeric hymn in which the poet says: 'I shall sing of Gaea, universal mother, firmly founded, the oldest of divinities.'

Gaea, 'the deep-breasted', whose soil nourishes all that exists, and by whose benevolence men are blessed with fair children and all the pleasant fruits of earth, was thus at one time the supreme goddess, whose majesty was acknowledged not only by men but by the gods themselves. Later, when the victorious dynasty of the Olympians was established, her prestige was not lessened. It was still Gaea whom the gods invoked when they made oaths: 'I swear by Gaea and the vast sky above her,' Hera proclaims when, in the *Iliad*, she answers Zeus' accusations.

Gaea the omnipotent not only created the universe and bore the first race of the gods, but also gave birth to the human race. Thus in the myth of Erichthonius she draws him forth from her own bosom and offers him to Athene: he was the first inhabitant of Attica.

The power of Gaea was also manifest in her gift of foretelling the future. The Oracle of Delphi, the chief

The mutilation of Uranus by Cronus, by Vasari and Gherardi. Palazzo Vecchio, Florence.

12

centre of divination in ancient Greece, had originally been sacred to Gaea, before it was won by Apollo.

Later, as other divinities rose in the estimation of men, the role of Gaea gradually became less important. Her cult, however, always continued in Greece. She presided over marriages and was honoured as pre-eminent among prophetesses. At Patras the sick came to consult her. She was particularly venerated at Aegae, at Delphi and at Olympia. She had sanctuaries at Dodona, Tegea, Sparta and at Athens, near the Areopagus. She was offered first fruits and grain; but when she was invoked as the guardian of the sanctity of oaths a black ewe was sacrificed in her honour. She was commonly represented in the form of a gigantic woman.

The Titans. The Titans, who formed the first divine race, had for the most part no very clearly defined personality. The etymology of their name which Hesiod gives (from a word meaning 'to stretch out', because they had stretched out their hand against their father) is fanciful. Their name probably derives from a Cretan word which meant 'king'.

In Greece the Titans were ultimately honoured as the ancestors of men. To them was attributed the invention of the arts and of magic.

Cyclopes and Hecatoncheires. In Hesiod the Cyclopes were storm deities, as their names indicate: Brontes, thunder; Steropes, lightning; Arges, thunderbolt.

As for the three Hecatoncheires or Centimanes, their names characterise them. Cottus, the Furious; Briareus, the Vigorous; Gyges, the Big-limbed.

Titans, Cyclopes and Hecatoncheires symbolised the tumultuous forces of nature.

Orphic Cosmogonies. The followers of Orphism opposed to the above primitive and popular cosmogony other explanations of the origin of things. They claimed as their authority the apocryphal writings attributed to Orpheus which seem actually to have been written by a priest named Onomacritus. The philosophic and scientific preoccupations which all these systems reflect, the subtleties in which they delight, and the many abstractions which they employ, remove them from the realm of the primitive. They are metaphysical systems rather than mythology. Broadly speaking, they state that the first principle was Cronus, or Time, from which came Chaos, which symbolised the infinite, and Ether, which symbolised the finite.

Chaos was surrounded by Night, which formed the enveloping cover under which, by the creative action of Ether, cosmic matter was slowly organised. This finally assumed the shape of an egg of which Night formed the shell.

In the centre of this gigantic egg, whose upper section formed the vault of the sky and whose lower section was the earth, was born the first being, Phanes —the Light. It was Phanes who, by union with Night, created Heaven and Earth. He was he also Zeus' father.

We shall not dwell longer on this brief summary of Orphic doctrine; for we shall meet it again when we come to the god Dionysus, who became the supreme god of Orphism. Let us return to Hesiod's account of the fate of the second divine dynasty.

Left, Gaea, the early Greek mother-goddess. Terracotta statuette from Tanagra. Borély Museum, Marseilles. Right, Cronus devouring his children, by Goya. The Prado, Madrid.

Cronus — the birth of Zeus

The Reign of Cronus. When Uranus was reduced to impotence, Cronus liberated his brothers, the Titans—with the exception of the Cyclopes and the Hecatoncheires—and became chief of the new dynasty.

Under his reign the work of creation continued. Night gave birth to Doom (Moros), to black Ker (Moera) and to Death; then to Sleep and his retinue of Dreams. She then bore bantering Gaiety (Momus) and wailing Misery (Oizus), and the Hesperides who guarded the golden apples beyond the Ocean. Then came the Fates: Clotho, Lachesis and Atropos, who apportioned to each mortal born his share of good and evil. Night also bore Nemesis, fearful to mortals, Fraud, Incontinence, Old Age and Eris (Strife) who in turn gave birth to Sorrow, Forgetfulness and Hunger, to Disease, Combat, Murder, Battles, Massacres, Quarrels, Lies and Equivocations, to Injustice and Oaths.

Pontus, the sea, united with Gaea, the earth, to produce Nereus the Truthful, Thaumas the Monstrous, Phorcys the Intrepid and pretty-cheeked Ceto and Eurybia with the heart of steel.

To Nereus and Doris, daughter of the Ocean, were born fifty daughters, the Nereids. To Thaumas and Electra were born Iris, the rainbow, and the Harpies with their fair tresses. By Phorcys Ceto bore the Graeae (the Old Ones), who came into the world with white hair, and the Gorgons, who lived beyond the Ocean in the land of the Hesperides.

The Titans also fathered children either by their sisters or by nymphs.

13

Oceanus and Tethys had three thousand sons, the Rivers, and three thousand daughters, the Water Nymphs, plus Metis (Wisdom), Tyche (Fortune), and Styx (the Infernal River). To Hyperion and Theia were born Helios (the Sun), Selene (the Moon) and Eos (the Dawn). Coeus and Phoebe were the parents of Leto and Asteria. By Eurybia Crius had Astraeus, Pallas and Perses. By the Oceanid Clymene or, according to others, by Asia, Iapetus fathered Atlas, Menoetius. Epimetheus and Prometheus. Finally Cronus married his sister Rhea, who gave him three daughters: Hestia, Demeter and Hera; and three sons: Hades, Poseidon and Zeus.

But whether it was that he feared, as it seems an oracle had predicted, that he would be supplanted by one of his children, or whether he had agreed with his older brothers, the Titans, to leave no posterity, Cronus swallowed each of this children as it was born. **The Birth and Childhood of Zeus.** Rhea, his wife, was overwhelmed with boundless grief. She asked herself in despair if she were condemned to see all her progeny thus disappear. When the time approached for her to give birth to Zeus she beseeched her own parents, Uranus and Gaea, to help her save this child. On their advice she went to Crete and there, in a deep cavern under the thick forests of Mount Aegeum, she brought forth her son. Gaea took the newborn baby and undertook to bring it up. There Rhea wrapped up an enormous stone in swaddling clothes and presented it to the unsuspecting Cronus, who swallowed it at once.

Meanwhile Gaea had carried her grandson to Mount Ida (others say to Mount Dicte) and given him for safe keeping into the hands of the nymphs Adrasteia and Ida, daughters of Melisseus, king of Crete. The two nymphs surrounded the young god with care and attention. The Curetes executed warlike dances around the cradle, beating their bronze shields with their swords, so that Cronus should not hear the baby crying.

Who exactly were these Curetes? In primitive times there had been a tribe of this name settled in Aetolia. On the other hand the Greeks gave them the epithet *Gegeneis* (children of the earth) or *Imbrogeneis* (children of the rain), so they may have been earth-spirits. Herodotus, however, calls them Phoenicians, followers of Cadmus, who had settled in Crete. Others say they came from Phrygia. Probably the Curetes were Cretan priests devoted to the orgiastic cult of the great goddess Rhea. They were distinguished by their half-warrior, half-sacerdotal character. To increase their prestige the first among them were deified and thus became the sacred Curetes, the protectors of Zeus. They had temples, notably in Messina, and they were invoked in making oaths—which tends to confirm their original identity as earth-spirits. The Curetes appear many times in the mythological history of Greece; on Hera's orders they spirited away at birth the young Epaphus, son of Zeus and Io, and were in consequence put to death by Zeus.

Thus sheltered from his father's cruelty the young Zeus grew up in the forests of Ida. The goat Amaltheia, a wonderful animal whose aspect terrified even the immortals, suckled the infant god. In gratitude Zeus later placed her among the constellations and from her hide, which no arrow could pierce, he made the redoubtable aegis. To the nymphs he gave one of her horns, conferring upon it the marvellous property of refilling itself inexhaustibly with whatever food or drink was wished for; this was the horn of plenty (cornucopia). According to certain authors Amaltheia was the wife of Melisseus and suckled the young god with her milk. Others make her a nymph who simply watched over the child Zeus, claiming that the god was fed on ambrosia and nectar brought to him by doves and an eagle. And if Adrasteia and Ida are called daughters of Melisseus (from the Greek *melissa*, a bee) was this not because the bees of Ida brought their scented honey to the divine child?

The oracle which had predicted to Cronus that he

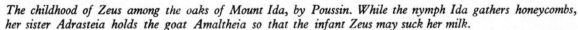

The childhood of Zeus among the oaks of Mount Ida, by Poussin. While the nymph Ida gathers honeycombs, her sister Adrasteia holds the goat Amaltheia so that the infant Zeus may suck her milk.

The War of the Titans and the Olympians, which raged for ten years. The Titans are here being crushed under boulders thrown by the Cyclopes and the Hecatoncheires. Painting by Giulio Romano.

would one day be overthrown by one of his sons had not lied. As soon as Zeus had reached manhood he planned to punish his father. Apollodorus tells us that he summoned to his aid Metis, daughter of Oceanus. Metis gave Cronus a draught that made him vomit up the stone and with it his children, the gods, whom he had swallowed. Vanquished by the might of Zeus, Cronus was driven from the sky and cast to the very depths of the universe and there enchained in the region which stretches beneath the earth and the sterile sea. This at least is what Homer says; according to others Cronus was sent to the ends of the earth to dwell in bliss, or plunged into mysterious slumber in distant Thule.

The era of the Olympians now began.

The Revolt of the Titans.   The Titans, with the exception of Oceanus, were jealous of the new gods and wished to reconquer the kingdom of which they had been dispossessed. Then began the terrible struggle. From their stronghold on Mount Othrys the Titans launched furious attacks upon Olympus. For ten years the outcome of the war remained doubtful. Zeus descended into Tartarus where, guarded by the monster Campe, the Hecatoncheires and the Cyclopes were kept prisoners. He set them free and made them his allies. The Cyclopes gave him the thunderbolt and the Hecatoncheires put their invincible arms at his service. Seizing in their enormous arms great boulders, they crushed the Titans. 'Sea and earth resounded with the horrifying clamour and the shaken firmament groaned aloud.' Zeus, too, was unable to curb his warlike rage and joined in the fray. From the heights of Olympus, Hesiod tells us, from the heights of the heavens he hurled thunder and lightning. With unwearying hand he flung bolt after bolt, and the air was rent with sound and fury. The fertile earth

shuddered and burned; vast forests flamed and all things melted and boiled: the River Ocean, the immense sea and the entire earth. Around the infernal Titans arose stifling mists and blazing air; their bold glances were blinded by flashes of lightning. The fire even reached Chaos, and from what the eye could behold and the ear distinguish one would have said that sky and earth were mingled, the earth shaken on its very foundations, the sky crashing down from its heights.

In spite of their pride and courage the Titans were finally defeated and, bound with chains, cast into the abysmal depths of the earth—as far below its surface as is the earth itself from the sky. It is there among impenetrable shadows and foul vapours, at the very end of the world, that the Titans 'are buried by the will of the king of the heavens'.

The War of the Giants.   Zeus had scarcely put down this dangerous revolt when he was forced to undergo a new struggle, this time against the Giants. The Giants had sprung from the blood of the mutilated Uranus and were not only distinguished for their size. For these monstrous sons of the Earth had legs like serpents and their feet were formed of reptiles' heads. At the instant that they emerged from the entrails of the ground at Phlegra, in the peninsula of Pallene, they appeared in glittering armour grasping enormous spears. Porphyrion and Alcyoneus were their leaders. They at once attacked Olympus, whose mass dominated the plain of Phlegra on the west. Islands, rivers, mountains, all gave way before them. 'While one,' says Claudian, 'with vigorous arm shook Mount Oeta of Thessaly in the air, another balanced the summits of Mount Pangaea in his powerful hand. One armed himself with the ice of Mount Athos, another seized Ossa and lifted it, while still another tore up Rhodope . . . From everywhere the horrible din echoed.' To reach the heights of Olympus the giants piled the surrounding mountains one upon another, Ossa on Pelion. But, grouped

The War between the Gods and the Giants. Athene striking down the giant Enceladus. The winged figure to the right is Nike. Detail from the frieze of the great altar of Zeus. Pergamum Museum, Berlin.

The War between the Gods and the Giants. In the centre, Zeus strikes the Giants with a thunderbolt. Greek amphora of the fourth century B.C., found at Melos. Louvre.

around Zeus, the gods—with the exception of Demeter who took no part in the struggle—stood their ground before the assailants. Apollo struck down Ephialtes. Clytius fell under the blows of Hecate or Hephaestus. The impetuous Ares pierced Pelorus and Mimas with his sword. Poseidon pursued Polybutes across the sea, flung the island of Nisyros on top of him and buried him.

The gods alone, however, could not triumph, for the oracle had declared that the sons of Gaea would succumb only to the blows of a mortal. This mortal was Hercules (Gk. Heracles), with whom Dionysus was sometimes associated. While Dionysus struck down Rhaetos (or Eurytus), Hercules attacked Alcyoneus. At first the giant resisted his blows. Hercules was astonished, but Athene revealed to him that Alcyoneus was invulnerable as long as he stood on the soil which had given him birth. The hero then seized the giant in his arms and carried him away from the territory of Pallene and at once slew him. Porphyrion wished to avenge his brother, but Zeus inspired in him a sudden passion for Hera. While the giant pursued Hera, Hercules pierced him with a deadly arrow. From that moment the defeat of the giants was assured. In vain Pallas and Enceladus attempted to struggle against Athene; one after the other they

were overcome. With the skin of Pallas Athene fashioned the aegis. As for Enceladus, she buried him under the island of Sicily. And even today when the giant turns over, the entire island quakes with volcanic eruptions.

Typhoeus. Gaea, however, could not resign herself to the defeat of her children. She raised up against Zeus a final monster, Typhoeus, whom she had borne to Tartarus. He was a terrifying creature whose hands worked ceaselessly and whose feet were never still. From his shoulders sprang a hundred horrible dragons' heads, each with a darting black tongue and eyes which spurted searing flame. From his thighs emerged innumerable vipers; his body was covered with feathers; thick bristles sprouted from his head and cheeks. He was taller than the tallest mountain. At sight of Typhoeus the gods were seized with fear and fled as far as Egypt. Only Zeus stood firm before the monster; but entwined in the myriad coils of the serpents he fell into the hands of Typhoeus who cut the tendons of his hands and feet and imprisoned him in his den in Cilicia. Rescued by Hermes, Zeus renewed the struggle. With his thunderbolts the god overwhelmed Typhoeus, who fled to Sicily, and there crushed him under Etna.

Thus in the first ages of the world, when the elements were not yet mastered and matter was still rebellious, there occurred terrifying cataclysms which threatened to overthrow everything. But the divine wisdom, regulator of the universe, finally imposed its will over the disorderly elements. Harmony was born anew and man, reassured, gave thanks to the god whose might had triumphed over the forces of evil.

The defeat of Typhoeus assured the final and lasting supremacy of Zeus; and among the Olympians gods and men acknowledged him as uncontested master.

Typhoeus or perhaps Typhon. The monster's three human torsos terminate in the triple body of a dragon. He holds birds and sparks of fire in his hands. Sculpture in porous limestone from the Hecatompedon. Period of Solon.

Opposite, Zeus, in the shape of a bull, carrying off Europa, one of several mortal women whom he loved and who bore him Minos, Rhadamanthys and Sarpedon. Red-figured krater by the Berlin Painter. National Museum, Tarquinia.

16

The origins of humanity

Prometheus. The Titan Iapetus was the father of four sons. Their mother, according to Hesiod, was the Oceanid Clymene; according to Aeschylus, she was Themis. Two of these sons, Menoetius and Atlas, were punished by Zeus, doubtless for having taken part in the Titans' revolt. Menoetius was plunged into darkest Erebus, as a punishment for 'his wickedness and boundless audacity'. As for Atlas, he was condemned to stand for ever before the Hesperides, on the edge of the world, and to bear upon his shoulders the vault of the heavens. The other two—Prometheus (who foresees) and Epimetheus (who reflects after the event)—had a different fate and played an important role in the legendary history of the origins of humanity.

Against the unchallengeable might of the Olympians, Prometheus had no weapon but cunning. During the revolt of the Titans he had kept a prudent neutrality and had even made overtures to Zeus when it seemed likely that the war would be won by him. Thus Prometheus had been admitted into Olympus and the circle of the Immortals. But he entertained a silent grudge against them as destroyers of his race.

He may have had other reasons for his interest in the human race; for a late tradition said that Prometheus was the creator of mankind. It was he who with earth and water—some said with his own tears—had fashioned the body of the first man, into which Athene breathed soul and life. In Phocis the author Pausanias saw bits of hardened clay which had the odour of human skin and which were plainly the residue of the slime employed by Prometheus.

But it seems that this creation took place only after the earlier race of man had been destroyed in the deluge. Current opinion actually attributed to man-

Prometheus and Atlas punished by Zeus. Atlas was condemned to support the vault of the heavens, and Prometheus was bound to a rock while an eagle fed upon his liver. Black-figured Cyrenaic kylix.

kind an older and nobler origin. 'Men and gods,' says Pindar, 'we are of the same family; we owe the breath of life to the same mother.'

The Four Ages of Man. The first men, who were contemporaries of Cronus, enjoyed complete happiness. It was the Golden Age. Hesiod says: 'They lived like gods, free from worry and fatigue; old age did not afflict them; they rejoiced in continual festivity.' Their lot did not include immortality, but at least 'they died as though overcome by sweet slumber. All the blessings of the world were theirs: the fruitful earth gave forth its treasures unbidden. At their death, men of the Golden Age became benevolent genii, 'protectors and tutelary guardians of the living'.

After the Golden Age came the Silver Age, which was peopled by a race of feeble and inept agriculturists who obeyed their mothers all their lives.

The creation of man. In the presence of the gods of Olympus (Poseidon, Hermes, Hera, Zeus, Apollo) Prometheus prepares to bring to life the body of the first man, whom he has just fashioned. Bas-relief from a sarcophagus in the National Museum, Naples.

Opposite, the Cyclops Polyphemus, blinded in his single eye by Odysseus and his followers, tries to capture them as they escape, clinging to the bellies of his ewes. Painting by Tibaldi. Palazzo Poggi, Bologna.

Pandora opens her box and lets loose all the afflictions of mankind. Nineteenth-century engraving.

The men of the Bronze Age were robust as ash trees and delighted only in oaths and warlike exploits. 'Their pitiless hearts were as hard as steel; their might was untameable, their arms invincible.' They ended by cutting each other's throats. From this generation, however, dated the discovery of the first metals and the first attempts at civilisation.

After the Bronze Age Hesiod places the Heroic Age, peopled by the valiant warriors who fought before Thebes and under the walls of Troy. But the more widespread opinion was that after the Bronze Age came the Iron Age—the contemporary age, a period of misery and crime 'when men respect neither their vows, nor justice, nor virtue'.

The Theft of Fire—Pandora.   As long as Cronus had reigned, gods and men had lived on terms of mutual understanding. Hesiod says: 'In those days meals were taken in common; men and the immortal gods sat down together.' Everything changed with the coming of the Olympians. Over men Zeus asserted his divine supremacy. A meeting of gods and men was held at Sicyon to determine which portion of victims offered in sacrifice was owed to the gods. Prometheus, who was in charge of the partition, laid out an enormous ox which he had cut up in his own way. He arranged the flesh, the entrails and the most succulent morsels in the skin and placed them on one side; on the other side he perfidiously laid the fleshless bones which he had covered with a rich layer of fat. Zeus, who was invited to take first choice, chose the bones; but when he had removed the white, gleaming fat and discovered nothing but the animal's bones he fell into a rage. In his anger he withheld fire from the unfortunate race who lived on earth. But the astute Prometheus went to the Island of Lemnos, where Hephaestus kept his forges. There he stole a brand of the holy fire which he enclosed in a hollow stalk and carried back to men.

Outraged by the theft, Zeus sent a fresh calamity to men. He ordered Hephaestus to fashion clay and water into a body, to give it vital force and human voice, and to make from it a virgin whose dazzling beauty would equal that of the immortal goddesses. All the divinities heaped their especial gifts on this new creature, who received the name of Pandora. Hermes, however, put perfidy into Pandora's heart and lies into her mouth and Zeus then sent her as a gift to Epimetheus. Although his brother Prometheus had warned him against accepting any gift from the ruler of Olympus, the imprudent Epimetheus was enchanted by Pandora's beauty, welcomed her, and made a place for her among men. Ill-fated imprudence! For Pandora brought in her arms a great vase— which is incorrectly called 'Pandora's Box'. She raised its lid, and the terrible afflictions with which the vase had been filled escaped and spread over the earth. Hope alone did not fly away.

The Deluge—Deucalion and Pyrrha.   Zeus' rage, however, was not appeased. In his anger he resolved to annihilate the human race by burying it beneath the waves of a deluge. But once again Prometheus was on guard. He warned his son Deucalion who, with his wife Pyrrha, daughter of Epimetheus and Pandora, then reigned in Thessaly. On the advice of his father, Deucalion constructed an ark and with his wife went aboard. For nine days and nine nights they floated on the waters. On the tenth day the downpour ceased and the two survivors disembarked on the crest of Mount Othrys or Mount Parnassus. Deucalion offered up sacrifice to Zeus Phyxius (protector of fugitives) and the god, touched by his piety, promised to grant him his first wish. Deucalion asked Zeus to renew the human race.

Another legend says that Deucalion and Pyrrha, having gone to Delphi, addressed their prayers to Themis. 'Veil your heads,' replied the goddess, 'remove the girdles of your robes and cast behind you the bones of your first ancestor'. Stricken at first with astonishment, Deucalion and Pyrrha at last solved the mystery of this ambiguous command. They veiled their heads and walked across the plain, throwing over their shoulders stones torn from the earth—for were they not descendants of Gaea, the earth, and were not the rocks her very bones? The stones which Deucalion threw were changed into men, those that Pyrrha cast were transformed into women.

The human race was renewed and Zeus recovered from his anger. Deucalion was regarded as the father of the Hellenes, the first king and founder of towns and temples. It was he, they said, who built the temple of Olympian Zeus at Athens, and near by the temple his tomb was pointed out.

The Torture of Prometheus.   Although peace had been concluded between Zeus and mankind, Prometheus had to pay cruelly for his trickery and thefts. At the command of Zeus, Hephaestus, assisted by Kratos and Bia, seized Prometheus and bound him with indestructible chains to one of the crests of Mount Caucasus. There, 'an eagle with outstretched wings, sent by Zeus, fed upon his immortal liver; as much as the winged monster devoured, during the day, that much grew again during the night'. In spite of the torture the Titan persisted in his attitude of revolt. Disdaining complaints and humiliating prayers he never ceased to defy the lord of Olympus and to express his hatred in violent outbursts. For was he not in possession of a secret which dangerously concerned the future of Zeus himself?

Finally after thirty years of suffering—others say thirty thousand years—he was with Zeus' permission rescued by the divine Hercules, who slew the eagle and broke the prisoner's chains. Prometheus then revealed to Zeus his famous secret and warned him that if he continued to pay court to Thetis, daughter of Nereus, he would run the risk of seeing a son born who would dethrone him. Not wishing to chance the same misadventure that had befallen his father and his grandfather, Zeus abandoned his amorous enterprise and allowed Thetis to marry a mortal, Peleus.

Prometheus, however, could not acquire divine immortality unless some immortal consented to exchange destinies with him. Now the centaur Chiron, whom Hercules had struck with a poisoned arrow, was in despair lest his wound never healed. To put an end to his suffering Chiron begged to be allowed to descend into Hades in the place of Prometheus. Zeus consented, and from then on the son of Iapetus took his permanent place on Olympus. And the Athenians, who saw in Prometheus the benefactor of mankind and the father of all the arts and sciences, raised an altar to him in the gardens of the Academy.

The Olympians

Mount Olympus. On the confines of Thessaly and Macedonia, along the shores of the Aegean Sea from which it is separated only by a narrow littoral, rises the chain of Olympus. While on the north the mountain group descends to the plain by a series of gentle hills, the south face—that which the Greeks saw—falls precipitously and the mountain offers the aspect of a rocky cliff. Above a sort of monster plateau, itself steeply flanked, which serves as a base, Mount Olympus soars up in one sweep to more than nine thousand feet. Down its sheer slopes, covered with dark woods, tumble numerous torrents which dig deep furrows, rather like the folds of a garment. Thus the poets called it 'Olympus of the innumerable folds'. The line of the mountain peaks is rounded into a kind of amphitheatre and the upper tiers of rock, formed by the heaping up of huge boulders round which cling shreds of cloud, look like gigantic seats arranged there for the use of supernatural beings.

The mariner who sailed into the gulf of Therme (today the gulf of Salonica) would feel himself filled with religious awe when he perceived against the hard blue line of sky the lofty profile of Mount Olympus. Everything conspired to reveal to him the fearful majesty of the gods. In the first place he had no doubt that Olympus was the highest mountain in the world. Then he would remember that the narrow Vale of Tempe, which separates Olympus from Ossa and cradles under its willows and plane-trees the peaceful stream of Peneus, had been hollowed out by Zeus during his struggle with the Titans. Finally he would scarcely dare raise his eyes towards the summits; for he knew that up there, behind the veil of clouds which hid them from mortal regard, dwelt the almighty gods. Bending over his oars he would repeat the words of Homer who, speaking of Olympus, had said: 'Never is it swept by the winds nor touched by snow; a purer air surrounds it, a white clarity envelops it and the gods there enjoy an eternal happiness.

Actually when the sons of Cronus drew lots for the partition of the empire of the world, Zeus received as his share the sublime regions of the Ether, Poseidon

The gods on Olympus. Dionysus, centre. Zeus and Athene, left; Hera and Aphrodite, right. Cup from the Municipal Museum, Tarquinia.

The gods on Olympus. Poseidon, Apollo and Artemis. Marble frieze from the east side of the Parthenon, Athens. British Museum.

the tumultuous sea, and Hades the sombre depths of the earth. But it was agreed that Olympus should be held in common by all the gods as a dwelling-place.

The Gods on Olympus. Assembled on Olympus, the gods formed a society with its own laws and hierarchy. First came the twelve great gods and goddesses: Zeus, Poseidon, Hephaestus, Hermes, Ares and Apollo; Hera, Athene, Artemis, Hestia, Aphrodite and Demeter. Beside them were ranged other divinities, some of whom claimed equal rank with the great twelve. Such were Helios, Selene, Leto, Dione, Dionysus, Themis and Eos. Then, of a lower rank, forming as it were the courtiers of the Olympians and sworn to their service: the Horae, the Moerae, Nemesis, the Graces, the Muses, Iris, Hebe, Ganymede. It must be pointed out that Hades, although a brother of Zeus, did not frequent Olympus and, with the goddesses Persephone and Hecate, remained in his subterranean empire.

Over this society Zeus reigned as sovereign ruler. If at times the gods were tempted by rebellious impulses, they were quickly reduced to obedience. In Homer we see how Zeus speaks to them: 'Let no god, let no goddess attempt to curb my will ... I shall seize him and cast him into darkest Tartarus. Then will he recognise how much mightier am I than all the gods! Come, then, try it, O gods! And you will discover with whom you have to deal. Hang from the heavens a golden chain and all of you, gods and goddesses, attach yourselves to it; no matter how hard you strive, you will not drag Zeus in his supreme wisdom from the sky down to earth. But when, afterwards, I begin to pull, I shall draw you, you and the earth and the sea together, I shall draw you up and wind the chain around the summit of Olympus and you will all remain there suspended in the air.' Without quite carrying out this threat Zeus nevertheless

inflicted severe penalties on gods who had displeased him. For instance he would make them servales slaves to mortals; such was the fate of Poseidon and Apollo. Therefore the gods did not resist him, even Hera counselling prudence. 'How foolish we are to become angry with Zeus ... He sits apart, for he boasts of being incontestably superior to the immortal gods in might. So resign yourselves.'

Above the gods, however, and above Zeus himself hovered a supreme power to whom all were subject: Moros, or Destiny. Son of the Night, Moros, invisible and dark like his mother, prepared his decrees in the shadows and extended his inescapable dominion over all. Zeus himself could not set aside his decisions and had to submit to them like the humblest mortal. He had, moreover, no desire to set aside the decisions of Destiny; for, being himself Supreme Wisdom, he was not unaware that in upsetting the destined course of events he would introduce confusion into the universe it was his mission to govern. Thus, even when it was a matter of saving the life of his own son Sarpedon, the hour of whose death the Fates had marked down, Zeus preferred to bow his head and let what was ordained be fulfilled.

The days of the gods passed in merrymaking and laughter. Sometimes, when they intervened in the affairs of men whose quarrels they wholeheartedly adopted, the gods would disagree. But these passing storms did not affect the normal serenity of Olympus. Seated around their golden tables the gods dined on celestial nectar and ambrosia, and savoured the rising fragrance of fatted cattle which mortals burned in their honour on their altars below. Even when Zeus called them together in counsel on the topmost peak of Olympus where he resided, the fair Hebe would move among them pouring nectar, and the golden cups would pass from hand to hand.

While they drank, Apollo would delight them with the harmony of his lyre and the Muses would sing in turn in their sweet voices.

Finally, 'when the brilliant torch of the sun had disappeared the gods would take their leave and return to the dwelling Hephaestus had built with marvellous cunning for each of them, there to rest.'

If the gods' daily life resembled that of men it was because, at least in appearance, their natures were not dissimilar. Their bodies were like mortal bodies, but superior in stature, strength and beauty. Ares' body, stretched on the ground, covered a length of seven plethra—well over two hundred yards—and when from the heights of Olympus Hera swore by the Styx, she could touch the earth with one hand and with the other reach the seas.

In the case of the gods, however, blood was replaced by a more fluid substance, the ichor, which rendered the body imperishable and incorruptible. This did not prevent the gods from being vulnerable to weapons used by men. But their wounds, no matter how painful, always healed and their bodies retained eternal youth.

Another privilege which the gods enjoyed was the power of metamorphosis, to change themselves if they wished into animals or even to take on the aspect of inanimate objects.

Like mortals the gods were subject to human passions. They were accessible to love, hate, anger, even to envy. They cruelly punished all who aroused their enmity, but showered favours on those who revered and honoured them with gifts.

Zeus

The very name Zeus, in which the Sanskrit root *dyaus* and the Latin *dies* (the day) are found, evokes the idea of the luminous sky. Originally, then, Zeus was the god of the sky and of atmospheric phenomena. He was lord of the winds, of the clouds, of rain both destructive and beneficial, of the thunder. He resided in the ether, the upper part of the air, and on mountain tops. He was literally the All-High. Hence he was worshipped in elevated spots such as Mount Lycaeus in Arcadia, Mount Apesas in Argolis, Parnassus and Hymettus in Attica, Helicon in Boeotia, Pelion in Thessaly, Olympus in Macedonia, Pangaea in Thrace, Ida in Crete, and so forth.

His Attributes. Later Zeus took on a moral personality and became the supreme god who united in himself all the attributes of divinity. He was omnipotent, he saw everything and knew everything. Thus he was the fountainhead of all divination, whether he spoke oracularly in person as on Olympus and at Dodona, or whether he had recourse as at Delphi to the intermediary of Apollo, his prophet. A wise sovereign, he ordained all according to the law of Fate with which his own will was merged. To mortals he dispensed good and evil; he was, moreover, kind and compassionate. Though he chastised the wicked he was capable of pity. He averted threatening dangers *(Alexikakos)*; he protected the weak, the indigent, the fugitive and, in general, all suppliants *(Milichios)*. His solicitude also extended to the family as god of the hearth *(Ephestios)*, of marriage *(Gamelios)*, of friendship *(Philios)*, and of the peoples' assemblies *(Agoraios)*. Finally he was the protector-god of all Greece—Panhellenic Zeus.

His Cult. The most famous sanctuary of Zeus was that of Dodona, in Epirus. It was also the oldest, dating back to the Pelasgians. People came there from all parts of Greece to consult the oracle of a sacred oak whose rustling and murmurs were regarded as the words of Zeus himself. On the origin of this oracle Herodotus, who claims to have heard it from the lips of the priestesses of Dodona says: 'Two black doves flew from Thebes in Egypt, one to Libya and the other to Dodona. The latter, alighting in an oak tree, began to speak in a human voice and to say that an oracle of Zeus should be founded in this place. The people of Dodona believed that they had received an order coming from the gods, and on the dove's advice founded the oracle.' The interpretation of the oracles of Dodona was entrusted to a college of priests, the Selli.

Among Zeus' other sanctuaries must be mentioned that of Mount Lycaeus in Arcadia on the summit of which was a mound of earth, fronted by two columns with engraved eagles. Here, it was said, human sacrifice was once practised. The root from which the word

Zeus with a thunderbolt. Figure in bronze from Dodona. About 470 B.C. The god is still nude and has none of the majestic serenity he later acquired in the classical representations. Former State Museum, Berlin.

Lycaeus was formed (it means 'light') reveals that Zeus was here originally a solar deity.

Finally there was the celebrated temple of Olympus with its famous statue of the god sculptured by Phidias. It rose on a richly ornamented pedestal which was about thirty feet high and twenty feet wide. The statue itself was more than forty feet in height. Seated on a throne of bronze, gold, ivory and ebony, the god held in his right hand a crowned Victory, while his left hand rested on a sceptre surmounted by an eagle. He was dressed in a golden mantle strewn with flowers. On his brow there was an olive wreath and his countenance, framed by a long beard, wore an expression of serene majesty.

Representations. The Olympian Zeus of Phidias represented the ideal which inspired subsequent artists. The god was normally depicted as a man in the fullness of maturity, of robust body, grave countenance and with a broad forehead jutting out above deeply set eyes. His face is framed by thick waving hair and a finely curled beard. Except in primitive images he is rarely nude. He usually wears a long mantle which leaves his chest and right arm free. His attributes are the sceptre in his left hand, in his right hand the thunderbolt and at his feet the eagle. Often on his brow he wears a crown of oak-leaves.

The Marriages of Zeus. Apart from the incidents which surrounded his birth, childhood and coming to the throne, the legends of Zeus are largely concerned with his many amorous adventures. Before marrying Hera and associating her officially with his sovereignty, Zeus, among whose many functions that of pro-creation was pre-eminent, had contracted numerous unions.

His first wife was Metis (Wisdom) who, Hesiod says, 'knew more things than all the gods and men

Zeus. This early representation shows him nude with his chlamys over his shoulder. Greek lecythus. Bibliothéque Nationale.

put together'. But Gaea and Uranus warned Zeus that if he had children by Metis they would be more powerful than he, and dethrone him. So, when Metis was about to give birth to Athene, Zeus, in order to forestall the danger, swallowed the mother and with her the unborn baby. By avoiding the risk of an embarrassing posterity in this manner he also now embodied supreme Wisdom—a double benefit.

Next he married Themis, daughter of Uranus and Gaea. Themis was the Law which regulates both physical and moral order. It is not surprising, then, that her children should be: the Horae or Seasons; Eunomia (Wise Legislation); Dike (Justice); Eirene (Peace), and finally the Fates or Moerae who were also said to be the daughters of Night. Even when she was replaced by Hera, Themis continued to remain near Zeus as an adviser, and she was always revered on Olympus.

Another Titaness, Mnemosyne, was the wife of Zeus. The god stayed nine nights with her, and when her time had come Mnemosyne gave birth to nine daughters, who were the Muses.

Zeus was also enamoured of Demeter, but the goddess repulsed his advances. He changed himself into a bull and took her by force, and from this union was born Kore, also called Persephone.

The Oceanid Eurynome was also among Zeus' wives and was the mother of the three Graces or Charites.

Zeus and Hera. And then Zeus married Hera. Actually their relationship was already long established. In the days when Cronus still reigned, the young

goddess grew up in the island of Euboea under the care of her nurse Macris. Zeus came to her one day and bore her to Mount Cithaeron on the confines of Attica and Boeotia, where he lay with her. Another legend places the first encounter between Zeus and Hera in the region of the Hesperides, while at Cnossus in Crete, near the River Theris, they also pointed out the exact spot where the marriage of the divine couple was consummated. Pausanias relates the adventure differently. In order not to awaken his sister's suspicions Zeus came to her in the form of a cuckoo. It was winter and the bird seemed to be frozen with the cold. Touched by pity, the young goddess warmed the cuckoo by holding it against her breast. Zeus then reassumed his natural form and attempted to take advantage of the situation. Hera resisted at first and gave way only after Zeus had promised to marry her. The marriage, solemnly celebrated on Olympus, did not, however, put an end to Zeus' amorous enterprises. Braving Hera's jealousy and ignoring the misfortunes which this jealousy could bring upon its victims, Zeus continued enthusiastically to pursue goddesses and mortal women.

Zeus and the Titanesses Zeus was not always successful. Thus, on the advice of Prometheus, he freely renounced Thetis for fear of begetting by her a son who would dethrone him. Nor could he overcome the resistance of the nymph Asteria, daughter of Coeus and Phoebe, who in order to escape him changed herself into a quail and threw herself into

Zeus, with the eagle, one of his attributes, at his side. Though his head is of classical type, he is depicted nude and with his chlamys over his shoulder. Greek statue in marble, from Anzio.

Zeus and Antiope, by Watteau. Louvre.

the sea where she became a floating island called, at first, Ortygia, and later Delos.

Leto was less shy than her sister Asteria and surrendered to Zeus' seductions. In this way she earned Hera's enmity and, as we shall later see, it was only after many misadventures that she was able to bring into the world her two children, Apollo and Artemis.

Maia, daughter of Atlas and Pleione, was more adroit and succeeded in evading Hera's jealous eye. She lived in Arcadia on Mount Cyllene. 'Escaping from the crowd of happy immortals,' says the Homeric hymn, 'Maia of the fair tresses lived in the depths of a dark cavern. It was here that the son of Cronus lay all night with the nymph whilst sweet sleep held alabaster-limbed Hera; sleep thus deceiving immortals and feeble men alike.' Maia gave birth to Hermes.

It was said that another daughter of Atlas, Electra, bore Zeus Harmonia—whom Hesiod, however, calls the daughter of Ares and Aphrodite — and Dardanus. Finally a third daughter of Atlas, Taygete, was pursued by Zeus. According to some accounts she was protected by Artemis, who turned her into a hind and only later restored her to her original form. In gratitude Taygete consecrated to the goddess a hind whose horns she had gilded and which we shall meet again during the labours of Hercules. According to other accounts Taygete submitted to Zeus and gave birth to Lacedaemon.

Zeus and the Nymphs. Among the nymphs loved by Zeus must also be mentioned Aegina and Antiope, the daughters of the river-god Asopus. The former had been carried off by Zeus who, assuming the shape of an eagle or a flame, had borne her to the island of Oenone or Oenopia, where she gave birth to Aeacus. Asopus set out in search of them. From Sisyphus he discovered the name of his daughter's ravisher and the place where she had hidden herself. He was on the point of finding her when Zeus struck him with a thunderbolt and forced him to return to his riverbed. Others relate how Asopus surprised the two lovers: to protect Aegina from the paternal fury Zeus changed her into an island and himself into a rock.

As for Antiope—who, according to Pausanias, was not the daughter of Asopus but of Nycteus—Zeus approached her in the form of a satyr and surprised her when she was asleep. To hide her shame Antiope fled to Sicyon, where she married the king, Epopeus. Her father Nycteus killed himself in despair, but before he died he charged his brother Lycus to avenge his honour. Lycus seized Sicyon, put Epopeus to death and brought Antiope back, a prisoner. At Eleuthere Antiope gave birth to twins, Amphion and Zethus, whom she exposed on Mount Cithaeron and who later figured among the chief heroes of Theban legend.

The nymph Callisto was a daughter of Lycaon. She was a companion of Artemis and had made a vow of chastity. But Zeus was captivated by her extraordinary beauty. One day while the nymph was resting in the woods Zeus presented himself to her in the form of Artemis. The young virgin welcomed him unsuspectingly, and when she realised her mistake it was already too late. She tried to hide her shame, but Artemis discovered what had occurred when one day she saw Callisto bathing with her companions. In order to shield the nymph from the rage of the goddess, Zeus changed Callisto into a bear. But Artemis pierced her with her arrows and she died giving birth to a son, Arcas, who was the ancestor of the Arcadians. As for Callisto, she was transformed into a constellation and became the Great Bear.

Zeus and Mortal Women. The first mortal woman whom Zeus loved was Niobe, daughter of Phoroneus and the nymph Laodice. She gave birth to Argos, founder of the city of that name. The same Phoroneus, son of Inachus, had a sister named Io who, in the former Heraeum, between Mycenae and Tiryns, exercised the functions of priestess of Hera. Zeus fell in love with her. In order to possess her he took the form of a cloud. In spite of this stratagem Hera's suspicions were aroused. Zeus pleaded innocence and, in order to put his wife off the scent, changed his mistress into a white heifer. Hera pretended to be deceived and asked him for the heifer as a gift. Once it was in her possession she placed the animal under the care of Argus Panoptes—'who sees all'. This Argus, son of Arestor, was a giant of redoubtable strength: he had once killed a bull which was ravaging Arcadia, and slain Echidna, daughter of Tartarus and Gaea. In addition he had one hundred eyes, of which fifty remained open while the other fifty closed in sleep. Zeus, however, ordered the cunning Hermes to set Io free. Hermes succeeded in charming the giant to sleep with the sound of his flute, and cut off his head. To honour Argus, who had served her, Hera distributed his eyes over the tail of her favourite bird, the peacock, whose plumage was thenceforth so brilliant. As for the unfortunate heifer, Hera sent a gadfly to torture her. Driven mad by the stinging insect, Io fled across the world. She swam the Thracian Bosporus, crossed the Ionian Sea which took her name and, having crossed Asia Minor, finally reached Egypt where, by a simple touch of the hand, Zeus restored her to her human form. She then bore a son, Epaphus —child of 'the touch'. But Hera was not disarmed. She ordered the Curetes to abduct the child. They obeyed and for this reason were slain by Zeus. Io at last found her child in Syria and returned to Egypt where she married the king, Telegonus. In later days

Hermes and Argus, by Rubens. Hermes, who has just lulled Argus to sleep with his flute, is about to kill him and set the cow Io free.

Zeus in the shape of Artemis seducing Callisto, by Boucher. Wallace Collection.

Io became confused with the Egyptian goddess Isis and her son Epaphus with Apis.

At Argos reigned Acrisius who had an only daughter, Danae. An oracle had told Acrisius that one day his daughter would bring into the world a son by whose hands he would perish. Acrisius thereupon had a chamber of bronze built underground—or some say a tower — and in it locked Danae with her nurse. But Zeus, who had been attracted by the girl's charms, found a way to enter the chamber in the form of a shower of gold and frequently visited Danae. The result was the birth of a son, Perseus. Acrisius was terrified when he learned of this miraculous birth, and shut up both mother and child in a chest which he cast into the sea. Tossed by the waves, the chest was finally carried to the island of Seriphus, where a fisherman, one Dictys, brother of King Polydectes, caught it in his nets. Danae and Perseus were thus saved. We shall see, when we come to Perseus, how this romantic adventure continued.

More terrible still was Hera's jealousy and the vengeance she took on another of Zeus' loves, Semele, daughter of Cadmus. When she learned of the relationship between her husband and this mortal girl Hera came to her rival in disguise and suggested that Semele ask her lover to appear before her in all the brilliance of his majesty. Zeus tried in vain to dissuade Semele from making such an unreasonable demand. Semele insisted. The god gave in, and visited her in his chariot of glory, surrounded by lightning and thunder. The sight of the great god in all his dazzling splendour was too much for mortal eyes and Semele perished, consumed by celestial flames. Zeus then took up the child she bore in her womb and enclosed it in his own thigh until the day set for its birth: it was to be Dionysus.

The rape of Europa had less tragic consequences. Daughter of Phoenix or of Agenor, King of Phoenicia, and of Telephassa, the young Europa was playing one day at the water's edge, gathering flowers with her companions. Her attention was caught by the sight of a bull with glistening hide who browsed peacefully among her father's herd. His air, gentle and at the same time majestic, struck her. She did not suspect that this bull was none other than the master of the gods, Zeus himself, who had assumed this shape to deceive the girl, of whom he had become enamoured. Trustingly Europa approached and caressed the animal, who very gallantly knelt before her. She climbed playfully on to his mighty back, and began to wreathe flowers around his powerful horns. Suddenly the bull reared to his feet, sprang into the waves, at a bound, and carried the weeping virgin across the vast sea. They finally reached the southern coast of Crete, at Gortyna. The plane tree under which Zeus made the young Phoenician his mistress was still pointed out in the days of Theophrastus. Because it had witnessed and sheltered the divine union this tree received the privilege of retaining its foliage in all seasons. Europa gave birth to Minos, Rhadamanthys and Sarpedon. All three were adopted by the King of Crete, Asterius, who subsequently became Europa's husband.

Although it was within his province to guard the sanctity of marriage, Zeus did not hesitate on occasion to pay court to married women. Thus he fell in love with Leda, the wife of Tyndareus. One evening when the young woman was bathing in a pool she saw floating majestically towards her a swan of dazzling whiteness. It was Zeus, who ravished her. The same night Leda also lay with her own husband; afterwards she was delivered of two eggs, one of which contained Pollux and Helen, children of Zeus, the other containing Castor and Clytemnestra, children of Tyndareus.

In order to seduce Alcmene, Zeus employed another stratagem. He wished, Hesiod says, 'to produce a son who would one day be a powerful protector for gods and men alike', and he had set his heart on the wife of the Theban chief, Amphitryon. But as he knew she was virtuous and incorruptible he took advantage of Amphitryon's absence to assume Amphitryon's own appearance. Alcmene welcomed Zeus in this disguise exactly as though he were her true husband. When the real Amphitryon returned a few hours later he was surprised by his wife's lack of enthusiasm while she, in her turn, was astonished that he had so quickly forgotten the marks of tenderness she had recently bestowed upon him. The mystery was finally cleared up by the soothsayer Teiresias. From the double union twins were born: Hercules, son of Zeus; and Iphicles, son of Amphitryon.

Such were the more memorable of Zeus' love affairs. But many more were attributed to him, and his progeny was enormous.

Leda and the swan, by Leonardo da Vinci. From the two eggs at Leda's feet have been hatched Pollux and Helen, Castor and Clytemnestra.

Danae and the shower of gold. From a red-figured vase after Harrison and MacColl.

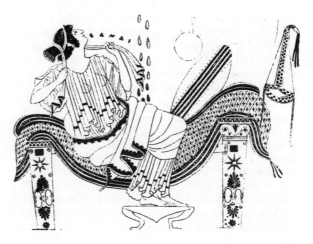

The huge list of Zeus' loves, both divine and mortal, and the list of the resultant progeny was enriched by the regional pride of various provinces of Greece or even small towns, eager to give themselves a divine ancestor. We have seen, in fact, how a number of Zeus' offspring became the ancestors of a tribe or the founders of cities. But some of these unions of the god can be explained in other ways. Some are solar myths: for instance the union of Zeus, god of the luminous ether, with Leto and Leda, who seem to have been deities of the night. Others are merely allegorical accounts of historical facts: the Phoenician Europa brought to Crete by a bull could represent the contribution of Asiatic civilisation to that of Crete, symbolised by the bull-god. Finally others are the romanticised expression of great natural phenomena: in the shower of gold which penetrates to the subterranean Danae it is easy to recognise the rays of the sun which germinate the seed buried in the ground.

In attributing to Zeus all these adventures, the Greeks then were not guilty of irreverence towards their god. They were only translating the emotions they felt in face of nature's great mysteries into gracious and poetic form. Or else, more naively, they were creating for themselves a noble ancestry.

Hera

The name Hera was once believed to be connected with the Latin root *herus* (master) and with an old Greek word which meant 'earth'. Today, however, it is agreed that the name is related to the Sanskrit *svar* (the Sky). Hera was then originally queen of the sky, the celestial virgin (hence her epithet Parthenia), and at first quite independent of Zeus. Their marriage was arranged afterwards, in order to explain the fusion of two cults which had at first been distinct. Some authorities even see in the hostility of Hera towards her husband a vestige of the resistance which the worshippers of Hera opposed to the rival cult of Zeus. Others interpret the noisy quarrels of the divine couple as a mythological translation of storms or the 'struggle of the meteors and atmospheric disturbances in revolt against the sky'.

Her Functions. Hera, however, soon lost her cosmic character and retained only her moral attributes. She was thought of as Woman deified. She presided over all phases of feminine existence. Thus Temenus, son of Pelasgus, consecrated three temples to her at Stymphalus: the first to the child-goddess, the second to the wife-goddess, the third to the widow-goddess. But primarily she was the goddess of marriage *(Gamelia)* and maternity. She represented the idealised type of wife.

Representations. Hera was depicted as a young woman, fully developed, of a chaste and rather severe beauty. Her forehead is normally crowned with a diadem or with a high crown of cylindrical shape, the *polos*. She wears a long tunic or *chiton* and is enveloped in a veil which adds to her noble bearing and her air of reserve and modesty. Her attributes are a sceptre surmounted by a cuckoo (an allusion to the circumstances of her nuptials) and a pomegranate,

Bust of Hera. Of oval shape, this is the classical Hera. Greek sculpture. National Museum, Naples.

symbol of conjugal love and fruitfulness. The bird sacred to her is the peacock, whose spangled plumage recalls the stars in the vault of heaven—and testifies to the service of hundred-eyed Argus.

Her Cult. Like Zeus, Hera was venerated on the summits of mountains. In Greece the chief centre of her cult was Argos. Here she had five or six temples, the oldest of which had been built by Phoroneus. It was the Heraeum at Argos which housed the famous statue of Hera in gold and ivory by Polycletus. The goddess was represented seated on a throne, her brow crowned by a diadem on which were depicted the Horae and the Graces. In her left hand she held a pomegranate and in her right a sceptre surmounted by a cuckoo. Near her stood her daughter Hebe.

Hera also possessed sanctuaries at Mycenae, Olympus, Sparta, in Attica, Boeotia and Euboea. She was particularly venerated in Crete and at Samos where the greatest of her temples stood; this was said to have been built by the Argonauts.

The Legend of Hera. Hera was the eldest daughter of Cronus and Rhea, and according to the Samians was born on the island of Samos, near a willow on the banks of the Imbrasos; this willow was still pointed out in the days of Pausanias. According to some, she had been brought up by Macris or by the daughters of the River Asterion; according to others, by the Horae or Seasons. Her childhood was spent on the isle of

Euboea and we have seen how her brother Zeus found her there and made her his wife. From then on Hera was associated with Zeus' sovereignty and became the chief feminine deity of Olympus. She sat on a golden throne beside her husband, and when she entered the assembly of the gods all rose in homage to her. On Olympus her marriage to Zeus had been the occasion of great rejoicing. All the Immortals had taken part in the wedding procession and the Fates themselves had chanted the hymeneal chorus.

But Hera's happiness was not unclouded. She had given Zeus four children: the gracious Hebe, Ilithyia, goddess of childbirth, the impetuous Ares, and the skilful Hephaestus. Her fidelity to her husband was exemplary. He, on the other hand, was constantly unfaithful.

It was not that she was lacking in charm. She took great care of her beauty. Every year she went to bathe in the spring Canathus at Nauplia and in these marvellous waters each time renewed her virginity. The 'white-armed goddess' was irresistible when she anointed her lovely body with an oil whose sweetness was such that it filled the whole earth and sky with its fragrance. When she had arranged her divine tresses, when she had pinned to her breast with golden clasps the robe Athene had woven for her with such art, put on her ear-rings, exquisitely worked and set with precious clusters of three drops, and draped from her head a glorious veil as white as the sun, Zeus himself, seeing her thus arrayed, cried: 'Never has love for goddess or mortal woman so flooded my senses and filled my heart!'

Hera would never have lacked suitors had she wished them. Ixion, King of the Lapithae, when invited to dine with the gods, had only to turn his eyes towards her to be inflamed with irresistible desire. In the madness of his passion he even embraced a cloud which Zeus had shaped to resemble Hera. Ixion was chastised for his insolence: he was bound to a fiery wheel which whirled him perpetually through the sky.

Hera, proud of her own virtue, did not endure the continual faithlessness of her husband without protest. Shortly after her marriage she left Olympus in vexation and returned to the isle of Euboea. In order to bring her back again Zeus employed a pleasant stratagem. He had a veiled statue carried around in a chariot and let it be known everywhere that this was the new fiancée of the master of the gods. In a transport of jealousy and wounded pride Hera waylaid the chariot, lacerated the robes of her supposed rival and, discovering the trick her husband had played on her, returned somewhat crestfallen to Olympus.

The renewed infidelities of Zeus incited her to avenge herself physically on his person. Assisted by Poseidon, Apollo and Athene, she once succeeded in binding him with thongs. This would have been the end of Zeus' power had not Thetis summoned to his rescue the hundred-armed giant whom the gods called Briareus and men called Aegaeon. 'Proud of his glory, he sat beside the son of Cronus; and the gods were struck with terror and did not enchain Zeus.' Hera considered it equally outrageous that Zeus

Above, the marriage of Hera and Zeus. Metope from Temple E, Selinus. The seated god looks at his new wife lovingly, while she slowly removes her nuptial veil. National Museum, Palermo.

Below, the bath of Hera. Ludovisi relief, believed to be remains of monumental bed sculpted by Polycletus for the Heraeum at Argos (fifth century B.C.). The goddess, attended by two nymphs, emerges from the spring of Canathus. This bas-relief was long held to show the birth of Aphrodite. Terme Museum, Rome.

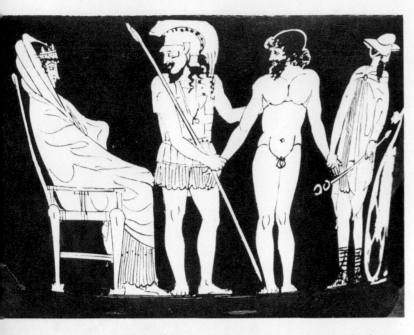

Ixion, about to be punished for aspiring to the favours of Hera. He is held before Hera's throne by Ares and Hermes. From a vase in the British Museum.

alone and unaided had given birth to Athene. In her rage she invoked the earth and the vast heavens and the Titans imprisoned in Tartarus, and implored their favour so that she, too, might bear unaided a child 'who should be in no way inferior in strength to Zeus'. Her wishes were granted and when her time came she gave birth 'not to a son who resembled gods or men, but to the frightful, the terrible Typhon, scourge of mankind'. This monster is confused with Typhoeus, son of Gaea and Tartarus, against whom Zeus had had so hard a struggle.

Hera was roughly punished for these vain attempts to revolt. One day Zeus beat and bruised her, and when Hephaestus tried to defend his mother Zeus seized his too-zealous son by one foot and flung him from the heights of Olympus. On another occasion Zeus attached an anvil to each of Hera's ankles, bound her hands with bracelets of unbreakable gold and suspended her from the sky, surrounded by clouds.

Though Hera was forced to submit she could at least vent her fury on her rivals. She caused Semele's death, for a long time persecuted Io, and tried to prevent the confinement of Leto and of Alcmene. She was equally remorseless towards the children of her rivals and towards their families. Hercules was her victim, and Ino, Semele's sister, was cruelly punished for having cared for the infant Dionysus.

The vindictive temper of the goddess was not only displayed when her conjugal honour was at stake. Because Antigone, daughter of Laomedon, had boasted of having hair more beautiful than Hera's, Hera turned her locks into serpents. Because they had treated a wooden statue of the goddess with contempt the daughters of Proetus, Lysippe and Iphianassa, were stricken with leprosy and madness. They went raging half-nude through the Peloponnese

and were cured only by the costly intervention of the seer Melampus. Melampus demanded as the price of his services a third of Proetus' kingdom. Proetus at first refused; but his daughters' madness became worse. He went again to Melampus, who raised his price and insisted on a second third of the kingdom for his brother Bias. Proetus consented, and Melampus obtained from Hera the two girls' restoration to health.

Finally Hera never forgave the Trojan Paris for having preferred Aphrodite on the occasion of the famous beauty contest on Mount Ida, and her rancour was satisfied only when the entire Trojan race had been annihilated.

Athene

Of the many derivations suggested for the name of Athene (or Athena) none is really satisfactory. The poetic epithet *Pallas* frequently joined to the name Athene comes either from the Greek 'to strike' or more probably from the Greek 'girl'.

Her Character and Functions. Although certain scholars have seen in Athene a personification of moisture, analogous to the Vedic Sarasvati, it seems more probable that she was in origin a storm- and lightning-goddess. Hence her normal attribute, the aegis—which in primitive times signified the stormy night—and her epithet as a goddess 'of the brilliant eyes'. She would thus be analogous to the Vedic goddess Vach. But Athene very quickly lost this meteorological character.

She had many aspects; ranked among the great divinities, she was venerated as a warrior-goddess, as goddess of the arts of peace and as goddess of prudent intelligence.

To Athene the warrior—her oldest manifestation—belong the epithets *Promachos* ('who fights in the foremost ranks') and *Alalcomeneis* ('who repulses the enemy'). She was the protectress of towns and the guardian of citadels.

The pacific Athene protected various industries. She was pre-eminently the *Ergane*, or working woman, and was the patron of architects and sculptors, as well as of spinners and weavers. She also protected horses *(Hippia)* and oxen *(Boarmia)*. The olive tree owed to her its fruit. Her wisdom, which earned her the epithet *Pronoia* (the Foreseeing), made her the counsellor-goddess *(Boulaia)* and the goddess of the Assembly *(Agoraia)*. Athene's emblem was the owl.

Her Cult. Though she was honoured throughout Greece Athene was the object of an especial cult in Athens. On the Acropolis she had, besides the Parthenon, two other temples: the temple of Athene Nike and the Erechtheum.

The chief festivals of the cult of Athene were the *Arrephoria*, in the course of which two little girls of noble family, from seven to eleven years old, descended from the Acropolis to deposit in an underground chamber near the sanctuary of Aphrodite mysterious objects which they carried in a basket; the *Scirophoria*, when priests and priestesses walked in solemn procession under a vast parasol *(sciron)*; and finally the *Panathenaea* which dated from the

Primitive terracotta Athene from Athens. Sixth century
B.C. *Berlin Museum.*

days of Theseus and consisted of a solemn procession
to the Acropolis in which a *peplos* made by the most
skilled workmen in Athens was carried to the goddess.
Taking part were not only priests and magistrates but
also girls carrying baskets, old men bearing olive
branches and young men on horseback. During the
Panathenaea races, gymnastic games and regattas
were held, and contests of music, singing and dancing
took place.

Representations. The oldest representations of
Athene were the *palladia*. Originally the palladia were
stones which were said to have fallen from the sky and
to which protective power was attributed. Later these
stones were replaced by statues in wood *(xoana)*
which had the same celestial origin. In them the
goddess was depicted with her body sheathed in
tight draperies, and in her hands she held a shield and
spear. The most celebrated statue of the warrior
Athene was that of the Parthenon, the work of
Phidias. The goddess, standing, wore a long chiton;
her head was helmeted, her breast covered with the
aegis, her right hand rested against a spear and in her
left hand she held a winged victory.

The Birth of Athene. When Zeus swallowed his
wife Metis she had been about to give birth to a child.
Shortly afterwards Zeus was tormented by an unbear-
able headache. To cure him Hephaestus—some said
Prometheus—split open his skull with a bronze
axe, and from the gaping wound, shouting a trium-
phant cry of victory, sprang Athene—'fully armed
and brandishing a sharp javelin'. At this sight all the
Immortals were struck with astonishment and filled
with awe. 'Great Olympus was profoundly shaken by
the dash and impetuosity of the bright-eyed goddess.
The earth echoed with a terrible sound, the sea
trembled and its dark waves rose . . .'

In Crete they said that the goddess had been hidden
in a cloud and that it was by striking this cloud with
his head that Zeus had caused Athene to emerge. The
event was supposed to have taken place near Cnossus
beside a stream, the Triton—whence the epithet
Tritogeneia (born of Triton) often given to Athene.
This epithet was also explained by making her the
daughter of Poseidon and of Lake Tritonis. Finally
some said that Athene's father was the giant Pallas,
whom she had killed because he wished to ravish her.
But these various relationships were dubious and it
was generally agreed that Athene was the daughter of
Zeus, engendered by the god himself.

Hera was infuriated by this birth of a daughter to
Zeus, in which she had played no part, and in attempted reprisal she herself had a child unassisted—but
it was a monster, Typhon.

Athene was Zeus' favourite child. His preference
for her was marked and his indulgence towards her so
extreme that it aroused the jealousy of the other gods.

'Thou hast fathered,' says Ares to Zeus, 'a rash and
foolish daughter who delights only in guilty acts. All
the other gods who live on Olympus obey thee and
each of us submits to thy will. But her thou curbest
neither by word nor deed; she does as she pleases.'

Athene, the Warrior Goddess. The manner in
which Athene made her first appearance revealed her
warlike proclivities. And, indeed, she delighted above
all in battle. We have seen her taking part in the war
against the giants, killing Pallas and hurling her
chariot against Enceladus, whom she finally crushed
under the island of Sicily. We find her again, equally
belligerent and ardent, in the battles which raged
beneath the ramparts of Troy. Not satisfied with
stimulating the ardour of the Greeks—whom she
favoured—she entered the skirmish herself. She put
on her head a helmet of gold with jutting crest 'vast
enough to cover the foot-soldiers of a hundred towns'.
Over her shoulder she slung the aegis, which she had
fashioned, according to some, from the skin of the

*Athene modelling a horse. Oinoche from Capua. About
460* B.C. *Athene was patron of architects and sculptors,
as well as of spinners. Former State Museum, Berlin.*

Athene Promachos, wearing her crested helmet and the aegis, with its head of Medusa and border of snakes. Statue of archaic style from Herculaneum. National Museum, Naples.

giant Pallas or which—as was more generally held—was made from the hide of the goat Amaltheia. Zeus had used it for the first time during the war with the Titans and afterwards presented it to his daughter. It was a sort of cuirass or breastplate, fringed and bordered with snakes and bearing in the centre the horrifying head of the Gorgon. Thus armed, Athene mounted the chariot of Diomedes, seized the whip and reins herself, and flung the horses against Ares, whom she stretched on the ground with one blow of the spear.

The memory of Athene's warlike prowess was perpetuated in Libya in annual festivals during which girls, divided into two camps, would stage a furious battle with sticks and stones.

Athene, Protectress of Heroes. Herself a warrior, Athene protected the brave and valorous. She stood beside Hercules, to help and comfort him, when as a victim of Hera's hostility he undertook his arduous labours. It was she who gave him the brazen cymbals whose sound frightened the birds of Lake Stymphalus. It was she who escorted him when he brought Cerberus from the Underworld. Finally it was she who, after his death, welcomed him on the threshold of Olympus. And so, when Hercules won the golden apples of the Hesperides, he offered them in homage to Athene.

In the same way Athene also guided Perseus on his expedition against the Gorgons. As the hero dared not look into the terrifying face of the Medusa she guided his arm so that he could strike the monster. In gratitude Perseus afterwards gave Athene the Gorgon's head, which she placed on her shield. Athene's part in the adventures of Perseus was so active that certain traditions say that she herself killed the Medusa by striking her during her sleep. This theory gave rise to several legends: for instance, that the battle between Athene and the Gorgon was the result of a beauty contest; and that the goddess gathered up the blood of her victim and made a gift of it either to Asclepius or to Erichthonius—blood from the left vein bringing death, blood from the right vein restoring life.

Athene was also kindly disposed towards Bellerophon: she appeared to him in a dream and gave him a golden bridle, thanks to which he was able to tame the horse Pegasus.

Finally she protected Odysseus successfully against all the perils which assailed him on his return from Troy, and in the guise of the sage Mentor she guided young Telemachus during his efforts to find his father.

Athene's Chastity. On all these occasions when Athene came to the aid of heroes it was because they were worthy of her esteem, not because of any amorous attraction. Athene was a striking exception to Olympian society because of her absolute chastity. In spite of calumny and insinuations about supposed relations with Helios, Hephaestus and even Hercules, her heart remained insensitive to the pangs of love and she defended her virginity fiercely. Woe to anyone who wounded her modesty!

One day when she was bathing with the nymph Chariclo, Teiresias happened to pass and saw her. Though his indiscretion had been involuntary, Athene nevertheless punished him by depriving him of his sight. In spite of her companion's plea for pity she refused to revoke her decision, but to soften the harshness of the punishment she conferred upon the unhappy Teiresias the gift of foretelling the future.

Hephaestus became enamoured of Athene. One day when the goddess came to see him about making a suit of armour for her he attempted to rape her. Athene fled, pursued by the limping god. He caught up with her, but she defended herself vigorously; Hephaestus, unable to accomplish his criminal design, scattered his seed on the earth, which shortly afterwards gave birth to a son, Erichthonius. The child was found by Athene, who brought him up unknown to the other gods. She enclosed the infant in a basket which she entrusted to the daughters of Cecrops, forbidding them to open it. One of them Pandrosos, obeyed; the other two, Herse and Aglauros, could not control their curiosity. But the moment they opened the basket they fled in terror; for around the infant was coiled a serpent. They were stricken with madness by Athene, and flung themselves

Athene taming a centaur, by Botticelli. Pitti Palace, Florence.

off the top of the Acropolis. Erichthonius grew to maturity and became king of Athens, where he established the solemn cult of Athene.

The Quarrel between Athene and Poseidon. Previously the goddess had already shown particular benevolence to the land of Athens. In the days of King Cecrops a dispute had arisen between her and Poseidon for the possession of Attica. To affirm his rights Poseidon struck the rock of the Acropolis with his trident and a salt water spring gushed forth. According to another tradition it was a horse which appeared under Poseidon's trident. Athene, in her turn, caused an olive tree to sprout on the Acropolis, a tree which could be seen in the time of Pericles, still alive in spite of having been burned by the Persians during the invasion of Xerxes. The gods were asked to settle the dispute and, on the evidence of Cecrops, pronounced in favour of Athene.

The Gifts of Athene. Athene was as benevolent in peace as she was redoubtable in war, and rendered valuable service to mankind. She taught the people of Cyrene the art of taming horses. She showed Erichthonius how to harness the first war chariots. She was present while Jason's companions were building the ship *Argo*. Her skill was revealed in the humblest handicrafts: she invented the potter's wheel and made the first vases. But above all she excelled in woman's work. The art of weaving cloth and embellishing it with wonderful embroidery held no secrets for her. The Immortals relied on her skill and it was she who embroidered Hera's veil. Jealous of her skill she allowed none to surpass her.

In Lydia there lived a girl named Arachne who was renowned for her skill in handling needle and spindle. One day she dared to challenge the goddess to compete with her. Athene arrived in the guise of an old woman and asked Arachne to withdraw her impious

Athene mourning the death of Achilles at Troy. Bas-relief in the Acropolis Museum, Athens.

challenge. Arachne refused. Athene reassumed her divine form and accepted the challenge. Arachne at once drew threads across her loom and with cunning hand guided the shuttle through the taut netting. As a subject, she had chosen to weave the loves of the gods. When she had finished she submitted her work to Athene for examination. The goddess tried in vain to discover any imperfection in it. Furious at her failure and unwilling to admit defeat, Athene changed Arachne into a spider and condemned her eternally to spin, and to draw from her own body the thread with which to weave her web.

Although Athene's activities were chiefly concerned with useful work she was not averse to artistic creation. Certain traditions originating in Boeotia, attributed to her the invention of the flute. They said that the goddess had thought of blowing into a stag's horn, pierced with holes, in order to imitate the plaintive whistling sound made by the Gorgon when Perseus cut its throat. But in Athens it was said that Athene had not persevered with her musical efforts because the Olympians had laughed at her when she blew out her cheeks and pursed her lips. So she had contemptuously tossed the flute aside and pronounced a curse on any person who picked it up. The satyr

The Temple of Athene Pronaia (the Foreseeing) at Delphi. Delphi was the foremost centre of divination in ancient Greece and its famous oracle was of ancient origin, having been associated with Gaea before it became specifically the sanctuary of Apollo.

Marsyas, who dared to take possession of the instrument, was cruelly punished for his imprudence.

Athene also at times took on the role of goddess of health: everyone knew how the architect Mnesicles, who had fallen while working on the construction of the Propylaea, and was in danger of death, had been miraculously healed by Athene, who was for this reason called Hygeia.

Athene extended her protection not only to individuals but also to entire cities. She was symbolised by the *Palladia* or statues of herself which, it was claimed had, fallen from heaven. The possession of a palladium was a pledge of security. Athens guarded one jealously in the Erechtheum. When Danaus fled from Egypt he was careful not to forget his palladium and carried it to Lindus in the island of Rhodes. The most celebrated palladium was that of Troy, which Zeus had presented to King Dardanus. According to others it had been made by Athene herself: heartbroken at having accidentally killed young Pallas, her playmate and the daughter of Tritonis, her foster-father, Athene carved from a tree trunk a statue reproducing the features of Pallas which she left with Zeus. Later Electra, whom Zeus seduced, took refuge behind this palladium. Zeus tossed it away and it fell on the land of Ilium, where Ilus had a temple built for it. When the Greeks laid siege to Troy they realised that they would never be victorious so long as the city retained its palladium. Diomedes and Odysseus therefore decided to steal the precious idol, and its theft spread discouragement among the Trojans. It seems, however, that Dardanus had taken the precaution of exposing to the faithful only a copy of the palladium, and had carefully concealed the original in the adytum—or innermost sanctuary—of the temple. Thus

it was the replica that the Greeks had stolen. As for the genuine palladium, after the fall of Troy it was taken to Italy by Aeneas. But it did not remain there. After many vicissitudes it was brought back to Amphissa in Locris, where it could be seen and venerated by all.

Apollo

The etymology of the name Apollo is uncertain. A connection has been suggested between the name and an old Greek verb which means 'to repel or set aside', and also an ancient form of a verb meaning 'to destroy'. (In the latter case Apollo would be the 'destroyer', as he appears to be in the *Iliad*.) A relationship between Apollo and the English word apple which would make of him a primitive apple-tree god is equally unsatisfactory.

Origin, Character and Functions. The same uncertainty surrounds Apollo's origin. Some authorities believe he came from Asia and was either a Hittite god, a Hellenic double of the Arab god Hobal, or a god of Lycia. Others, because of his close relations with the Hyperboreans, think that he was a Nordic divinity, brought by the Greeks from the North in the course of their migrations. It is difficult to decide between these two opposing schools of thought because, though both have plausible arguments, neither is conclusive.

The difficulty is that the legends of Apollo and his functions reveal divergences which are sometimes even contradictory. How is it, for example, that this pre-eminently Greek god was, in the *Iliad*, the ally of the Trojans—that is to say, the Asiatics? And if he was in fact of Asiatic origin, how can we explain his retreat in the Vale of Tempe and among the Hyperboreans? In this it is tempting to see a return of the god to the land of his origin.

As to his functions, they are so multiple and complex that it is often hard to connect one with another.

Apollo was first of all a god of the light, a sun-god—without, however, being the sun itself, which was represented by a special divinity, Helios. From this arose his epithets: Phoebus, the 'brilliant'; Xanthus, the 'fair'; Chrysocomes, 'of the golden locks'; as such he delighted in 'high places, the frowning peaks of high mountains, wave-lapped, beetling promontories'. This god of the light was the son of Latona or Leto—probably a double of the Asiatic Lada—who was undoubtedly a divinity of the night.

As a solar god Apollo caused the fruits of the earth to ripen, and at Delos and Delphi the first crops were therefore consecrated to him. In addition he protected

Opposite, Athene, helmeted and carrying a spear and shield decorated with her attribute, the owl, as she watches Hercules performing the first of his twelve labours, the killing of the Nemean Lion. Black-figured amphora by Psiax. Brescia Museum.

Opposite, the birth of Athene. Athene, daughter of Zeus
alone and embodiment of wisdom, springs fully armed
from her father's brow, which Hephaestus has just split
with an axe. Poseidon and the two Illithyias, goddesses
of childbirth, look on. Vase in the British Museum.

Above, Athene pouring a libation for Hercules, one of
the heroes whom she protected. Interior of a red-figured
cup in the Munich Museum.

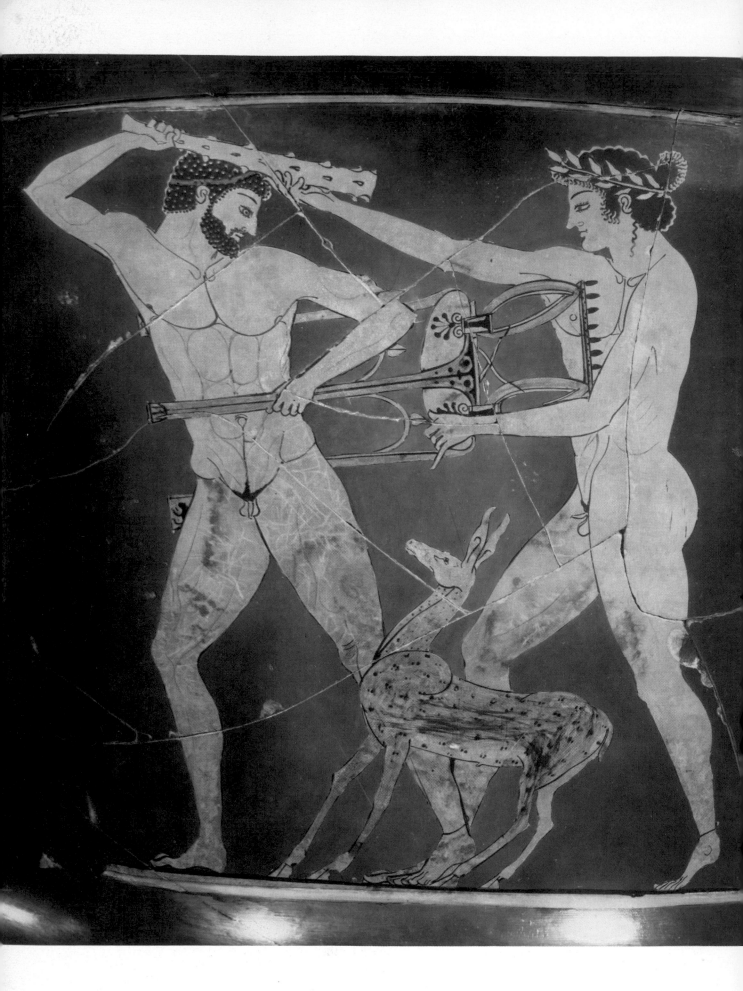

the crops by destroying the mice which infested the fields *(Apollo Smintheus)* and drove off the locusts which devastated the harvest *(Apollo Parnopius)*.

Because the sun is murderous when its rays strike like darts, and at the same time beneficent because of its prophylactic powers, Apollo was thought of as an archer-god who shot his arrows from afar *(Hecatebolos)*, as the god of sudden death; but also as a healer-god who drove away illness *(Alexikakos)*. In this latter function he had apparently supplanted a primitive deity Paeon (the healer) whose name is closely related to the divinity whom Homer calls the gods' physician.

Apollo was also the god of divination and prophecy. Apart from the many early oracles he possessed in Asia Minor, at Thymbra, Clarus, Grynia, Didymus, he had sanctuaries all over Greece where men came to consult him and where he pronounced judgment through the intermediary of priestesses, the Sibyls. Famous ones were those of Tegyra, near Orchomenus, and of Thebes in Boeotia, which was presided over by Teiresias' own daughter, Manto. At Thebes in the days of Pausanias the stone from which the priestess delivered her oracles could still be seen. It was called the Seat of Manto. Manto was afterwards led to Delphi, where she devoted herself to the cult of Apollo. The god, it was said, sent her to Asia Minor to found the oracle of Clarus.

But of all the sanctuaries of Apollo the most celebrated was that of Delphi, situated in a deep cavern from which emanated prophetic vapours. The priestess, or Pythia, sat on a tripod placed on the threshold of the cavern. Soon, under the god's influence, she would fall into a trance and, possessed by prophetic delirium, begin to pour forth broken phrases and

Apollo as a sun-god. In this role Apollo gradually supplanted the underworld divinities in their prophetic functions. Second-century bust found in the Temple of Mitra. Church of St. Clement, Rome.

obscure words which were then interpreted by the priest and members of the sacred counsel of Delphi.

This role of prophecy conferred on a sun-god is surprising in view of the fact that in Greece divination was reserved for underworld divinities. It is a fact, however, that Apollo ousted them all little by little. We must then assume that he already possessed this function when he came to Greece from Asia.

Apollo was also a shepherd-god *(Nomius)* whose mission it was to protect the flocks. We shall see later that flocks are often associated with Apollo. His epithet, Lycian—unless it simply signifies that he was of Lycian origin—can clearly be derived from the root *lux*, light, and would then be a qualifying epithet for a solar deity. But 'Lycian' is also related to the Greek word meaning wolf. The primitive Apollo could then have been a wolf-god (as Reinach conjectured) or else a god who killed wolves *(Lukoktonos)*—both equally applicable to a rural divinity. Apollo Nomius may be linked with Apollo Carneios (the ram-god of the Dorians) who was also a pastoral divinity.

Apollo is a musician-god as well, the god of song and the lyre. This is how Homer shows him when he described the gods listening to 'the sound of the gracious lyre which Apollo held'.

He is also a builder and a colonising-god who, as Callimachus says, 'delights in the constructions of town of which he himself lays the foundations'.

So many varying functions lead one to suspect that in Apollo there were many personalities, and the problem of his origin would be clarified by considering him to be a solar god from Asia who was merged with a pastoral god, the chief god of the Dorians.

Left, Head of the so-called Citharist Apollo, a classical portrayal of the god. National Museum, Naples. Right, Detail from an early statue of Apollo, the Apollo of Veio. Etruscan terracotta. Villa Giulia, Rome.

Opposite, Apollo and Hercules fighting over possession of the tripod from the oracle at Delphi. The Pythia had refused to answer Hercules when he went to Delphi for purification after murdering Iphitus, and he therefore seized the tripod. Zeus had to intervene to settle the dispute. Vase in the British Museum.

Apollo with his lyre. National Museum, Rome.

Representations. In spite of his multiple character Apollo always appears as a single type in the representations which were made of him. He was depicted as a young man of idealised beauty, with a vigorous body, a broad chest and slim hips. His beardless face with its delicate features is surmounted by a high forehead and thick, long hair which sometimes falls freely behind him, sometimes is knotted on top or at the nape of his neck so that only a few curls fall to his shoulders. He is generally nude or wears only a chlamys thrown over his shoulder. Sometimes, particularly when he is represented as a musician, he wears a long tunic with loose folds.

His attributes are the bow, the quiver, the shepherd's crook, the lyre. The animals which are sacred to him are the swan, the vulture, the crow, the cock, the hawk, the cicada, the wolf and the serpent. His favourite plants are the laurel, the palm, the olive and the tamarisk.

The Birth of Apollo. According to the oldest traditions Apollo's mother, Leto, daughter of Coeus and Phoebe, was the wife of Zeus before Zeus was married to Hera. This is how she appears in the *Iliad* where, like her son—and doubtless because of her Asiatic origin—she protects the Trojans. Hesiod also depicts her in this role and represents her as enveloped in a veil of sombre hue, a garment natural to a goddess of the night. Only later was Leto made a mistress of Zeus and a victim of Hera's

jealousy; and it is chiefly the history of her misfortunes which enriches her legend.

When Leto was pregnant with the twins Zeus had given her she wandered the earth in search of a place to give birth to them. But she was pursued by Hera's jealous fury and ranged Attica, Euboea, Thrace and the islands of the Aegean sea, in vain begging of each of these countries to receive her. All feared the anger of Hera and all 'were seized with dread and terror' and none dared receive her. But Leto at last found shelter. It will be remembered that Leto's sister, Asteria, had been changed into a quail because she had resisted the ardours of Zeus, then into the floating island of Ortygia. On the promise that Apollo would erect a splendid temple on its stony and barren soil, the island of Ortygia consented to receive Leto. Hera, however, had sworn that her rival would give birth only in a place where the sun's rays never penetrated. In order that this vow should not be broken Poseidon raised the waves like a dome over the isle of Ortygia which, at the same time, he anchored to the depths of the sea with four pillars. After the birth of Apollo, Ortygia was called by a new name, Delos—'the Brilliant'.

No longer able to prevent the birth she abhorred, Hera attempted at least to delay it. While all the other Immortals hastened to Delos to be with Leto, Hera detained Ilithyia, the goddess of childbirth. During nine days and nine nights Leto was the victim of atrocious suffering. Finally Iris was dispatched to Olympus and succeeded in fetching Ilithyia. Then, says a Homeric hymn to Apollo, 'Leto clasped a palm-tree in her arms, pressed the soft ground with her knees, and the earth beneath her smiled as the child leapt into the light. All the goddesses cried out with joy. Then, O Phoebus, the goddesses washed thee in sweet water, limpid and pure, and they gave thee for swaddling clothes a white veil of tissue, light and fresh, which they tied with a golden girdle.'

Leto gave birth at the same time to Artemis.

Owing to the similarity of place-names the birth of Apollo is sometimes placed in the sacred grove of Ortygia, in the neighbourhood of Ephesus.

Leto's tribulations did not end with the birth of Apollo. For fear of Hera she left Delos in haste and went to Asia Minor, to the land which later became Lycia. There one day she paused at the edge of a pool. She wished to quench her thirst but was prevented from doing so by rude shepherds who stirred the water to make it muddy. Leto punished them by turning them into frogs.

The Childhood of Apollo. The Serpent Python. Unlike other children Apollo was not nourished on his mother's milk. Themis put nectar and sweet ambrosia to his lips. Immediately the newborn baby threw off his swaddling clothes and was endowed with manly vigour, which he proved without delay in doing battle with the serpent Python.

This monster was a female dragon which the earth had given birth to and which had acted as nurse to Typhon. Hera, who was resolved to exterminate her rival, sent Python against Leto at the moment of Apollo's birth. But thanks to Poseidon, who had

40

The childhood of Apollo. Four days after his birth Apollo, held in the arms of Leto, lets fly an arrow at the serpent Python which has been sent by the jealous Hera. This event was said to have occurred at what was later to be called Delphi, but the palm trees in the centre symbolise the tree on Delos which Leto was supposed to have clutched during her nine-day labour. Black-figured Attic vase.

hidden Leto's retreat among the waves, Leto was saved and the serpent Python returned to its lair on the wooded slopes of Parnassus. Now, four days after his birth, Apollo set forth in search of a place to establish his sanctuary. Armed with the arrows which Hephaestus had forged for him, he descended from the heights of Olympus, crossed Pieria, Euboea, Boeotia, and arrived in the valley of Crissa. On the treacherous advice of the nymph Telphousa, who reigned over this region and wished to retain her position, Apollo wandered into the savage gorge of Parnassus which was the serpent Python's lair. The serpent saw the god and sprang at him. But Apollo let fly an arrow. 'Torn with cruel pain the monster lies shuddering: he rolls in the sand. He plunges into the forest and twists on the ground, now here, now there, until the moment when, with poisonous breath, he exhales his life in a torrent of blood.' Apollo contemptuously pushed his victim aside with one foot and said: 'Now rot where you lie.' And in memory of the occasion the spot where this dramatic encounter took place was called by the name *Pytho*—from the Greek 'to rot'. It was later changed to Delphi. As for Telphousa, the god punished her treachery by smothering her under a rock.

In order to purify himself from the stains he had got when killing the serpent, Apollo exiled himself to Thessaly, in the Vale of Tempe. When his period of expiation was concluded he returned to Delphi, his head crowned with sacred laurel, and escorted by a procession of priests, chanting hymns of triumph.

The memory of these events was perpetuated at Delphi by the festival of the *Septeria* (or Veneration) which was celebrated every nine years.

The Foundation of Delphi. Delphi was in fact Apollo's chosen land. Soon after his victory over the serpent Python he built an altar in harsh Pytho, in the midst of a sacred grove. The place was deserted and Apollo was wondering where he would find priests for his new cult when he perceived in the

distance on the dark sea a ship manned by some Cretans. Immediately assuming the form of a dolphin, he sped after the ship and leapt on to the deck, to the great terror of the sailors, who were even more terrified when their ship suddenly ceased to obey the oars and, deviating from its course, rounded the Peloponnese, entered the Gulf of Corinth and ran aground on the shores of Crissa. Apollo then reassumed his divine appearance and told the Cretans his will. 'From now on none of you will again return to your pleasant city. You will see your rich dwellings and your cherished wives no more; but you will guard my temple. You will know the designs of the immortal gods and, by their will, you will be perpetually honoured. You will have in abundance all that the illustrious tribes of men bring to me. And since you first beheld me on the dark sea in the shape of a dolphin, you shall invoke me by the name of the Delphinian.' Such was the origin of Delphi. The same episode explains the role of Apollo as god of navigation and marine expeditions, particularly colonisation.

But Apollo did not always remain at Delphi. Every year at the end of autumn he went away, beyond the Rhipaei mountains where the impetuous Boreas reigned, towards the mysterious land of the Hyperboreans. There, under a sky eternally bright, lived a happy and virtuous race of men devoted to the cult of Apollo. Leto herself, they said, was a native of this blessed land, which she had left in the guise of a she-wolf to come to Delos. With the return of the good weather Apollo would come to Delphi again in a chariot drawn by white swans or monstrous griffins. Some placed this annual exile of the god in Lycia.

The Exploits of Apollo. Apollo, the celestial archer whose arrows were long-ranged and infallible, was distinguished for many exploits. He fought against the Aloadae, Ephialtes and Otus. These two giants, sons of Aloeus or Poseidon, aspired to the hands of Hera and Artemis, and repeating the

The arrival of Hyperborean Apollo. Apollo came back from the land of the Hyperboreans with the annual return of good weather to Delphi. He arrived in a chariot drawn by griffins. Red-figured vase. British Museum.

Apollo as a pastoral god. During his servitude, Apollo tended the flocks of Admetus, King of Pherae. Black-figured Attic vase. Louvre.

audacious attempt of the Titans to scale Olympus, piled Pelion on Ossa to achieve their daring objective. They would have succeeded had not Apollo struck them down with his arrows. It is true that another tradition attributes the death of the Aloadae to Artemis. In the same way, Apollo slew the giant Tityus who had tried to rape Leto, his mother.

The god was no less ruthless towards mortals. In Phocis there was a man of extraordinary strength named Phorbas, chief of the Phlegyians. He would lie in wait beside the road which led to the temple of Delphi and force the passing pilgrims to fight with him. Having vanquished them he would then put them painfully to death. Apollo, disguised as an athlete, appeared one day and felled Phorbas with a mighty blow of the fist. Apollo even measured his strength against Hercules. Hercules had come to Delphi, but, not obtaining from the Pythia the oracle he hoped for, he seized the sacred tripod and carried it away. Apollo hastened after him, overtook him and prepared to fight it out. It required the intervention of Zeus himself to put an end to the combat. Zeus obliged Hercules to restore the tripod and reconciled the two adversaries. Indeed, Apollo tolerated no insult to his person or his cult. The archer Eurytus, who had dared to challenge him, perished for his presumption; and because at Troy Agamemnon had gravely offended his priest Chryses, Apollo let fly his exterminating arrows for nine days against the Greek army, sending innumerable warriors to the kingdom of Hades.

Among the Olympians Apollo enjoyed especial consideration. When he entered, the assembly of the gods all rose in sign of respect. Leto, his mother, would relieve him of bow and quiver, which she would hang from a golden nail. Zeus would welcome his son and give him nectar in a golden cup. The Immortals would then resume their places. Leto was proud to have borne this illustrious son who wielded the redoubtable bow.

Only the cunning Hermes dared to play tricks on his half-brother.

Apollo's Servitude. In spite of the marked favour which the master of the gods showed him, Apollo twice aroused the wrath of Zeus. The first time was when Apollo took part in the plot which Hera formed against her husband and which failed thanks to Thetis. In fury Zeus condemned Apollo, together with Poseidon, to go to Troy, there to enter the service of King Laomedon for a year. While Poseidon worked on the construction of the Trojan ramparts, Apollo pastured the royal oxen on the slopes and in the wooded gorges of Mount Ida. When the year had run its course Laomedon refused to pay the two gods the wages which had been agreed upon and even threatened to cut off their ears. In revenge Apollo spread plague through the country and Poseidon summoned a monster from the sea which killed men in the fields.

The second time Apollo incurred his father's anger was when, in order to avenge the murder of his son, Asclepius, whom Zeus had struck with a thunderbolt, Apollo killed the Cyclopes who had made the thunderbolt. Zeus punished him by sending him to serve Admetus, King of Pherae. Apollo tended his mares and ewes. He showed devotion to his mortal master, helped him to get married and even saved his life. These two episodes demonstrate the pastoral character of Apollo Nomius.

While he watched his flocks Apollo would play his lyre, for he was the most important of musician-gods. Attracted by the divine music, the fallow deer and hinds would come to frisk, and even the savage beasts of the forest joined in. Did Apollo invent the lyre? According to some he did; though it seems more likely that he received the instrument from Hermes.

Apollo would have it that no instrument could compare in beauty with the lyre or the cithara. One day while strolling on Mount Tmolus he was challenged to a musical contest by the satyr Marsyas, who had acquired a remarkable virtuosity on the flute which Athene had once cast aside. A jury was constituted among whom sat the Muses and Midas, King of Phrygia. When the tournament was finished Apollo was declared the victor. Only Midas voted for Marsyas. The god punished Midas by bestowing upon him a pair of ass's ears. As for his unfortunate rival, he attached him to a tree trunk, flayed him alive and suspended his body at the entrance of a cavern which could be seen in the neighbourhood of Celaenae in Phrygia. According to other traditions the contest took place between Apollo and Pan.

The Loves of Apollo.   It would seem that a god endowed with all the charms of youth, strength and grace would find few to resist him. Indeed the amorous adventures of Apollo were numerous; but several of them were singularly unfortunate—his mistresses were unwilling and the dénouements were tragic.

To be sure, he was loved by the Oceanid Melia, whom he made mother of Ismenius, by Corycia who gave him a son Lycoreus, and by Acacallis, mother of Phylacides and Philandros; but he tried in vain to seduce Daphne. This nymph, daughter of the River Peneius, was as chaste as she was beautiful. When she refused to submit to Apollo he attempted to take her by force; but she fled. He overtook her and she already felt the eager arms of the god around her when she called upon the venerable Gaea to aid her. Immediately the earth gaped open. Daphne disappeared, and in her place a laurel tree sprang from the ground. Apollo made it the plant sacred to him.

The nymph Cyrene, who was said to be the daughter of King Hypseus, was a huntress. Apollo saw her one day on the wooded slopes of Mount Pelion, wrestling with a lion. Charmed by her beauty

The contest of Apollo and Marsyas. Antique bas-relief. National Museum, Athens.

and courage, he carried her away in a golden chariot to Libya, where she gave birth to Aristaeus.

Nor did all mortal women submit to Apollo's desires. There was Castalia, a girl of Delphi, who, in order to escape the god's pursuit, threw herself into the fountain which afterwards took her name.

Acacallis—who must not be confused with the nymph of the same name—and Chione were loved simultaneously by Hermes and Apollo. Chione, daughter of Daedalion, had Autolycus by Hermes and Philammon by Apollo. Very proud of the beauty of her sons, she had the imprudence to scoff at the barrenness of Artemis, who in punishment pierced her with arrows. Acacallis, also called Deione, was the daughter of Minos. Her father had sent her to Libya, where she was seduced by Apollo. She had two sons by him, Amphithemis or Garamas and Miletus. When Miletus was born his mother, fearing Minos, had him carried into a forest and here, thanks to Apollo's protection, the wolves took care of the newly born babe who grew up among them. Shepherds discovered him and removed him from this savage existence. Later Miletus aroused the suspicions of Minos and fled to Asia Minor, where he founded the town of Miletus. Less fortunate was Linus, Apollo's son by Psamathe, daughter of Crotopus, King of Argos. Linus had been exposed by his mother, who wished to conceal his birth, and he was devoured by dogs. At the news Psamathe was overcome with grief and betrayed herself. Her father had her put to death. Apollo immediately struck the city of Argos with a terrible plague which ceased only when Crotopus was exiled. This Linus, who died in infancy, is not the musician hero whom Apollo had by Urania.

The adventure of Apollo and Coronis had a tragic sequel. Coronis, daughter of Phlegyas, King of the Lapiths, had yielded to Apollo and conceived a son. When she was on the point of giving birth to the child, she married the Arcadian Ischys. A crow, that Apollo had left with Coronis to watch over her, came at once to tell Apollo of the girl's infidelity. In his rage Apollo cursed the crow, whose plumage suddenly turned black, and put Coronis and Ischys to death. According to others he let Artemis avenge him. The

Apollo and Daphne. Villa Borghese, Rome.

two bodies were placed on the funeral pyre and the body of Coronis was already half consumed when Apollo arrived and tore from the flames the child who was about to be born. The child became the god of medicine, Asclepius. When Phlegyas learned who was responsible for the tragedy he marched on Delphi and burnt the temple of Apollo. But he perished, under the blows of the god and was thrown into Tartarus, cruelly tortured for his sacrilege.

One day while gathering flowers on the slopes of the Acropolis, Creusa, daughter of Erechtheus and Praxithea, was surprised by Apollo. She yielded to him in a neighbouring cavern. Here she later gave birth to a son, Ion. Apollo sent Hermes to fetch the child and bring him to Delphi, where he entered the service of the temple. Meanwhile Creusa had married Xuthus, but their union remained childless. The couple came to Delphi, where the oracle proclaimed that the first being whom they beheld would be their son. As they emerged from the temple the first person they encountered was the young Ion. Xuthus adopted him. Creusa, jealous, attempted to poison Ion, and Ion himself tried to kill Creusa. Then Pythia herself cleared up the misunderstanding and revealed to Creusa and Ion that they were mother and son. Athene also told Xuthus the truth, and from Apollo Xuthus received the promise that he would become the father of two sons, Dorus and Achaeus, who, with Ion, were the ancestors of the Greek race.

By Thyria Apollo had a son Cycnus, a youth of rare beauty who was attached by a tender affection to his companion of the chase, Phylius. When Phylius abandoned him, Cycnus in despair threw himself into Lake Canopus. Thyria, his mother, threw herself in after him; and Apollo changed them both into swans.

By a certain Cyrene, sometimes also called Asteria, Apollo had another son, Idmon, whom he endowed with the gift of foreseeing the future. When he was invited to take part in the expedition of the Argonauts, Idmon foresaw that he would die in the course of the voyage. He went, nevertheless, and was in fact killed by the bite of a snake.

Rhesus, son of Euterpe and Strymon, with two rearing horses. The oracle had said that if these horses drank the waters of the Xanthus Troy would become impregnable. Black-figured vase in the British Museum.

Evadne bore Apollo Iamus, a celebrated soothsayer and chief of the family of the Iamidae at Olympia.

Divination naturally plays an important role in the legends of Apollo. Thus, when Apollo fell in love with Cassandra, daughter of King Priam, he conferred upon her the gift of foretelling the future on her promising to yield herself to him. But Cassandra refused to fulfil her part of the bargain. Apollo then begged a single kiss. In this way he breathed into her mouth and, though he left her with the power of foretelling the future, he took from her the power of persuasion so that from then onwards no one would believe what Cassandra predicted.

Several youths were also loved by Apollo. Such was Cyparissus, whom the god changed into a cypress because the young man was heartbroken at having carelessly killed a favourite stag. Such also was Hyacinthus, son of Amyclas, King of Laconia. Now Hyacinthus was loved not only by Apollo but also by Boreas and Zephyrus. One day when Hyacinthus and Apollo were throwing the discus, Boreas and Zephyrus out of jealousy directed the discus which Apollo had just thrown so that it struck Hyacinthus on the head and immediately killed him. From the blood which gushed from the wound sprang the flower which bears his name, the hyacinth.

The retinue of Apollo

The Muses. In his aspect of god of music, Apollo's habitual companions were the Muses. Thus he was called *Apollo Musagetes*.

Originally the Muses, like the Nymphs, seem to have been deities of springs. Afterwards they became goddesses of memory, and then of poetic inspiration.

Their number varied. The first Muses worshipped on Mount Helicon were three in number: Melete, Mneme and Aoide. They were also three at Sicyon, as well as at Delphi, where their names—Nete, Mese and Hypate—personified the three strings of the lyre. There were seven Muses in Lesbos and in Sicily, eight for the Pythagoreans and in primitive Athens. It was finally agreed that there were nine Muses: Clio, Euterpe, Thalia, Melpomene, Terpsichore, Erato, Polyhymnia, Urania and Calliope.

Functions. The Muses were for long merged in an indissoluble choir which presided over music and poetry in general. It was only later that a special province was assigned to each.

Clio thus became the Muse of History. Her attributes were the heroic trumpet and the clepsydra, a time-measuring device.

Euterpe presided over flute-playing and her attribute was the flute.

Thalia, who was at first considered a bucolic Muse, became the Muse of Comedy. In her hands she carried the shepherd's staff and the comic mask.

Melpomene was the Muse of Tragedy. Her attributes were the tragic mask and also the club of Hercules.

Terpsichore, whose attribute was the cithara, was the Muse of Lyric Poetry and of the Dance.

Erato was the Muse of Love Poetry.

The Muses. Each is shown with her attributes. From left to right: Calliope, Thalia, Erato, Euterpe, Polyhymnia, Clio, Terpsichore, Urania and Melpomene. Sarcophagus in the Louvre.

Polyhymnia, after having been the Muse of heroic hymns, became the Muse of Mimic Art. She was represented in an attitude of meditation with a finger on her mouth.

Urania was the Muse of Astronomy and her attributes were the celestial globe and a compass.

Calliope, who was first in rank among her sisters, was considered in turn to be the Muse of Epic Poetry and Eloquence. Her attributes were the stylus and tablets.

Places of Cult and Representations. The cult of the Muses originated in Thrace, or more precisely in Pieria, as their oldest sanctuary testifies. It was established at Libethrum on the eastern slopes of Olympus, and then spread to Boeotia where, around Helicon, the centres of the cult were the towns of Ascra and Thespiae. In the rest of Greece the cult of the Muses was no less fervent. In Athens a hill near the Acropolis was consecrated to them and they were worshipped on the banks of the Ilissus. At Delphi they were venerated with Apollo.

Their former character of spring nymphs explains why numerous fountains were sacred to the Muses.

The Muses are represented as young women with faces smiling, grave or thoughtful, according to their function. They are dressed in long floating robes, covered by a mantle. Urania and Clio are normally depicted sitting. They are otherwise distinguished by their individual attributes.

The Legend of the Muses. As to the origin of the Muses traditions vary. Hesiod's opinion was, however, generally accepted, and he called them the daughters of Zeus and the Titaness Mnemosyne (or Memory).

It was told how after the defeat of the Titans the gods had asked Zeus to create divinities who were capable of celebrating the victory of the Olympians. The master of the gods then went to Pieria, where he shared Mnemosyne's couch for nine consecutive nights. When her time had come Mnemosyne gave birth to nine daughters, the choir of the Muses.

Although the Muses often frequented Olympus, where they added gaiety to the feasts of the Immortals with their singing, they preferred to dwell on Helicon, a high mountain in Boeotia whose wooded slopes were covered with fragrant plants which had the property of depriving snakes of their venom. Here

The Muses dancing with Apollo on Parnassus, by Giulio Romano. Pitti Palace, Florence.

numerous springs caused an agreeable freshness: the most celebrated were Aganippe and Hippocrene, which gushed forth under the hoof of Pegasus. Both had the virtue of conferring poetic inspiration on those who drank their waters. On the tender greensward which bordered these fountains the Muses 'with tireless feet would trace the graceful figures of a dance, full of charm, while they displayed the harmony of their brilliant voices', and when they were tired they would restore the freshness of their complexions in the azure waters of Hippocrene. When night came they would abandon the summits of Helicon and, wrapped in a thick cloud, draw near the habitations of men, who could then hear their melodious voices.

The Muses also liked to visit Parnassus in Phocis where they shared the company of Apollo. From the flank of this mountain came forth a spring, the fountain Castalia, which was sacred to them and whose waters also gave poetic inspiration. This fountain was said to communicate with the Cephisus— which also had its source on Parnassus—and was regarded as a mouth of the River Styx. The waters of Castalia were used in purification rites in the temple at Delphi, and they were given to the Pythia to drink. The Muses were thus closely connected with the cult of Apollo and as well as being patrons of poetry were guardians of the oracle of Delphi. They themselves, moreover, had the gift of prophecy: 'they said what is, what will be, and what has been'. It was they who taught Aristaeus the art of divination.

But their legend is chiefly concerned with their function as goddesses of song. Hesiod shows us the Muses on Olympus charming the great soul of Zeus. 'Their tireless voices flow from their mouth in sweet accents, and this bewitching harmony as it spreads afar brings smiles to their father's palace, their father who wields the thunderbolt.'

Like all goddesses the Muses were easily offended and punished those who dared compete with them. When the Thracian bard Thamyris boasted that he surpassed them, they struck him blind and dumb.

Pierus, King of Emathia in Macedonia, had nine daughters, the Pierides, who dared to challenge the Muses for the prize of poetry. They were changed into magpies by Apollo and the Muses took over their name.

Finally, the Sirens paid dearly for their presumption. Having issued a challenge to the Muses they were vanquished in spite of the irresistible sweetness of their voices, and in consequence were deprived of their wings.

Originally the Muses were represented as virgins of the strictest chastity. They had taken shelter one day with Pyreneos, King of Daulis in Phocis, when the king attempted to violate them. The Muses then took to wings and flew away. Pyreneos tried to follow, but he fell from the top of his palace and was killed.

Later all the Muses became less shy, and numerous love-affairs were attributed to them.

Calliope was not only loved by Apollo, by whom she had two sons, Hymenaeus and Ialemus; she also married Oeagrus, to whom she bore Orpheus, the celebrated singer of Thrace.

Melpomene lay with the river-god Achelous and became the mother of the Sirens.

Euterpe—others say it was Calliope or Terpsichore—had a son, Rhesus, by Strymon, the river-god of Thrace; Rhesus was slain by Odysseus and Diomedes during the Trojan war while he was leading a body of Thracians to the support of Troy, for an oracle had said that if the horses of Rhesus drank the waters of the Xanthus Troy would become impregnable.

Clio, having reproached Aphrodite for her passion for Adonis, was punished by Aphrodite, who roused in her heart an irresistible love for Pierus, King of Macedonia. By him Clio had Hyacinthus, whose unfortunate history, has already been described.

Thalia gave birth to the Corybantes after lying with Apollo.

By Amphimarus, the musician, Urania had Linus, who was also said to be the son of Apollo and Calliope or Terpsichore. To Linus was attributed the invention of melody and rhythm. It was told how he challenged Apollo to a singing contest and how Apollo killed him. Linus had a statue on Helicon where he was honoured as an equal of the Muses. Thebes claimed to possess his tomb.

Finally, Thamyris was supposed to be the son of Erato, and Triptolemus the son of Polyhymnia.

Artemis, as a huntress, accompanied by a hind. Louvre.

Artemis

The etymology of the name Artemis is obscure and gives us no precise indication of her complex character, in which, it would seem, different divinities are merged, as in the case of Apollo.

Character and Functions. The primitive Artemis, probably a replica of *Apollo Nomius*, was an agricultural deity, worshipped especially in Arcadia. She was the goddess of the chase and of forests *(Agrotera)*. Her symbol was a she-bear, which suggests that she was originally confused with Callisto, who was later made her companion. One is tempted to connect the Arcadian Artemis with Artio, the Celtic goddess of Berne, whose symbol was also a she-bear.

From the beginning Artemis was associated with Apollo and could not fail to participate in his nature: thus she is also a divinity of the light (Phoebe), though of the moon's light. Similarly, her lunar character gradually became less marked, as the appearance of a special moon-goddess, Selene, testifies. In her aspect of light-goddess she has the same functions as Apollo. Armed like him with bow and quiver, she bore the epithet *Apollousa*, the destructress; or *Iocheaira*, who liked to let fly with arrows, strike down mortals with her fearful darts, and afflict their flocks with deadly disease. Like Apollo she was the deity of sudden death, though it was usually women whom she struck. Like him, however, she brought prosperity to those who honoured her.

In her capacity of moon-goddess Artemis presided over childbirth, jointly with Ilithyia.

Finally Artemis was likened to other divinities who had no connection with her, such as the moon-goddess of Tauris, the Cretan goddess Britomartis, and Hecate, a Thracian divinity who was at the same time a moon-goddess and a goddess of the Underworld. There is even less connection between the Greek Artemis and the Artemis or Diana of Ephesus, a personification of fecundity, one of the forms of the great mother-goddess of the Orient.

Artemis was particularly venerated in Arcadia, but was worshipped throughout Greece, notably in the Peloponnese, at Sparta, at Caryae in Laconia, at Athens, Aegina, Olympia and Delos, where the laurel was consecrated to her and where Hyperborean girls brought their offerings to her. She was revered, too, in Crete, Asia Minor and Magna Graecia.

Representations. Although the lunar character of Artemis is sometimes recalled on coins by a torch held in her hand, or by the moon and the stars which surround her head, sculptors have chiefly emphasised her rural aspect. She appears to us as a young virgin, slim and supple, with narrow hips and regular features. Her beauty is a little severe, with her hair drawn back or partly gathered in 'a knot on her head. She wears a short tunic which does not fall below her knees: this is, in fact, the Dorian chiton which has been turned up and the folds held by a girdle. Her feet are shod with the cothurnus or laced buskin. She is usually accompanied by a hind or a dog.

Very different is the appearance of the crowned Artemis of Ephesus, whose body is tightly sheathed

Artemis, on the right, with Apollo and their mother Leto. Red-figured vase in the British Museum.

in a robe covered with animal heads which leaves her bosom with its multiple breasts exposed: a striking image of a fertility-goddess who has nothing to do with the Greek Artemis.

The Legend of Artemis. Artemis was occasionally presented as the daughter of Zeus and Demeter or Persephone; or else of Dionysus and Isis. But according to the tradition general among the Greeks she was the daughter of Leto, and Apollo's twin sister.

She was born, they said, on the sixth day of the month of Thargelion—a day before her brother—on the isle of Ortygia which took the name Delos only after the birth of Apollo. She shared the vicissitudes which marked the childhood of her brother, accompanying him on his expedition against the serpent Python and during his exile in Thessaly. Then Arcadia became her favourite abode. In this savage and mountainous region, where torrents tumbled down the woody slopes and plunged through narrow gorges, Artemis devoted herself to the pleasures of hunting, accompanied by sixty young Oceanids and twenty nymphs appointed to care for her pack of swift hounds. As soon as she was born she had, in fact, gone to find her father Zeus and, embracing his knees, begged from him, not ornaments or jewellery, but a short tunic, hunting boots, a bow and a quiver full of arrows.

When she had tired of tracking wild beasts or pursuing the light-footed roebuck she would pause beside the clear waters of a fountain and bathe with her companions until the freshness of the waters had assuaged her fatigue.

In this rude, outdoor existence there was no place for love. To the virgin huntress even the legitimate joys of marriage were repugnant, and she made chastity a strict law which she imposed on her com-

Artemis setting her hounds upon Actaeon. From a red-figured vase in the Berlin Museum.

Artemis and Apollo killing the children of Niobe. Kylix krater from Orvieto. Louvre.

panions. Woe to the nymph who had joined Artemis' band and then so far forgot her duty as to taste of forbidden pleasures! Even were she a victim of some god's trickery she was none the less cruelly chastised. The unfortunate Callisto, who had been approached by Zeus in the guise of the goddess herself and seduced, fell beneath Artemis' arrows when her disgrace became known.

Woe, also, to the imprudent man who gave way to his curiosity! Actaeon, son of Aristaeus and Autonoë, was himself a passionate huntsman. One day, accompanied by his hounds, he was chasing a stag when he came to the valley of Gargaphia, near the fountain Parthenius, where at that moment Artemis and her companions happened to be bathing. Ravished by the beauty of the goddess. Actaeon paused to contemplate her. He was observed. Enraged that a mortal should have seen her in her nakedness, Artemis changed Actaeon into a stag and set his own pack on him. The hounds tore Actaeon to pieces and devoured him.

But on one occasion, it would seem, Artemis' own heart was stirred by the hunter Orion. Perhaps she might even have married him had not Apollo intervened. One day when Orion, a strong swimmer, was bathing in the sea, he had swum far from shore and had nearly vanished on the horizon when Apollo challenged his sister to hit the scarcely perceptible point which, far out to sea, moved on the surface of the waves. Artemis, not realising that the distant object was Orion, accepted the challenge, bent her bow and shot an arrow. It pierced Orion's temple. Did Apollo wish to safeguard his sister's honour, or was he motivated by secret jealousy? Certain traditions do, indeed, claim that he had ravished Artemis on his own altar at Delos.

Elsewhere it was told that Orion perished for having dared to touch the goddess one day when they were hunting together in the island of Chios. Artemis summoned a deadly scorpion from the earth which stung Orion on the heel.

This version tallies better with what we know of the dark and vindictive character of Artemis. When Apollo punished Tityus for the outrage done to Leto,

his mother, Artemis seconded him. The death of the Aloadae was also sometimes attributed to her: the two giants having attempted to violate her, Artemis turned herself into a white doe and got between them in such a way that, trying to strike the beast with their javelins, they ran each other through instead.

We have seen how Artemis killed Chione whom her brother loved, because Chione was vain of her children's beauty. Niobe was punished still more harshly. Daughter of Tantalus, Niobe had six sons and six daughters by her husband Amphion. In her maternal pride she dared to disparage Leto, who had brought only two children into the world. To punish this insolence Apollo and Artemis struck down all twelve of Niobe's children with their arrows and Niobe, heartbroken, at last persuaded Zeus to change her into a rock.

The slightest negligence towards Artemis was apt to be punished. Admetus, who had omitted to offer sacrifice to the goddess on his marriage, had when he entered the bridal chamber the disagreeable surprise of finding it full of snakes. Oeneus, who reigned at Calydon in Aetolia, forgot to consecrate the first fruits of his crop to Artemis: his territory was ravaged by a prodigious boar and, in the course of the adventures which accompanied and followed the capture of the monster, his whole family perished.

It was also for offending the goddess, either by killing a stag in a wood that was sacred to her or by boasting that he was a more skilled hunter than she, that Agamemnon was wind-bound in the port of Aulis, together with the Greek fleet. He could obtain the return of favourable winds only by sacrificing to Artemis his own daughter, Iphigenia. But the goddess took pity on the innocent victim and snatched Iphigenia away at the moment of sacrifice, bearing her to Tauris where she was made a priestess of Artemis' cult.

In the Tauric Chersonese there existed, in fact, a local divinity who was later identified with the Hellenic Artemis and who was honoured by blood sacrifices. All strangers who were shipwrecked on the coasts of Tauris were sacrificed to her. Iphigenia presided over the sacrifices. One day her brother Orestes approached these inhospitable shores. He was condemned to death, but he revealed himself to his sister and together they fled, carrying with them the statue of the goddess, which was deposited in the town of Brauron in Attica and later transferred to a sanctuary on the Acropolis in Athens. It was venerated under the name of *Artemis Brauronia*, the bear being sacred to her. The story was told that a tame bear which wandered freely through the villages of Attica one day lacerated a girl with its claws. It was killed by the girl's brothers. Artemis in anger at once sent a deadly plague to Athens. The oracle, when consulted, replied that the scourge would cease only if the inhabitants consecrated their daughters to Artemis, and this they did every five years.

The town of Limnaion in Laconia also gloried in the possession of the true Taurian Artemis. The statue had been found standing upright in the middle of a thicket—for this reason it was called *Artemis Orthia* (the upright)—and the discovery had been accompanied among the inhabitants of Limnaion and the neighbouring villages by an outbreak of madness, murders and epidemics. They succeeded in appeasing the bloodthirsty goddess by human sacrifices, later replaced by the flagellation of youths in front of the statue of Artemis. The statue was carried by the priestess, and it became heavier whenever the zeal of those performing the flagellation slackened.

We should be wrong, however, to consider the daughter of Leto only under this rough and barbarous aspect. Though she loved to roam the mountains and the valleys, she also permitted herself more gentle amusements. She was the sister of Apollo, god of the cithara, and she too was a musician-goddess: singing and dancing were pleasing to *Artemis Hymnia*. 'When the chase has rejoiced her heart she unbends her bow and enters the vast dwelling-place of her

Left, Artemis of Ephesus, goddess of fertility. Capitoline Museum, Rome.
Right, An Amazon. Vatican Museum, Rome.

brother in the rich land of Delphi and joins the lovely choir of the Muses and the Graces. There she hangs up her bow and arrows and, gracefully dressed, leads and directs the choir.'

Artemis of Ephesus and the Amazons. We have said above that by a rather strange confusion the name of Artemis had been given to a fertility-goddess particularly venerated at Ephesus. The origin of this cult was said to go back to the Amazons, a mythical people of female warriors who had come from the region of the Caucasus to settle in Cappadocia on the banks of the Thermodon. There the Amazons founded a state whose capital was Themiscyra and which was ruled over by a queen. Men were not admitted. Once a year the Amazons would go to their neighbours the Gargarensians to form temporary unions. Of the resulting children they would keep only the girls who were trained from infancy for the chase and for war.

To the Amazons was attributed the foundation of many towns: Smyrna, Ephesus, Cyme, Myrina and Paphos. From Cappadocia they reached the islands, landed at Lesbos and Samothrace, and had even penetrated Boeotia and Attica. The motive for this invasion of Attica was to avenge the abduction or the abandonment—one does not know exactly which—of Antiope by Theseus. Antiope was the sister of the Amazon queen, Hippolyta. In Athens they used to show the tombs of the Amazons who had perished in the course of the war, and every year the Athenians offered sacrifices to the *manes* of their enemies. The Amazons also fought in Lycia against Bellerophon, and against Hercules, who slew Hippolyta, their queen. During the Trojan war they came to the aid of Troy and saw their young queen, Penthesileia, fall beneath the blows of Achilles. It was also told how they sent an expedition against the island of Leuce

Achilles killing Penthesileia, Queen of the Amazons, during the Trojan War. Red-figured Attic cup, about 460 B.C. Munich Museum.

in the Black Sea, where they were put to flight by the shade of Achilles, whose sanctuary they were about to sack.

By their warlike habits and their horror of men the Amazons offer some resemblance to the Greek Artemis, which is doubtless the reason why their great goddess was given the same name.

Hermes

As in the case of the other Greek gods, many etymologies have been put forward for the name Hermes. Some suggest a connection with the Vedic Sarameya, derived from Sarama, god of the storm or of the dawn; others relate Hermes to a Greek word which conveys the idea of movement; still others—thinking of the early representations of the god—suggest the word for 'stone' or 'rock', and also the verb which means 'to protect'.

Character and Functions. Certain details of Hermes' legend suggest that he was either a god of

Hermes of Andros. School of Praxiteles. National Museum, Athens.

the twilight or of the wind. Such are his birth, his theft of Apollo's heifers—analogous to the cows of the Vedic Indra, which personified the clouds, the myth of his slaying Argus, later thought to explain the epithet *Argephontes*, a probable corruption of *Argeiphantes*, 'he who makes the sky clear'. It is, however, more probable that Hermes was a very ancient Pelasgian divinity, of Thracian origin, who was particularly honoured by the shepherds of Arcadia and whose mission was to watch over their flocks and protect their huts. From this doubtless arose the Greek habit of placing at the doors of houses a more or less crude image of this god. The Dorian invasion lessened the prestige of Hermes. Apollo Nomius took his place, and the primitive Hermes of the shepherds and of animal fertility took on another character.

Hermes was above all thought of as the god of travellers, whom he guided on their perilous ways. His images were placed where country roads branched and at crossroads in towns. It is without doubt a natural extension of this role that Hermes was also charged with conducting the souls of the dead to the Underworld. But this *Hermes Psychopompus* (conductor of souls), who is sometimes differentiated from the celestial Hermes, may have been a substitute for some older subterranean divinity, a kind of *Zeus Plutos*.

Since in primitive times voyages were scarcely undertaken except for commercial purposes, Hermes was consequently the god of commerce, the god of profit—lawful and unlawful—and the god of games of chance. And, since buying and selling require much discussion, and the art of the trader is to overcome the buyer's hesitation by subtle persuasive words, Hermes became the god of eloquence, the god *Logios*.

To these various functions Hermes added that of being the messenger of Zeus. This is how he appears in Homer, where he is qualified with the epithet *Diactoros* (the messenger). He comes to earth ceaselessly with orders from the king of the gods and undertakes the most delicate missions. In Hesiod, Hermes is the god who brings to men's hearts the impressions and sentiments which Zeus has inspired.

This indefatigable runner could scarcely fail to be honoured by athletes. Thus he had the epithet *Agonios*, 'who presides over contests', especially in Boeotia. His statue stood at the entrance to the stadium at Olympia, and the invention of boxing and racing was attributed to him.

Representations. The classic aspect of Hermes is that of an athlete-god. In primitive times he had been represented as a mature man with a thick, long beard, his hair bound with a fillet and falling in curls to his shoulders. Afterwards he became the idealised type of the *ephebe* or young gymnast, with lithe and graceful body. His hair is short and crisp, his features fine; he carries his head slightly inclined as though listening with friendly interest. His nervous and supple body is largely exposed by the chlamys tossed over his shoulder or wound round his left arm. He often wears a round, winged hat—a *petasus*—and on his feet there are winged sandals. In his hand he

The Hermes of Ammon. This representation of Hermes, with its ram's horns and ears, is symbolic of the god's pastoral associations. National Museum, Naples.

holds a winged staff around which serpents are entwined; this is the *caduceus*.

The Theft of Apollo's Heifers. Hermes, son of Zeus and Maia, was born in the depths of a cave on Mount Cyllene in Arcadia. On the day of his birth Hermes displayed his mischievousness by stealing the cattle entrusted to Apollo. Sneaking furtively from his cradle, the infant god climbed the mountains of Pieria, where he found the divine herd. From it he separated fifty lowing heifers which he drove before him under cover of the night to the banks of the Alpheus. He made them walk backwards so that their hoofmarks should not betray the direction they had taken. He himself had cautiously put enormous sandals of tamarisk and myrtle twigs on his delicate feet. Before shutting up the heifers in a cavern he picked out two of the fattest and, having ingeniously produced fire by rubbing twigs of laurel together, he roasted them, dividing the flesh into twelve equal portions in honour of the twelve great gods. After which he regained the heights of Cyllene, re-entered his cave through the keyhole, 'like vapour or a breath of autumn', and crawled into his cradle again. On the following day Apollo noticed the disappearance of his heifers. He grasped—by divination—what had occurred and went at once to Cyllene, where Hermes stubbornly denied all knowledge of the theft. Apollo seized the infant in his arms and carried him to the tribunal of Zeus on Olympus. The master of the gods could not but laugh at the cunning of his newborn child but, as he also cherished Apollo, he instructed Hermes to return the heifers.

The Invention of the Lyre. Reconciliation between the two gods was completed by the gift Hermes made to Apollo of a musical instrument he had ingeniously devised. When he had set out on his nocturnal adventure, Hermes found a tortoise in his path. He picked it up and, with a bright chisel, emptied the shell. Around it he stretched oxhide

with the aid of reeds and arranged over a bridge seven strings made from sheep gut which then gave out harmonious sounds. It was the first lyre.

When Apollo, still annoyed by the theft of his heifers continued bitterly to reproach him, Hermes struck the strings of the instrument he had just fashioned. Apollo was charmed by the sound and his anger died—'while the delightful sound of the divine music penetrated his senses, a sweet desire took possession of him'. Hermes guessed that Apollo coveted the lyre and spontaneously gave it to him. In exchange Apollo gave Hermes a bright whip or a golden wand—a prototype of the caduceus—and entrusted him with the care of the celestial herd. From then on Apollo became the god of music and Hermes the protector of flocks and herds. The friendship of the two gods was never broken. On many occasions Hermes was of service to Apollo and, in particular, took charge at their birth of several of Apollo's children.

The Good Offices of Hermes. In spite of his playfulness and pranks Hermes won the sympathy of all the gods. Even the vindictive Hera forgot her jealousy where Hermes was concerned. Alone among the illegitimate children of Zeus, the son of Maia found favour with her and the august goddess even consented to suckle him.

Hermes was always willing to be helpful, and his ingenuity made him a valuable ally. During the war against the giants he put on the helmet of Hades—which made him invisible—and killed the giant Hippolytus. We have already seen how he freed Zeus, when Zeus was a prisoner of Typhoeus. He restored Zeus' strength by replacing the nerves which the giant had cut. During Zeus' amorous adventures, Hermes' aid was invaluable: he put the giant Argus

Hermes speeding across the waves and holding a lyre — the instrument which he invented and gave to Apollo in exchange for a golden whip, symbol of his role as protector of herds. This exchange sealed the friendship between the two gods. Red-figured cup in the British Museum.

Above, Hermes as god of travellers leading four horses. Black-figured vase in the British Museum.
Below, Hermes, wearing his winged hat and sandals, carries a wine jar and drinking cup and is accompanied by a satyr carrying a lyre. Red-figured vase painting.

to sleep with the sound of his flute and then, in order to free Io, killed him. When Dionysus was born it was Hermes who carried the child to Orchomenus and delivered him into the hands of Ino, Semele's sister. Zeus moreover made him his messenger. In order to cross the celestial spaces rapidly Hermes wore winged sandals which bore him 'over the watery sea or over the vast earth like a breath of wind'. To aid his flight he sometimes added wings to his hat.

When Ares fell into the hands of the Aloadae and was kept captive for thirteen months without anyone's knowing the place of his captivity, it was Hermes who finally discovered his prison and set him free. Again it was Hermes who found in the abode of Tantalus the golden dog Pandareus had stolen from Zeus.

Hermes' protection was also extended to heroes: when Perseus faltered he restored his courage, and he accompanied Hercules down to the underworld.

Hermes was a benefactor of mankind, and protected their flocks, guided them on their voyages, presided over their business affairs and inspired in them melodious speech and eloquence. Often he also took a direct part in their affairs. He plunged the Greeks into deep slumber with the aid of his magic wand 'with which he made drowsy the eyes of mortals or, if he so desired, roused them from sleep'. In doing this he made it possible for Priam to bring the body of his son Hector back into the walls of Troy. He gave Odysseus a magic plant which made him immune to the enchantments of Circe.

Hermes, as we have seen, was also concerned with the Underworld; for it was he who conducted the souls of the dead to their final dwelling-place. For this reason he was called *Psychopompus*.

Homer shows us the souls of Penelope's suitors slain by Odysseus as they fly after Hermes, rustling like bats, until they reach the 'fields of asphodel where dwell the phantoms of those who are no longer'. Hermes could also lead back the souls of the dead into the world of light. When Tantalus cut his own son into pieces and served them as a feast for the gods, Hermes, on the instructions of Zeus, reassembled the pieces and restored the young man to life. Hermes also accompanied Orpheus on his search for Eurydice.

The Sons of Hermes. Hermes, like the other gods, had many amorous adventures. Among the goddesses he was, it appears, the lover of Persephone, Hecate and Aphrodite. Among nymphs, whom he pursued in the shady depths of forests, his conquests were wider. By them he had a numerous progeny among whom it is sufficient to mention: Saon, son of the nymph Phene, who colonised Samothrace; Polydorus, son of the Thessalian nymph Polymele; Daphnis, the beautiful and unhappy shepherd of Sicily, who was born in the neighbourhood of Etna; and above all Pan, the rustic god of Arcadia. While tending the flocks of Dryops on the slopes of Mount Cyllene, Hermes saw Dryops' daughter and loved her. She brought into the world a son who was covered with hair and had the horns and feet of a goat. In horror she abandoned him, but Hermes picked him up, wrapped him in the skin of a hare and then carried him to Olympus where the gods delighted in the spectacle. According to another tradition, Pan was the son of a mortal, Penelope, whom Hermes came to in the guise of a he-goat.

Among the mortals whom Hermes loved were Akakallis, daughter of Minos, whom he made mother of Cydon, founder of the Cretan town of Cydonia, and Chione, who also bore him a son, Autolycus. Autolycus received from his father the gift of rendering what he touched invisible. In this way he was able to commit numerous thefts until one day Sisyphus, whose oxen he had stolen, caught him.

Ares

Should we connect the name Ares—like Mars—with the Sanskrit root *mar*, from which derive the Vedic *maruts*, storm-divinities? Or with the Greek root which means 'carry away, destroy'? Both hypotheses are equally ingenious but neither seems very plausible.

Character and Representations. Ares originated in Thrace. He was always thought of by the Greeks with more terror than sympathy, and his role was strictly limited. He was simply the god of war, of blind, brutal courage, of bloody rage and carnage. Hypotheses which would make him primitively a fertility-god or a solar deity seem to be unfounded.

Actually we know little more about this god than what the poets tell us. He was, however, honoured throughout Greece and his cult was particularly developed in Thrace and Scythia. He had a temple in Athens. Olympia honoured him under the name

Ares and Aphrodite feasting on Olympus. Red-figured cup in the British Museum.

Ares Hippios, and Sparta under that of Ares Enyalius (the warlike). A spring was consecrated to him near Thebes, beneath the temple of Apollo.

In Greek sculpture Ares was not represented by any especially fixed type. We scarcely know him except from vase paintings. At first he was depicted as a bearded warrior wearing a helmet with a tall crest and dressed in heavy armour. Later he appears as a young man, almost nude, who has retained few of his warlike attributes except the spear and helmet.

The Rages of Ares. 'Of all the gods who live on Olympus', says Zeus in the *Iliad* to Ares, 'thou art the most odious to me; for thou enjoyest nothing but strife, war and battles. Thou hast the obstinate and unmanageable disposition of thy mother Hera, whom I can scarcely control with my words.'

In expressing these hostile sentiments to his son, the master of the gods exactly defines the character of Ares, 'a furious god, by nature wicked and fickle', who in the immortal society of Olympus apparently found very little sympathy.

As god of war it was natural that he enjoyed fighting. Mounted on a chariot drawn by swift horses with golden brow-bands, clad in bronze armour and grasping in his hands an enormous spear, Ares ranged the battlefield, striking deadly blows on all sides. His two squires, Deimos (Fear) and Phobos (Fright)—sometimes said to be his sons—accompanied him, together with Eris (Strife), 'insatiable in her fury', Enyo, 'destroyer of cities', and the Keres, sombre divinities, eager to drink the black blood of the dying.

Though none disputed his warlike ardour, Ares was disliked not only for his perpetual thirst for blood and slaughter which made him the 'scourge of mortals', but for his brutality and blind violence. It was in this, especially, that he differed from Athene who, as a warrior-goddess, represented cool and intelligent courage. Ares and Athene were thus constantly opposed. Many times they encountered each other

Ares Ludovisi, an example of the later, softened representations. While the god rests, Eros plays at his feet. Terme Museum, Rome.

53

on the plains of Ilium where they fought on opposite sides. The very sight of Athene set Ares in a rage. 'Why, then, shameless fly, dost thine insatiable audacity enflame the war between the gods? What ardour carries thee away? I think that today thou shalt pay for all thou hast done to me!' With these words he struck the terrible aegis which even the thunderbolt of Zeus could not break. Athene, drawing back, took up a stone which was lying on the plain: a black stone, rugged and enormous, which men of past ages had put there to serve as a boundary stone for the field. She hurled it at the neck of the impetuous Ares. His knees gave way and when he fell his body covered seven acres. Dust soiled his hair and his armour jangled about him. Pallas Athene smiled and, glorying in her exploit, addressed to him winged words: 'Vain fool! Hast thou not yet learned how superior my strength is to thine?'

Indeed the impetuous Ares, contrary to what one might expect, rarely emerged victorious from combat. Nor was it only the immortal gods who got the better of him. Otus and Ephialtes, the two Aloadae, succeeded in binding and keeping him captive for thirteen months. When he challenged Hercules, who had just killed his son Cycnus, Ares was wounded by the hero and forced to return groaning to Olympus. According to others, Zeus, who did not wish to see his two sons quarrel, put an end to the fight by dropping a thunderbolt between the two combatants.

The Loves of Ares. He was scarcely more happy in his love affairs. Impressed by the glamour of the handsome warrior whom she doubtless compared with Hephaestus, her ill-favoured husband, Aphrodite fell in love with Ares. The sentiment was quickly reciprocated. Ares took unscrupulous advantage of Hephaestus' absence to dishonour the marital couch; but Helios, who had observed the two lovers, reported the matter to the smith-god. Although a deceived husband is usually an object of ridicule, Hephaestus was able to parry the laughter by an ingenious artifice. Secretly he forged a net so fine that it could not be seen, but so strong that it could not be broken. He arranged this net above the couch where the lovers normally frolicked, and pretended to leave for Lemnos.

Ares and Aphrodite. Mural painting from Pompeii. National Museum, Naples.

As soon as Ares saw the industrious Hephaestus depart he made his way towards the dwelling-place of the illustrious god, burning with love for Cytheraea of the fair crown. She was seated. He took her hand and said. 'Come, my dear, let us lie on the couch of Hephaestus, for thy good man has gone to Lemnos, the land of the barbarous-tongued Sintians.' Thus he spoke, and his words were pleasing to the goddess. Soon they fell asleep and the invisible net of the ingenious Hephaestus spread over them. Then the limping god, who had retraced his steps, cried out in a terrible voice to all the gods:

'Zeus and ye Immortals! Come in haste and see this intolerable thing, worthy of your laughter. Because I am lame Aphrodite despises me. She loves the fatal Ares because he is agile and handsome. See them both, asleep on my couch. Soon they will no longer care to sleep; for these cords will keep them bound together until Zeus returns the gifts I made him in order to obtain this impudent wench who cannot restrain her lust!'

Then the gods gathered together in the palace of bronze and from their throats rose roars of uncontrollable laughter which threw Ares and Aphrodite into a state of extreme confusion. Hephaestus at last consented to free the two guilty ones when Ares promised to pay him the price of the adultery. The guilty wife fled to Paphos in the island of Cyprus and the seducer retired into the mountains of Thrace. From the union of Ares and Aphrodite a daughter was born, Harmonia, who later became the wife of Cadmus, King of Thebes.

The combat of Ares and Hephaestus over Aphrodite. They are watched by Hera on her throne. Satirical vase-painting in the British Museum.

Opposite, Artemis, goddess of hunting, shooting a stag with her bow and arrow. She is accompanied by her retinue of Nymphs. Vase in the British Museum.

54

Opposite, an Amazon wearing armour and carrying a spear. The best-known exploits of these female warriors, who were connected with the cult of Artemis of Ephesus, occurred during the Trojan War and in battles against Bellerophon and Hercules. Red-figured vase in the Munich Museum.

This page, Helios, god of the Sun, rising at dawn from the sea. The boys plunging into the sea in front of his chariot represent the fading stars. Vase in the British Museum. The white winged horses of Helios, which drew his chariot across the skies. Greek sculpture.

Whether Ares had other misadventures of this nature is unknown, but he had little luck with his children.

By the nymph Aglauros Ares had a daughter, Alcippe. One day Halirrhothius, son of Poseidon, ravished her and Ares killed him. For this murder Poseidon summoned him before the tribunal of the twelve great gods, which met on a hill situated in front of the Acropolis in Athens. Ares was acquitted. In memory of this event the hill received the name of the Areopagus, and afterwards criminal cases continued to be judged there.

Among the other children of Ares who came to unhappy ends it is sufficient to mention: Phlegyas, son of Chryse, who was killed by Apollo; Diomedes, King of the Bistones of Thrace, who was put to death by Hercules; Cycnus, son of Pelopeia or of Pyrene, who was also killed by Hercules.

Having seduced Harpina, daughter of the river-god Asopus, Ares had by her a son, Oenomaus, who reigned near Olympia, and himself had a daughter, Hippodameia. Since an oracle had predicted that he would be killed by his son-in-law, Oenomaus, in order to get rid of her suitors, announced that he would give his daughter only to the man who beat him in a chariot race. He was certain he would always win, because Ares his father had made him a gift of winged steeds. Pelops, however, carried away the prize, thanks to a treacherous ruse of Hippodameia herself, which caused Oenomaus to be thrown from his chariot and killed.

Hephaestus

Origin, Functions and Representations. Whether we see in the name Hephaestus the Greek form of the Sanskrit *Yavishtha* (the very young), an epithet of Agni, the Vedic god of fire, or whether we derive it

Hephaestus during the battle between the gods and giants, with Doris and a giant. Pergamum Museum, Berlin.

Opposite, Nereus, an ocean god and prophetic divinity, who knew of the secret route to the Garden of the Hesperides. He is struggling with Hercules, who is trying to wrest the secret from him. Vase. British Museum.

from the Greek words for 'hearth' and 'to kindle', there is no doubt that Hephaestus was, from remotest times, the personification of terrestrial fire, of which volcanoes were the most terrifying manifestation.

Thus the cult of Hephaestus, who was perhaps an Asiatic divinity, a native of Lycia, first arose on the volcanic island of Lemnos. From there it was brought to Attica and introduced into Sicily through the Greek colonies there.

It is possible that in primitive times Hephaestus personified celestial fire and that he had thus been a thunder-god; his limping gait would then symbolise the zigzag of the lightning. If fire is of celestial origin then there is no reason why Hephaestus should not have had such a character.

The fire which he represents is not, however, the destroying element, but rather the beneficent element which permits men to work metal and foster civilisation. Thus Hephaestus appears as the divine blacksmith, the artisan-god, the demiurge who has created admirable works and taught men the mechanical arts.

That is why Hephaestus—who was at first depicted as a beardless young man—was afterwards traditionally represented as a robust smith, with bearded face, powerful neck and hairy chest. His short and sleeveless chiton leaves his right shoulder bare; on his head he wears a conical bonnet and in his hands he grasps a hammer and tongs.

The Birth of Hephaestus. Although Hesiod's genealogy claims that Hephaestus was, like Typhon, engendered by Hera alone, it was generally considered that he was the son of Hera and Zeus. At most one was sometimes given to understand that he was conceived before the official marriage of the two deities and that Hera had invented this legend of a miraculous birth in order to conceal her shame.

In contrast with the other Immortals, who were distinguished by beauty and the symmetry of their bodies, Hephaestus was ill-made and lame in both legs. His feet were twisted. His stumbling gait and dislocated hip aroused the 'unquenchable laughter of the Immortals' when he walked among them.

His Misadventures. Contrary to what was often said, Hephaestus' infirmity was not the result of an accident. He was lame from birth. Homer, in fact, recounts that Hera, ashamed of the ugliness of her son, tried to hide him from the Immortals 'because he was lame'. She threw him from the heights of Olympus into the sea, where he was taken in by Thetis, daughter of Nereus, and Eurynome, daughter of the old Ocean. For nine years he remained concealed in their deep grotto, 'forging a thousand ingenious objects for the two nymphs', and at the same time preparing a cunning revenge. One day Hera received a gift from her son, a golden throne artistically wrought. She sat on it with delight, but when she tried to rise again she was suddenly gripped by invisible bands. The Immortals tried in vain to extricate her from the throne. Only Hephaestus was capable of releasing her, but he refused to leave the depths of the Ocean. Ares tried to drag him up by force, but was put to flight by Hephaestus who threw burning brands at him. Dionysus was more successful: he

59

made Hephaestus drunk and, while he was drunk, perched him astride a mule and thus brought him back to Olympus. But they still had to meet his demands: Hephaestus refused to set Hera free unless they gave him the loveliest of the goddesses, Aphrodite—though some say Athene—for a bride. According to another tradition the reason why Hephaestus bound up Hera was to make her tell him the secret of his birth.

From then on there was peace between Hera and her son. Indeed, forgetting his former rancour, and at the peril of his life, Hephaestus attempted to defend his mother when she was beaten by Zeus. Irritated by his son, Zeus seized him by one foot and flung him from the courts of heaven. All day long he tumbled through space and, at sunset, fell more dead than alive on to the island of Lemnos.

The Blacksmith of Olympus. Under this graceless exterior, however, lurked a subtle and inventive spirit. Hephaestus excelled in the art of working metals. On Olympus he built palaces for the gods. For himself he constructed a 'sparkling dwelling of glittering and incorruptible bronze'. In it he had his workshop. There he could be seen beside the flaming furnaces, bathed in sweat, bustling about his bellows, poking the fires under twenty crucibles at a time, or hammering out the molten metal on an enormous anvil. When some god came to visit him, the gigantic blacksmith would pause to sponge his face, his hands, his powerful neck and hairy chest. He would put on a tunic and, leaning against a heavy staff, reach his gleaming throne. In order to steady his unsure footsteps—for his frail legs supported his massive body with difficulty—he had even fashioned two golden statues which resembled living girls. They had been endowed with movement and hastened to his side to aid him as he walked.

The Earthly Dwellings of Hephaestus. Homer places the workshop of Hephaestus on Olympus. But the fire-god also haunted the earth, where he maintained various underground places of residence. He had done his apprenticeship as a blacksmith in the

Hephaestus forging new arms for Achilles at the request of his mother, the Nereid Thetis, by Giulio Romano. Ducal Palace, Mantua.

Hephaestus being led back to Olympus by Dionysus after his nine-year exile. Attic vase. Munich Museum.

isle of Naxos and it was said that he unsuccessfully disputed the possession of the island with Dionysus. If so, understanding between the two gods was quickly re-established, and they always remained on excellent terms. Often the Sileni and the Satyrs helped Hephaestus in his work. It was said that to initiate him in the art of the forge Hera had confided Hephaestus to the dwarf Cedalion, whose identity is rather mysterious. Some call him the son, others the father of Hephaestus. All that is known is that he always remained attached to the fire-god and followed him to Lemnos when Hephaestus set up an establishment there.

Hephaestus, indeed, had never forgotten the welcome the Sintians had given him on the occasion of his fall from Olympus and, in gratitude, settled in this volcanic island. His presence there was attested by the flaming vapours which escaped from Mount Moschylus to the accompanying sound of dull rumbling. This was the sound of the divine blacksmith's hammers from the workshop he had set up in the bowels of the mountain. Beside him worked the faithful Cedalion from whom he was never separated, except on the occasion when he lent him as a guide to the blind giant Orion who wished to be conducted to the West in order to recover his eyesight. Hephaestus was also helped by the Cabeiri, who were probably his sons. It was to Lemnos, according to one

Hephaestus in his forge, with his wife Aphrodite, by Boucher. Wallace Collection, London.

tradition, that Prometheus had come in order to steal the divine fire which he then gave to mankind.

Later on Hephaestus emigrated to Sicily. At first we find him in the volcanic archipelago of the Lipari Islands. He was doubtless the mysterious and obliging blacksmith, who at night wrought the metal which was left in the evening on the edge of a crevasse and found there again next morning wonderfully wrought. Subterranean ramifications connected the Lipari Islands with Mount Etna in Sicily, where Hephaestus finally settled. He dislodged an indigenous demon called Adranus. In Etna Hephaestus also acted as a gaoler to Typhoeus who, it will be remembered, had been crushed under this mountain by Zeus. Earth-

quakes and eruptions of lava were caused by the monster's convulsions when he attempted to break from his prison. But he could not escape, for Hephaestus had placed on his head heavy anvils on which he energetically hammered bronze and iron. When sailors skirted the coasts of Sicily and saw long streamers of smoke escaping from the crest of Etna they had no doubt that it was Hephaestus lighting his forge. The god was helped in his task by the Palici, twins whom he had had by the Oceanid Etna (though others say that the Palici were sons of Zeus and the nymph Aethalia, daughter of Hephaestus). The giant Cyclopes also assisted him.

His Works. The activity of Hephaestus was prodigious and only equalled by his skill. He was ceaselessly employed on some work of great delicacy. As well as the palaces on Olympus with their bronze trimmings, he fashioned Zeus' golden throne, sceptre and thunderbolts, the fearful aegis, the winged chariot of Helios, the arrows of Apollo and Artemis, Demeter's sickle, Hercules' cuirass, the arms of Peleus, the armour of Achilles, the necklace which Harmonia, wife of Cadmus, wore for her nuptials, Ariadne's diadem, Agamemnon's sceptre, the hypogeum or underground chamber of Oenopion. Nor should one forget the golden goblet which Zeus presented to Aphrodite, a vase given by Dionysus to Ariadne, the *harpe* of Perseus and Adonis' hunting equipment.

Hephaestus was also credited with the manufacture of such works of wonder as the tripods with golden wheels which rolled of their own accord into the assembly of the gods, the bronze bulls whose nostrils spurted forth flame, the golden and silver dogs of Alcinous' palace, and even the giant Talos 'that man of bronze' whose duty it was to guard the Cretan tree.

Nothing was impossible to him. It was to Hephaestus that Zeus turned when, in order to punish men, he decided to create the first woman, Pandora. He ordered Hephaestus to mould the body of a woman with water and clay, to give it life and a human voice, and to form from it a virgin of ravishing beauty. To perfect his work Hephaestus encircled Pandora's brow with a golden crown which he himself had engraved.

On many other occasions Hephaestus gave assistance to Zeus. He split his skull with an axe in order that Athene might spring out. On Zeus' orders he bound Prometheus to the Caucasus. Doubtless Hephaestus remembered the harsh lesson his father had given him when he had dared to cross Zeus' will. For this reason Hephaestus would pacify the other gods on Olympus, and especially Hera, when they were angry with Zeus. To all he preached submission.

His Loves. Hephaestus was addicted to all pleasures. In spite of his ugliness he became the husband of Aphrodite. The position was not without its compensations, nor without its risks: his wife was continually unfaithful to him, especially with Ares. We have already seen with what spirit Hephaestus avenged himself by imprisoning the two lovers in a net and exposing them thus to the laughter of the Olympians. This misadventure did not prevent Hephaestus himself from aspiring to the love of the

61

Aphrodite leaving the drunken Hephaestus with Dionysus; one of her many infidelities. Engraving by Bonaventura Genelli. Dresden, Print Room.

wise Athene. But the goddess successfully resisted him and he tried in vain to ravish her in the plain of Marathon. Certain legends say that Hephaestus' passion for Athene dated from the very moment of her birth. Before he struck Zeus with the axe which would liberate Athene from his head, Hephaestus had demanded the hand of the virgin who was about to appear. Zeus, they said, consented; but Athene herself refused to keep her father's promise.

Hephaestus was also said to have married the beautiful Charis and Aglaia, one of the Graces. By Cabeiro, daughter of Proteus, he was the father of the Cabeiri. The Oceanid Etna bore him twins, the Palici, the Dioscuri of Sicily; though another tradition says that they were sons of Zeus and the nymph Aethalia, daughter of Hephaestus. To escape Hera's vengeance Aethalia begged the earth to conceal her until the day of her delivery. Her prayers were granted and when her time came the two children sprang from the earth, whence their name: 'They who return to the light'. Two small lakes at the foot of Etna, always full of boiling sulphur water, marked the place where they had appeared. Their temple was there, and there they delivered oracles.

The Companions of Hephaestus. We have seen that Hephaestus was aided in his work by a certain number of subterranean divinities or fire genii. The best known were the Cyclopes, who assisted him at the forges under Etna. The first Cyclopes who appear in Greek mythology were the three sons of Uranus and Gaea: Arges, Steropes and Brontes. It may be remembered how after their father had cast them into Tartarus they were delivered by Zeus, whom they helped in his struggle against the Titans. Apart from thunder, the thunderbolt and the lightning which they gave Zeus, they presented Hades with a bronze helmet and Poseidon with a trident. They were put to death by Apollo, who took his vengeance on them for the death of his son Asclepius.

These earlier Cyclopes had nothing in common with the Cyclopes whom Homer introduces us to in the Odyssey. The latter were men of gigantic stature and repellent ugliness with their single eye in the middle of their forehead, who inhabited the south-west coast of Sicily. Given to a pastoral existence, they were gross and ill-mannered, living in isolated caverns, slaughtering and devouring any strangers who approached their shores. The best known among them was Polyphemus, who took Odysseus and his companions prisoner. In order to escape, the Greek hero made Polyphemus drunk and put out his single eye by means of a sharpened, burning stake; Odysseus and his companions then escaped from the cavern by tying themselves under the bellies of rams. Before this misfortune Polyphemus had fallen in love with the Nereid Galatea. He paid court to her by sending her a daily present of a bear or an elephant. To this inelegant suitor Galatea preferred the shepherd Acis, son of the nymph Symoethis. Jealous of this rival, Polyphemus crushed him beneath a rock and Acis was changed by the gods into a river.

When tradition made Mount Etna the abode of Hephaestus he was given the Cyclopes as companions. They borrowed their features from the Cyclopes of Hesiod and Homer. They were, says Callimachus, 'enormous giants, as big as mountains, and their single eye, under a bushy eyebrow, glittered menacingly. Some made the vast bellows roar, others one by one laboriously raising their heavy hammers, struck great blows at the molten bronze and iron they drew from the furnace.' Their number was not stated. Among the names which were given to them we find those of Brontes, Steropes, Acamas and Pyracmon.

At Lemnos the Cyclopes were replaced by the Cabeiri, divinities whose origin and nature have remained rather mysterious, especially since they occur in various regions with quite distinct characters. The Cabeiri of Lemnos, said to be the sons of Hephaestus, were benevolent genii, underground smiths evidently associated with the volcanic nature of the island's structure. At Samothrace the Cabeiri were a kind of inferior god, sworn to the service of the great gods of the island; tradition made them the sons of Zeus and Calliope. At Thebes in Boeotia the Cabeiri appear to have been associated with the cult of Demeter and Kore, since their temple was situated near a grove sacred to these two goddesses. In Thessaly they spoke of a Cabeire who was put to death by his two brothers and buried at the foot of Olympus. Finally we find Cabeiri at Pergamum and in Phoenicia, and Herodotus believed he recognised them in Egypt. From all this it would seem that the Cabeiri, were in primitive times underground spirits, originating in Phrygia, who in the volcanic islands naturally took on the character of fire genii. They were reputed to be the first metal-workers.

The Greeks, however, recognised other metallurgical genii who, without being directly concerned with the cult of Hephaestus, must be mentioned here.

In the forests of Phrygian Ida there lived cunning magicians called the Dactyls. Originally there were three of them: Celmis, Damnameneus and the powerful Acmon, 'who in the caves of the mountains was the first to practise the art of Hephaestus, and who knew how to work blue iron, casting it into the burning furnace'. Later their number increased. From Phrygia they went to Crete, where they taught the inhabitants the use of iron and how to work metals. In addition the invention of arithmetic and the letters of the alphabet was attributed to them.

Genii who also played a civilising role but afterwards assumed a malign character were the Telchines, said to be the sons of Poseidon and Thalassa, though another tradition makes them Poseidon's guardians. The centre of their cult was the island of Rhodes, whence they spread to Crete and Boeotia. They were great metal-workers, as the names of three of them suggest: Chryson, Argyron and Chalcon. They forged the first statues of the gods, and among their works were the sickle of Cronus and the trident of Poseidon. But they were feared for their enchantments. They could cast the evil eye and, by sprinkling the ground with the waters of the Styx mixed with sulphur, they blighted the harvest and killed the flocks.

Aphrodite

Origin and Character. Though the primitive Greeks certainly had a goddess of love it would seem she was not Aphrodite. We must not be misled by the legend which arose later to justify an etymology based on a sort of pun which connects her name with the Greek word for 'foam'. In reality the name Aphrodite seems to be of oriental origin, probably Phoenician, like the goddess herself—sister of the Assyro-Babylonian Ishtar and the Syro-Phoenician Astarte. From

Polyphemus observing Acis and Galatea, by Giulio Romano. Palazzo del Te, Mantua.

Phoenicia the cult of Aphrodite passed to Cythera, a Phoenician trading-post, and to Cyprus (whence the epithets Cytheraean and Cyprian which the goddess has in Homer); then it spread throughout Greece and even reached Sicily.

In origin Aphrodite—like the great Asiatic goddesses—was obviously a fertility goddess whose domain embraced all nature, vegetable and animal as well as human. Afterwards she became the goddess of love in its noblest aspect as well as in its most degraded.

Aphrodite Urania, or the celestial Aphrodite, was the goddess of pure and ideal love. Aphrodite Genetrix or Nymphia favoured and protected marriage; unmarried girls and widows prayed to her in order to obtain husbands. Aphrodite Pandemos (common) or Aphrodite Porne (courtesan) was the goddess of lust and venal love, the patroness of prostitutes. Under the influence of her legend Aphrodite later became a marine deity (Pelagia, Pontia).

Cult and Representations. The chief centres of the cult of Aphrodite were Paphos in Cyprus and Cythera in Crete. Among her most famous sanctuaries were the temple of Cnidus in Caria and the temple on the island of Cos. Aphrodite Pandemos was venerated at Thebes, where there was a statue of the goddess reputedly made of the battering-rams of the ships which had brought Cadmus to Greece. In Athens there was a temple of Aphrodite Hetaera, in which the goddess was represented sitting on a he-goat. She was venerated at Abydos, at Ephesus and above all at Corinth, where the prostitutes of the town acted as her priestesses. Aphrodite Genetrix was worshipped at Sparta and at Naupactus. Aphrodite Urania had temples at Sicyon, Argos and Athens. Finally, the marine Aphrodite Pelagia was especially honoured at Hermione. In Thessaly they venerated an Aphrodite Anosia (the impious) in memory of the murder of the courtesan Lais by the wives of the region. In Sicily Aphrodite had a celebrated temple on Mount Eryx.

The representations of Aphrodite vary according to the character in which she was envisaged.

At Sicyon they venerated an ivory-adorned statue in which the goddess was crowned by a *polos*. Nobility and modesty characterised this statue, which evidently depicted Aphrodite Urania or Genetrix.

The note of sensuality is emphasised in the later effigies of Aphrodite. Indeed, the models whom the sculptors employed were often courtesans like Cratina, Phryne or Cambyse, the mistress of Alexander. Such were the nude Aphrodites of Praxiteles which, it is said, shocked the piety of the inhabitants of Cos. The Aphrodite which was honoured at Cnidos was particularly voluptuous.

Hesiod's myth of the birth of Aphrodite inspired the various types of Aphrodite *anadyomene*—i.e., rising from the waters—like the celebrated Aphrodite (or Venus) de' Medici, and the Aphrodites at the bath so popular in statuary.

A type rather different from the preceding is Aphrodite the Warrior, represented armed and wearing a helmet. She was particularly venerated at

Aphrodite Anadyomene or 'rising from the waters'. Antique sculpture. Vatican Museum, Rome.

Sparta. The Venus de Milo was a warrior Aphrodite.

The Birth of Aphrodite. Homer describes Aphrodite as the daughter of Zeus and Dione—a rather vague divinity who was said to be the daughter of Oceanus and Tethys and of whom we know only that she was closely associated with the cult of Zeus at Dodona. Even her name, which is merely the feminine form of Zeus, suggests her lack of defined personality. Popular imagination could scarcely be satisfied with so poor a legend, and the Homeric tradition was thus supplanted by another, richer in popular appeal.

At the instigation of Gaea, his mother, Cronus castrated his father, Uranus, and cast the severed genitals into the sea. They floated on the surface of the waters, producing a white foam out of which rose Aphrodite. Carried across the tumultuos sea by Zephyrus, the West Wind, the goddess was borne along the coast of Cythera and finally landed on the shores of Cyprus.

She was greeted by the Horae, who dressed her richly, adorned her with precious jewels and conducted her to the assembly of the Immortals. Beside her walked Love and Himeros, tender Desire. When they saw her the gods were struck with admiration for such beauty and each, says the poet, 'wished in his heart to take her as a wife and lead her to his abode'.

It was natural that they should be moved; for Aphrodite was the essence of feminine beauty. From her gleaming fair hair to her silvery feet everything about her was pure charm and harmony. To be sure Hera and Athene were also very lovely, but the haughty beauty of Hera imposed respect and the severe beauty of Athene arrested desire. Aphrodite exuded an aura of seduction. To the perfection of her figure and the purity of her features she added the grace which attracted and conquered.

The Judgment of Paris. One can imagine that the other goddesses did not accept without resentment the presence on Olympus of this redoubtable rival. They were determined to dispute the prize of beauty with her. Now all the Immortals had been invited to the nuptials of Thetis and Peleus except Eris, or Discord. Infuriated by the omission, Eris tossed into the hall where the guests were gathered a golden apple with this inscription: *For the fairest.* Hera, Athene and Aphrodite each claimed it. To settle the affair Zeus ordered them to submit the dispute to the judgment of a mortal. Choice fell upon one Paris, son of King Priam of Troy. Hermes then conducted the three goddesses to Phrygia where Paris was tending his father's flocks on the slopes of Mount Ida. Paris was acutely embarrassed and tried to refuse, but he had to submit to the will of Zeus, expressed by Hermes. One by one the three goddesses appeared before him and attempted to influence his decision by reinforcing the power of their charms with alluring promises. 'If you award the prize to me,' said Hera, 'I shall make you lord over all Asia.' Athene promised to see that the young shepherd was always victorious in battle. Aphrodite, who could offer neither sceptres nor victories, merely loosened the clasps by which her tunic was fastened and unknotted her girdle; then she promised to give Paris the most beautiful of mortal women. The verdict was then delivered, and the shepherd of Mount Ida awarded the coveted apple to Aphrodite. In this way Paris won possession of Helen, wife of Menelaus; but neither Hera nor Athene forgave him the wound to their pride, and avenged themselves cruelly by delivering his country, his family and his people to devastation and making sure that he, too, fell beneath the blows of the Greeks.

But from that time Aphrodite's supremacy remained uncontested. Even Hera, when she wished to recapture her husband's wayward love, did not hesitate to run to her former rival to borrow the magic girdle which was endowed with the power of enslaving the hearts of gods and men alike.

Head of Aphrodite, by Praxiteles. Vatican Museum, Rome.

Goddess of love, Aphrodite was mistress of seductive conversation, 'gracious laughter, sweet deceits, the charms and delights of love'. This was her empire, though, like the other gods, she sometimes espoused the quarrels of mankind. On such occasions she too threw herself into the fray and we see her defending the Trojans and taking part in the battles which raged beneath the walls of Ilium with, it may be added, little success. On day, when she had come to the aid of her son Aeneas and was shielding him against the Greek arrows with a fold of her sparkling veil, Diomedes recognised her. Well aware that she was a divinity without courage, he attacked her, and with the sharp point of his spear lightly wounded her delicate hand. Aphrodite retired hastily to Olympus, watched mockingly by Athene who said: 'Doubtless the Cyprian has been persuading some Greek woman to fight for her dearly beloved Trojans, and while she was caressing the woman a golden clasp has scratched her delicate hand!' Aphrodite complained bitterly to the father of the gods. Zeus smiled and said to her: 'You, my child, were not meant to concern yourself with war. Go, attend to the sweet tasks of love.'

The Loves of Aphrodite. Aphrodite's beauty had stirred all the gods; but it was Hephaestus, the ugliest and most graceless among them, who obtained her for a wife. Such an ill-matched union could not be happy, and even on Olympus Aphrodite found those to console her, among others Ares, with whom she was surprised by her husband, and Hermes who, it seemed, was more adroit. Aphrodite, moreover, took a wicked delight in rousing the passionate desires of the Immortals and launching them on amorous adventures. With the exception of Athene, Artemis and Hestia, all came under her influence. The master of the gods himself yielded to her power. 'She distracts the mind

Aphrodite hunted down by Athene, by Tintoretto. Aphrodite was notoriously cowardly, and never forgave Diomedes, who was protected by Athene, for taking advantage of this and wounding her during the Trojan War. She is accompanied by the Horae, whose task it was to guard the entrance to heaven. The Prado, Madrid.

of Zeus, deceives his prudent soul, and sends him chasing after mortal women.'

To avenge himself 'Zeus, in his turn, inspired in Aphrodite the sweet desire to lie with a mortal man'. And so the goddess was seized by an irresistible passion for the Trojan Anchises, whose beauty rivalled that of the gods. One day when Anchises was pasturing his flocks on Mount Ida Aphrodite came to join him. First she had visited her sanctuary at Paphos where the Graces had anointed her body with fragrant and incorruptible oil and adorned her in her most precious jewels.

When she came to Anchises she explained that she was the daughter of Otreus, King of Phrygia, and confessed her desire to become his spouse. Without further ado Anchises conducted Aphrodite to his well-prepared couch, covered with the skins of bears and lions. And there 'a mortal man, by the will of the gods and destiny, slept with an immortal goddess without knowing who she was'.

Upon awaking Aphrodite appeared before Anchises in all her divine splendour. The shepherd beheld her in terror, fearing the premature old age with which a man who has lain with an immortal goddess is

Aphrodite and Zeus, by Raphael. As goddess of love, Aphrodite was able to influence even the father of the gods. Farnese Palace, Rome.

stricken. But Aphrodite reassured him and promised him a son who would be like a god. She asked of him only that he should never reveal the name of the child's mother. The child was later the pious Aeneas.

Anchises was not the only mortal loved by Aphrodite. The Phoenicians who frequented the isles of the Aegean and the ports of the Peloponnese had brought with them the tale of the love of their own goddess Astarte for Adonis. The Greeks naturally retold it of Aphrodite, and this story of Aphrodite and Adonis was one of the episodes most often treated by poets and artists.

Among Aphrodite's favourites must be mentioned Phaethon, son of Eos and Cephalus, who was carried off as a child by the goddess and became 'the nocturnal guardian of her sacred temples'. There was also Cinyras, sometimes described as the father of Myrrha—and consequently of Adonis. He was usually regarded as the founder of the cult of Aphrodite in the island of Cyprus over which he reigned.

In this same island of Cyprus, in Amathus, there lived a sculptor named Pygmalion. Passionately devoted to his art, Pygmalion was happy only in the silent world of statues which his chisel had created. His misanthropy was attributed to the disgust he felt at the conduct of the Propoetides. These were girls in Amathus who rashly denied the divinity of Aphrodite. To punish them Aphrodite inspired in them such immodesty that, losing all sense of shame, they would prostitute themselves to all comers. In the end they were turned into rocks. Thus Pygmalion shunned the society of women, but none the less fervently venerated Aphrodite. Now it came about that he made an ivory statue of a woman of such extraordinary beauty that he fell in love with it. Alas! the cold image did not respond to his transports of love. Aphrodite took pity on this singular lover. One day

The Judgment of Paris, by Cima da Conegliano. A fourteenth-century interpretation of the Tuscan school. National Museum, Florence.

while pressing the inert statue in his arms Pygmalion felt the ivory suddenly moving; his kisses were returned. The statue was miraculously alive.

This prodigy is only an example of the sovereign power of Aphrodite over all creation. Throughout all nature she spread her life-bringing joy: at her appearance, Lucretius says, 'the heavens are assuaged and pour forth torrents of light; the waves of the sea smile on her'. Aphrodite was also, however, the terrifying divinity who filled women's hearts with the frenzy of passion. Unhappy were they whom Aphrodite chose for her victims for they would betray their own fathers, like Medea or Ariadne; they would abandon their homes, like Helen, to follow a stranger; they would be overcome, like Myrrha or Phaedra, with incestuous desires, or, like Pasiphaë, be torn by monstrous and bestial passions.

The Judgment of Paris. Hermes leads the three goddesses, Athene, Hera and Aphrodite, accompanied by Erotes, to the shepherd Paris, who seated on a rock, plays the lyre and is surrounded by goats. From a red-figured kylix by Heiron. Berlin Museum.

Hermaphroditus asleep. National Museum, Rome.

The Venus of Rhodes. Rhodes Museum.

The same Aphrodite nevertheless protected legitimate unions and figured among the divinities who presided over the sanctity of marriage. Spartan mothers offered a sacrifice to her when their daughters were married. It was Aphrodite who cared for the daughters of Pandareus, Merope and Cleothera, after the death of their parents, fed them on milk and honey and delectable wine and, when they had grown up, asked the almighty Zeus that their nuptials should be blessed. Had it depended on Aphrodite alone, Merope and Cleothera would have become happy and respected wives; but the two unfortunate young women, at the moment of their marriage, were carried off by the Harpies and made into followers of the odious Furies.

Hermaphroditus. Among Aphrodite's children were Harmonia, a daughter, whom she bore to Ares and who married Cadmus, and a son, Hermaphroditus, whose father was Hermes.

To conceal his birth Aphrodite immediately entrusted Hermaphroditus to the nymphs of Mount Ida who brought him up in the forests. At the age of fifteen he was a wild and savage youth whose chief pleasure was to hunt in the wooded mountains. One day in Caria he arrived at the banks of a limpid lake whose freshness tempted him to bathe. The nymph Salmacis who ruled the lake saw him and was enamoured of his beauty. She told him so, and in vain the shy youth attempted to repulse her. Salmacis threw her arms around him and covered him with kisses. He continued to resist and the nymph cried out: 'Cruel youth! You struggle in vain. O ye gods! Grant that nothing may ever separate him from me, or me from him!' Immediately their two bodies were united and became as one. 'In their double form they are neither man nor woman; they seem to have no sex yet to be of both sexes.'

Following this event the waters of the lake acquired the property of causing those who bathed in it to lose their virility. This fulfilled the final wish expressed by Hermaphroditus just before Salmacis drew him down into the depths of the water.

Some have interpreted this strange fable as a survival of the cult of the Bearded Aphrodite of Cyprus.

The retinue of Aphrodite

Eros. Among Aphrodite's customary companions the most important was Eros. Unknown in Homeric times, he appears in Hesiod's *Theogony* as the son of Erebus and the Night. His role was to co-ordinate the elements which constitute the universe. It is he who 'brings harmony to chaos', and permits life to develop. This primitive deity, a semi-abstract personification of cosmic force, has little resemblance to the traditional Eros whose physiognomy was developed only in later times.

About his origin there is little agreement. Some say his mother was the goddess Ilithyia; others say he was born to Iris and Zephyrus. Sometimes he is supposed to have been born before Aphrodite, whom he and the Horae welcomed on the shores of Cyprus. Sometimes—and this was the most widespread tradition—he was considered to be the son of Aphrodite. As to his father, the ancients hesitated between Ares, Hermes and Zeus.

Eros was the youngest of the gods; he was a winged child, gracious though rebellious, whose pranks and caprices caused much suffering among men and gods. He was armed with a bow and arrows whose prick stirred the fires of passion in all hearts. In his mischievousness he respected not even his own mother, and Aphrodite sometimes had to punish him by taking away his wings and quiver. Normally, however, he was her zealous servant. He helped with her toilet and accompanied her abroad. While the goddess lingered in the arms of Ares, Eros amused himself by handling the war-god's heavy weapons and trying on his helmet with its gleaming plume. In much the same way we see him later playing with the weapons of Hercules.

This cruel and charming young god who delighted in torturing men and who, according to Anacreon, repaid hospitality offered to him by an artfully released dart, was himself sometimes a victim of the passions he inspired in others. This is illustrated by the charming tale of Psyche, although the story is of late invention and more philosophical than mythological.

Eros and Psyche. Psyche (in Greek the word means 'soul') was a princess of such remarkable beauty that Aphrodite herself was jealous of her. She instructed her son Eros to punish the audacious mortal. Shortly afterwards an oracle commanded Psyche's father, under threat of terrifying calamities, to conduct his daughter to the summit of a mountain where she would become the prey of a monster. Trembling but resigned, Psyche was awaiting the fulfilment of the oracle on a solitary rock, when suddenly she felt herself gently lifted in the arms of Zephyrus, who carried her to a magnificent palace. When night fell Psyche was on the verge of sleep when a mysterious being joined her in the darkness, explaining that he was the husband for whom she was destined. She could not see his features, but his voice was soft and his conversation full of tenderness. Before the return of dawn the strange visitor disappeared, first making Psyche swear never to attempt to see his face. In spite of the oddness of the adventure, Psyche was not discontented with her new life; in the palace nothing she could desire was lacking except the constant presence of her delightful husband, who came to visit her only during the dark hours of night. Her happiness could have continued in this way had not her sisters—who were consumed by envy—sown the seeds of suspicion in her heart. 'If your husband is afraid to let you see his face,' they said, 'it is because he must really be some hideous monster.' They nagged her so much that one night Psyche, in spite of her promise, rose from the couch she shared with her husband, stealthily lighted a lamp and held it above the mysterious face. Instead of a fearful monster she beheld the most charming person in the world—Eros himself. At the foot of the couch lay his bow and arrows. In her delight Psyche held the lamp nearer in order to study her husband's features more closely. A drop of scalding oil fell on the god's bare shoulder. He awakened at once, reproached Psyche for her lack of faith and immediately vanished.

The palace vanished at the same time, and poor Psyche found herself on the lonely rock again in the midst of terrifying solitude. At first she considered suicide and threw herself into a near-by river; but the waters bore her gently to the opposite bank. From then on she was pursued by Aphrodite's anger and submitted to a series of terrible ordeals. She succeeded, however, in overcoming them one by one, thanks to mysterious assistance. She even had to descend into the underworld. Finally, touched by the re-

Eros. Terracotta statuette from Myrina.

69

pentance of his unhappy spouse, whom he had never
ceased to love and protect, Eros went to Zeus and
implored permission for Psyche to rejoin him. Zeus
consented and conferred immortality on Psyche.
Aphrodite forgot her rancour, and the wedding of the
two lovers was celebrated on Olympus with great
rejoicing.

Other divinities were often seen at the side of Eros;
chief among these were Himeras and Pothos, both
personifications of amorous desire.

The Graces. Aphrodite's retinue was usually
completed by the Graces. Though sometimes said
to be the daughters of Helios and Aegle, the Graces
were more generally considered to have been born
to the Oceanid Eurynome and fathered by Zeus.
They were smiling divinities whose presence spread
joy not only throughout the external world but also
in the hearts of men. The most widely accepted
tradition fixed their number as three and their names
as Aglaia, Euphrosyne and Thalia. As Aphrodite's
companions they attended to her toilet.

With the return of Spring the Graces delighted in
mingling with the nymphs, forming with them groups
of dancers who tripped the ground with nimble step.
This was because these divinities—in whom some
have seen a personification of the sun's rays, but who
were originally nature-goddesses—also presided over
the budding of plant-life and the ripening of fruits.
Aglaia was 'the brilliant'. Thalia was 'she who
brought flowers'. The joy which results from the sun's
blessings is revealed in Euphrosyne's name: 'she who
rejoices the heart'. In origin as well as function the
Graces were closely connected with Apollo: hence
they often form part of his retinue.

They were also considered to be the goddesses of

*The three Graces at their toilet. Red-figured cup in the
British Museum.*
*Eros and Psyche. Classical group. Capitoline Museum,
Rome.*

*Amphitrite presenting Theseus with a crown. Theseus,
son of Poseidon, had descended to the realm of his father
to recover a ring which Minos had thrown into the sea.*

70

Apollo and the three Graces. Classical relief.

gratitude. Their mother was sometimes said to be Lethe (oblivion) because gratitude is quickly forgotten.

The most celebrated sanctuary of the Graces was at Orchomenus in Boeotia, where they were worshipped in the form of aeroliths or meteorites. They also had two sanctuaries in Athens.

The Graces were at first clad in long chitons and wore crowns, but from the end of the fourth century B.C. they were represented as three nude young women holding each other by the shoulder.

Poseidon

Character and Functions. Although Poseidon's dominion was the sea, he held his own appointed position among the great gods on Olympus.

Far from being a Libyan importation, as Herodotus claims, he was actually a very ancient Pelasgian deity, older even than Zeus. His province, later confined to the waters, was in primitive times much wider.

The etymology which the ancients gave his name, connecting it with 'drink' and 'river', is doubtful. The name Poseidon seems rather to derive from the root meaning 'to be master.

It is not impossible that this primitive Poseidon, this sovereign 'master', had once been a celestial god, as his attribute, the trident—probably a symbol for the thunderbolt—seems to indicate. Though supplanted by Zeus, Poseidon continued to exercise his empire over the entire earth, as is proved by those struggles he had with other divinities who contested with him the mastery of various parts of Greece, and also by the titles Homer gives him, such as *Enosichthon*—'earth-shaker'. Poseidon was, indeed, the god of earthquakes. Even when his sphere was more narrowly confined to the sea Poseidon retained his

character of a great god: he remained the equal of the celestial Zeus, the Zeus Elalios (marine), whose power extended over the whole physical universe.

As a personification of the watery element Poseidon was always considered a god of fecundity and vegetation.

Cult and Representations. Poseidon was a national god of the Ionians of the Peloponnese, who brought him with them when they emigrated from Asia, and he was particularly worshipped in this part of Greece. At Sparta he was even called *Genethlios*, the creator. But his cult was spread throughout Greece, especially in maritime towns. In Corinth, Rhodes and Taenarus he actually succeeded in supplanting the local divinity.

Animals which were sacred to him were the horse, symbol of gushing springs, and the bull, emblem either of his power to fertilise or of his impetuosity. In the course of certain festivals dedicated to Poseidon and called Taureia, black bulls were thrown into the waves.

In the same way horse races were celebrated in honour of Poseidon. This custom originated in Thessaly where the god was said to have created the horse with a blow of his trident.

In the art of classical antiquity Poseidon very much resembles Zeus: he has a similar majesty when he is depicted standing, his chest bare, grasping his trident. But normally his features are less serene and, with his thick beard and disorderly hair, bear a careworn expression.

The Legend of Poseidon. Poseidon was a son of Cronus and Rhea. He shared the fate of his brothers and sisters, and at birth was swallowed by his father. He was disgorged with the others when Zeus, on the advice of Metis, gave Cronus the draught which made him vomit up his children. According to another tradition Rhea managed to shelter Poseidon from his father's voracity by giving Cronus a young foal to swallow, meanwhile hiding her son in the midst of a flock of lambs near Mantinea. Poseidon was then entrusted to a nurse named Arne and grew up without his father's knowledge. It was also said tha Rhea gave Poseidon to Capheira, a daughter of Oceanus who, with the aid of the Telchines, brought him up in Rhodes.

When Zeus fought the Titans and the Giants, Poseidon fought at his side and killed the giant Polybutes by hurling at him a fragment of cliff torn from the island of Cos, which later became the islet of Nisyros. After their common victory the paternal heritage was, as we remember, divided into three parts: Zeus took the vast heavens, Hades the murky underworld, and Poseidon obtained the immense sea.

Although he was the equal of Zeus by birth and dignity Poseidon was nevertheless subject to his brother's sovereign power. The sea-god complained and grumbled at times. Once he went so far as to conspire with Hera and Athene to dethrone Zeus. Zeus was the stronger and Poseidon was forced to pay

Poseidon. Detail from a statue once thought to be of Zeus himself, such is its majesty. Bronze of the first half of the fifth century B.C. National Museum, Athens.

for his attempted revolt by spending a year in the service of the haughty Laomedon, for whom he constructed the walls of Troy.

Poseidon's empire, however, was not unworthy of his ambitions. He was master not only of the sea but of the lakes and rivers. In a sense even the earth belonged to him, since it was sustained by his waters and he could shake it at will. Indeed, during the war with the Giants he split mountains with his trident and rolled them into the sea to make the first islands. And it was he who, in the days when Thessaly was merely a huge lake, had cleared the road for the River Peneius by splitting the mass of Mount Ossa in two.

Poseidon's thirst for possession was so keen that he often found himself in conflict with the other gods.

We have already mentioned the dispute he had with Athene for the possession of Attica, a dispute which ended to Athene's advantage. Out of spite Poseidon flooded Attica. Nor could he win Troezen from the same goddess; Zeus awarded it to them in common.

Poseidon was no more fortunate with Hera, with whom he contested the dominion of Argolis. The decision was submitted to the judgment of the river-god Inachus, assisted by the rivers Asterion and Cephissus. It was unfavourable to Poseidon, who avenged himself by drying up the three rivers and with them Argolis.

There was also a contest between Poseidon and Helios over the isthmus of Corinth. Briareus, chosen to arbitrate, awarded the Corinthian Acropolis to Helios and left the rest of the isthmus to Poseidon. This was the origin of the cult in which Poseidon was honoured in the isthmus of Corinth; during his festivals the celebrated Isthmian Games were held.

Finally Poseidon unsuccessfully disputed Aegina with Zeus, and Naxos with Dionysus. He had to cede to Apollo the territory of Delphi, which until then he had held in common with Gaea, receiving in exchange the island of Calauria.

On the other hand no one ever disputed Poseidon's rule over the sea. He established his abode in the depths of the Aegean Sea where 'there had been built for him a magnificent palace, glittering with gold, which would endure for ever'. When he left the palace he would harness to his chariot swift steeds with golden manes and shod with bronze. Clad in golden armour he would seize a cunningly wrought whip in his hand and hurl his chariot across the watery plain. Around him would frolic sea monsters, come up from the abysmal depths to render homage to their sovereign. The joyful sea would open before him as his chariot flew lightly across waves, which did not so much as wet the bronze axle. More often, however, the appearance of Poseidon was accompanied by wild tempests, a manifestation of the god's furious rage.

Amphitritè. Poseidon's wife was Amphitrite, who was in origin the feminine personification of the sea. She was a daughter of Oceanus or of Nereus. Poseidon picked her out one day when she was dancing with her sisters on the island of Naxos. When he asked for her hand in marriage Amphitrite at first refused and

Poseidon in his classical pose, grasping his trident and with a careworn expression. Lateran Museum, Rome.

Athene and Poseidon during their contest for the patronage over Athens. From an amphora by Amasis. Cabinet des Médailles, Paris.

fled to Atlas. Poseidon sent a dolphin to look for her. The dolphin discovered where she had taken refuge and brought her back to his master; as a reward Poseidon placed him among the constellations.

From then on Amphitrite shared Poseidon's kingdom. We see her at her husband's side on the divine chariot drawn by Tritons blowing conch-shells. In her hand she sometimes holds the trident, insignia of Poseidon's sovereignty.

From the union of Poseidon and Amphitrite were born a son, Triton, and two daughters: Rhode, who gave her name to the island of Rhodes and was the mother of the Heliades; and Benthesicyme, who settled in Ethiopia.

Amphitrite was an accommodating wife and put up patiently with her husband's frequent infidelity. Only once did she show jealousy: this was with regard to Scylla, who was originally a nymph of rare beauty. Enraged by the love Poseidon showed her, Amphitrite threw magic herbs in the pool where Scylla used to bathe, and the nymph was changed into a frightful monster. Her metamorphosis is sometimes attributed to Circe.

The Loves of Poseidon. Of Poseidon's innumerable mistresses we shall mention only the principal ones.

Among the goddesses there was Gaea, whom he made mother of the fearful giant Antaeus. There was Demeter, who changed herself into a mare in order to escape him. But Poseidon took the form of a stallion and from their union was born—apart from a daughter whose name remains mysterious (perhaps it was Despoena)—the wild horse Arion, whose right feet were those of a man and who was endowed with the power of speech.

It was also in the shape of a horse—though others

say a bird—that Poseidon succeeded in seducing Medusa, in the very temple of Athene. Infuriated by this profanation, Athene turned Medusa's hair into snakes. When Perseus decapitated Medusa, the blood which escaped from the wound gave birth to Chrysaor and the horse Pegasus.

By Alcyone, one of the Pleiades, Poseidon had a daughter, Aethusa, who was loved by Apollo, and two sons: Hyperenor and Hyrieus. The latter reigned in Boeotia and by the blessing of the gods became father of the giant Orion.

By the harpy Celaeno, Poseidon had two sons: Lycus, who reigned over the Fortunate Isles, and Eurypylus, who distinguished himself at the siege of Troy and took part in the expedition of the Argonauts.

Another Eurypylus, who reigned over the isle of Cos and was killed by Hercules, and the Argonaut Ancaeus were born to Poseidon and Astypalaea, sister of Europa.

Chione, daughter of Boreas, was seduced by Poseidon and had a son, Eumolpus. To hide her shame she threw the child into the sea; but Poseidon saved it and carried it to Ethiopia where he entrusted it to his daughter Benthesicyme, who later became Eumolpus' mother-in-law.

Aethra was the daughter of Pittheus, King of Troezen. Athene ordered her in a dream to go to the isle of Sphaeria and there on the tomb of Sphaerus to offer a sacrifice. Aethra was surprised in the temple by Poseidon and ravished. She afterwards married Aegeus and became the mother of Theseus.

Because of her great beauty Theophane, daughter of Bisaltes, was besieged by suitors. To protect her from their attentions Poseidon, who loved her himself, carried her to the isle of Crinissa (Crumissa). The

Amphitrite with Eumolpus, son of Chione and Poseidon. Vase in the British Museum.

suitors followed her. Poseidon then turned her into a ewe, the inhabitants of the island into sheep, and himself into a ram. Theophane gave birth to the famous ram with the golden fleece.

Alope, daughter of Cercyon, had a son by Poseidon. She left him in an exposed place, after having covered him with a rich robe. The infant was suckled by a mare and found by herdsmen who carried him to Cercyon, who at once recognised the rich robe and discovered his daughter's disgrace. He condemned her to perpetual imprisonment and once more abandoned the infant in the open. But the faithful mare again came to suckle him. For this reason he was named Hippothous. Later, when Cercyon was slain by Theseus, Hippothous ascended the throne of his grandfather.

For having plundered a grove sacred to Demeter, Erysichthon, King of Thessaly, was afflicted with insatiable hunger. To appease it he was obliged to sell everything he possessed. At the end of his resources he finally put his own daughter Mestra up for sale. Now Poseidon loved Mestra and granted her the gift of metamorphosis, so that each time she was able to escape her purchasers. This stratagem allowed Erysichthon to sell his daughter over and over again, until at last the ruse was discovered and he had no alternative but to devour himself.

During the drought in Argolis which was the result of Poseidon's fury with Inachus, Danaus sent his daughters in search of water. One of them, Amymone,

carelessly wounded a sleeping satyr who then leapt at her. Others say that Amymone was surprised by the satyr while she herself was asleep. In either case Poseidon arrived, put the satyr to flight and rescued Amymone, whose favours he then enjoyed. In gratitude the god struck a rock with his trident and the springs of Lerna gushed forth. By this union Amymone had a son, Nauplius, who later founded Nauplia and was swallowed by the waves for blaspheming the gods. The origin of the fountain of Pirene, near Corinth, was also connected with a legend of Poseidon. By the nymph Pirene, daughter of Achelous or Asopus, the god had two sons who perished miserably. Pirene was inconsolable and her tears which gave birth to the celebrated fountain.

The nymph Tyro, daughter of Salmoneus and Acidice, had conceived a passion for the River Enipeus. Poseidon, who loved her, despaired of moving her heart. One day when Tyro was strolling along the banks of the Enipeus Poseidon assumed the appearance of the river-god and approached her. The nymph was deceived by this disguise and yielded. She bore two sons, Pelias and Neleus, whom she abandoned. They were found by shepherds and brought up among herds of horses. Meanwhile Tyro had married Cretheus, King of Iolcus, and was ill-treated by Sidero, her mother-in-law. When Pelias and Neleus returned to their mother they killed the wicked Sidero.

The Posterity of Poseidon. Among Poseidon's numerous offspring we shall limit ourselves to mentioning a few names:

Euphemus, son of Europa, who received from his father the power of walking on the waters and who was the second pilot during the expedition of the Argonauts.

Hallirrhothius, son of the nymph Euryte, who was put to death by Ares for having ravished his daughter Alcippe. This murder gave rise to a quarrel between Ares and Poseidon, to settle which the tribunal of the Areopagus was instituted at Athens.

Evadne, daughter of Pitane, who at her birth was entrusted to Aepytus, King of Phoesane in Arcadia, and who afterwards bore a son to Apollo, Iamus.

The Molionids, twin sons of Molione, who were born of a silver egg and who so resembled each other that later tradition said they had but a single body with two heads, four arms and four legs. It was they who commanded the troops of Augeias against Hercules, who killed them.

Cycnus, son of Calyce or Harpale, who was exposed on the seashore at birth and taken in by fishermen. He became king of Colonae in the Troad, and

Opposite, Poseidon and his wife Amphitrite riding in triumph through the waves, accompanied by various divinities of the sea. Mosaic from the Villa Stabia, Pompeii. Louvre.

Page 76, Meleager, hero of Aetolia, whose most famous exploit was the killing of the Calydonian Boar, sent by Artemis to ravage Aetolia. Bronze and gold statue by Antico. Victoria and Albert Museum, London.

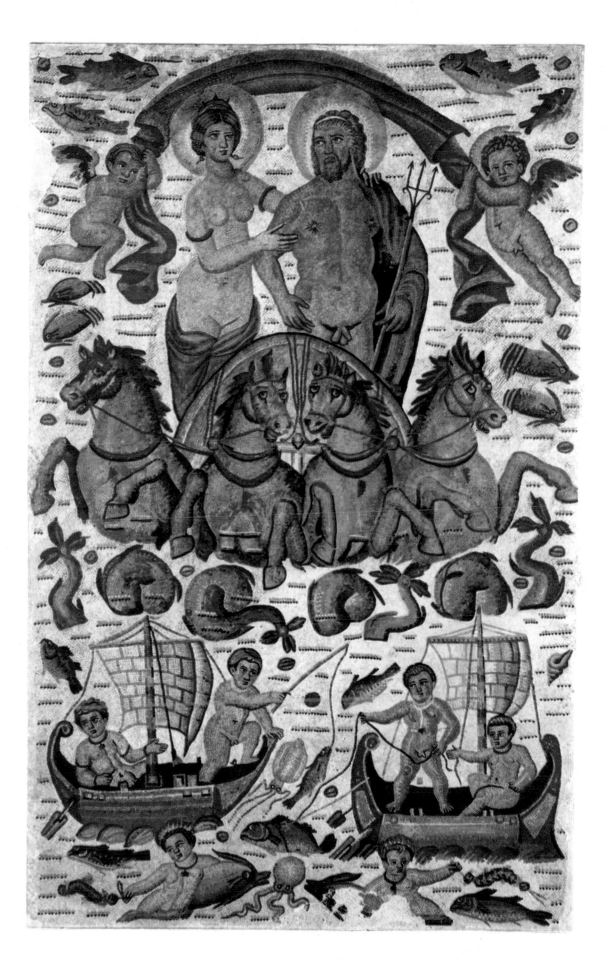

by his first wife, Procleia, had two children, Tenes and Hemithea. His second wife, Phylonome, conceived a passion for her stepson Tenes but, unable to seduce him, slandered him to his father. Cycnus had Tenes and his sister Hemithea locked up in a chest and set them adrift on the sea. But the two young people were saved by Poseidon, and Tenes, landing at Tenedos, became its king. When Cycnus learned the truth he killed Phylonome and went to join his son. Both fought in the Trojan ranks against the Greeks and perished by the hand of Achilles. Since Cycnus was invulnerable, Achilles strangled him with the strap which secured his helmet; but when he attempted to despoil him of his arms the body of Cycnus changed into a swan.

Finally we mention a certain number of monstrous and malignant beings who were also among Poseidon's progeny.

Amycus, born of the nymph Melia, reigned in Bithynia. He was of prodigious strength and challenged all strangers who approached his kingdom to a fatal boxing match. When the Argonauts arrived in Bithynia he at once defied them, but Pollux accepted the challenge and killed him.

The Aloadae were children of Poseidon by Iphimedeia, wife of Aloeus. They were twin brothers, Ephialtes and Otus, who each year grew so fast that at the age of nine they were nearly twenty yards high. We have seen how they attempted to scale Olympus, kept Ares captive for thirteen months and finally perished either beneath Apollo's blows or through a stratagem of Artemis. They were thrown into Tartarus for their crimes and there bound, back to back, to a column by means of a chain made of interlaced serpents. To them were attributed the foundation of Ascra and the institution of the cult of the Muses on Mount Helicon.

Cercyon, son of a daughter of Amphictyon, lived in Eleusis. He forced all travellers to wrestle with him and he killed the vanquished. Only Theseus succeeded in beating him, and put him to death. Cercyon was the father of Alope, who was herself loved by Poseidon.

Another son of Poseidon was also killed by Theseus. This was the brigand Sinis, who lived in the isthmus of Corinth. He submitted all passers-by to an odious torture: he tied them to the tops of two pine- trees which he had bent down. When the trees were released the victims were torn asunder. Theseus made him suffer the same torture.

No less cruel was the King of Egypt, Busiris, son of Poseidon and Anippe. When drought devastated his kingdom Busiris consulted a soothsayer of Cyprus,

Poseidon, riding a dolphin, with Triton. Drawing by Adam Elsheimer, 1578 - 1610. Dresden Print Room.

who declared that the scourge would cease only if each year he immolated a stranger. Busiris began by immolating the soothsayer and continued this bloody practice until the day when Hercules arrived in Egypt and was chosen as a victim. They were about to cut his throat when Hercules burst from the chains which bound him and killed Busiris and his attendants. From that day human sacrifice was no longer practised in Egypt.

To this list of monsters may be added the Cyclops Polyphemus, son of Poseidon and the nymph Thoösa.

In this monstrous progeny attributed to Poseidon may perhaps be seen a survival of the impression of terror felt by primitive men at the rages of the stormy sea. Similarly it was said that Poseidon often summoned up fearful monsters against his enemies. He sent such a monster to ravage the Troad to revenge himself on Laomedon; another, at the prayers of the Nereids, desolated Ethiopia in order to punish the pride of Cassiopeia, mother of Andromeda. He sent a wild bull to devastate the plain of Marathon and a dragon which caused the death of the son of Theseus, Hippolytus.

Hestia

Character and Functions. The Greek word 'hestia' means the hearth, the place in the house where the fire was maintained. The difficulty which primitive man experienced in procuring fire easily explains why he tended it with care and also venerated it. Moreover, it was around the hearth that the family gathered. When one of its members departed to found a new family he took with him a parcel of fire from

Opposite, Perseus holding up the severed head of the Gorgon Medusa. Bronze statue by Benvenuto Cellini. Bargello, Florence.
Page 77, Demeter with her daughter Kore and Triptolemus: the Eleusinian divinities. These goddesses of the Earth and agriculture entrusted Triptolemus with the mission of teaching mortals to cultivate the soil and make bread. Bas-relief of the fifth century B.C. National Museum, Athens.

his parents' hearth, which thus symbolised the continuity of the family. When families began to form groups in towns, each town had its communal hearth where the public fire was maintained. Finally the fire of the *hestia* was used in sacrifices. For these various reasons the *hestia*, like the Vedic Agni, very early took on a sacred character. This character was afterwards personified in a deity who took the actual name of the object she symbolised.

Hestia, then, was, like Hephaestus, a fire-divinity. But while Hephaestus represented the fiery element in its celestial and subterranean manifestations, Hestia symbolised the household fire—fire, as it were, domesticated. Hence the homely and social character of this goddess, whose province was to protect not only the house and the family but also the city. Later Hestia, by analogy, represented the fire in the centre of the earth and the earth itself; but this conception was less mythological than philosophical.

Hestia was venerated in all Greek towns; she had her altar in every prytaneum—or Public Hearth. The Hestia of Delphi was the object of an especial cult, because Delphi was believed to occupy the centre of the universe and its hearth was therefore the common hearth of all Greece. Temples of Hestia were characterised by their circular form.

Representations of Hestia are rare. Glaucus of Argos sculpted one for Olympia. There was also a very celebrated one in Paros. The goddess was depicted sometimes seated, sometimes standing, but always in an attitude of immobility.

Hestia did not spring, like the other divinities, from popular imagination, and consequently legends about her are few.

According to Hesiod—for Homer, before him, did not know of the goddess Hestia—she was the first child born to Cronus and Rhea. Thus she was the oldest of the Olympians and always maintained her precedence. Men understood this well, and when they offered sacrifices consecrated the first morsels of the victims to Hestia and in festivals poured her the first and last libations. On Olympus Hestia's dignity was unquestioned and her rights as the eldest were recognised. She seems to have taken little advantage of this and played a minor role in Olympian drama. 'In the dwelling of the gods,' says Plato, 'Hestia alone maintains repose.' We know of her only that both Poseidon and Apollo sought her hand in marriage. She would have neither one nor the other. In order to put an end to their attentions she placed herself under Zeus' protection and made a solemn vow, touching the head of the master of the gods, to remain a virgin for ever. Zeus accepted her vow and 'instead of marriage offered her a handsome recompense: seated in the midst of the celestial dwelling-place she receives the richest part of sacrifices, and among men she is of all the deities the most highly venerated'.

Hestia thus shared with Athene and Artemis the prerogative of chastity. She was one of those over whom Aphrodite never succeeded in exercising her power.

The lesser gods of Olympus

Olympian society was made in the image of human society and beneath the great gods there were lesser gods who held various positions.

Themis. Of these Themis may be said to be the most important. She was the daughter of Uranus and Gaea and belonged to the race of Titans which the Olympians had supplanted. Far from sharing the disgrace of her brothers, however, Themis never ceased to be honoured on Olympus. Indeed, at the beginning of his reign Zeus had chosen her for his wife. The Moerae, they said, had brought her to Zeus from the far-off regions where Uranus dwelt. Later, when Hera became the wife of Zeus, Themis remained at his side to offer counsel and service. It seems that Hera took no offence at this; when Hera arrived in the assembly of the gods it was from the hand of Themis that she received the cup of nectar.

Themis' mission on Olympus was not only to maintain order but also to regulate the ceremonial; she invited the gods to forgather and prepared their feasts.

Hestia Justiniani. Torlonia Museum, Rome.

She was moreover helpful and obliging. It was she, they said, who had received the infant Zeus from Rhea when Rhea wished to shelter him from the voracity of his father, Cronus. Later she presided over the laborious birth of Apollo and Artemis. It was also said that she made Apollo a present of the oracle at Delphi which she had inherited from her mother, Gaea.

On earth her province was also extensive; above all she was the goddess of justice. She protected the just—whence her epithet *Soteira*, the protectress—and punished the guilty. In her name and according to her advice judges gave their verdicts. Themis was also goddess of wisdom and was called *Euboulos*, the good counsellor; under this title she presided over public assemblies. Finally, since she was the interpreter of the gods' will, she had the gift of delivering oracles. It was she who, after the deluge, suggested to Deucalion the means of repeopling the earth. We have just seen that she once possessed the oracle of Delphi.

From her union with Zeus, Themis had several children: the Horae, and the Moerae or Fates. The Hesperides were also sometimes said to be her daughters.

The cult of Themis was spread throughout Greece; a temple was consecrated to her in the citadel of Athens. She also had sanctuaries at Troezen, Tanagra, Olympia and at Thebes, where she was worshipped with Zeus Agoraios.

She is represented as a woman of grave countenance and austere features. Her attribute is a pair of scales.

Iris. Pontus and Gaea had had, among other children, a son Thaumas who united with Electra, daughter of Oceanus and Tethys. From this union were born the Harpies and Iris. On Olympus Iris, who to the ancients personified the rainbow, was the messenger of the gods. She was assigned in particular to the service of Zeus. When Zeus had an order to give another Immortal, Iris delivered it. If he wished to make his will known to men, Iris flew lightly down to earth where she either borrowed mortal shape or appeared in her divine form. In her divine form she wore a long, full tunic, her hair encircled by a bandeau, and in her hand held the caduceus. She could be recognised by the golden wings attached to her shoulders. Occasionally, like Hermes, she wore winged sandals. Sometimes she cleaved the air as swiftly as the wind, at others glided down the rainbow which bridged sky and earth. She sped through the waters with equal ease. When Zeus sent her in search of the marine-goddess Thetis, Homer tells us how she dived into the dark waves between Samos and the cliffs of Imbros, making the gulf itself groan aloud. Even the Underworld opened before Iris when, at the command of Zeus, she went to refill her golden cup with the waters of the Styx by which the Immortals bound themselves with fearful oaths.

Iris was devoted to Zeus but even more so to Hera. She not only delivered Hera's messages but also effected her vengeance, such as the time when she went to Sicily and, in the guise of Beroe, set fire to Aeneas' fleet. Iris also fulfilled the role of Hera's faithful servant. She prepared Hera's bath, helped her with her toilet, and night and day stood at the foot of her mistress's throne, never falling asleep or even loosening her girdle or sandals.

She also waited on the other gods. When they returned to Olympus in their chariots she would unharness steeds and give them nectar and ambrosia. When Aphrodite was wounded by Diomedes, Iris 'took the overwhelmed goddess and led her away from the battle', helped her to mount the chariot of Ares, and took the reins and whip into her own hands.

Even mortals benefited from her good nature. When she heard Achilles bitterly complain that the flames of the pyre were slow in consuming the body of Patroclus she immediately went to find the Winds—who had just forgathered in the dwelling of the violent Zephyrus for a solemn feast—and begged Boreas and Zephyrus to come and fan the funeral pyre.

Some said that this same Zephyrus was the husband of Iris and claimed that Eros was the fruit of their union.

Hebe, goddess of youth. She is shown here carrying the nectar and ambrosia which it was her task to serve to the gods. Vase detail. Jatta Museum, Ruvo.

On earth Iris was particularly honoured at Delos, where she was offered dried figs and cakes of wheat and honey.

Hebe. Hebe was worshipped by the Greeks as the goddess of youth. She had an altar in the Cynosarges at Athens. At Phlius a grove of cypresses which possessed the right of asylum was sacred to her. She also had a sanctuary at Sicyon.

Hebe was the daughter of Zeus and Hera. She had the gift of eternal youth and represented the deified type of young maiden who in the primitive family was devoted to domestic occupations. Thus on Olympus she performed many duties.

She assisted her brother Ares to dress, bathed him and clad him in magnificent robes. When her mother Hera wished to go forth from Olympus, Hebe prepared the chariot, 'rapidly fixing the curved wheels to the iron axle, tying to the end of the shaft a handsome golden yoke to which she attached reins of gold'. But her chief duty was to hand around nectar and ambrosia to the gods during their feasts. She would move among them, bearing the ewer with the divine draught with which she would fill their goblets. It was claimed that as a result of a fall in which Hebe exposed herself to the eyes of all in a rather indecent posture, she was replaced in this function by Ganymede.

When Hercules, having at last appeased Hera's wrath, was admitted on his death to Olympus with the rank of a god, he was given the gracious Hebe for a wife. They had two children, Alexiares and Anicetus.

Ganymede. In primitive times Ganymede seems to have been conceived as the deity responsible for sprinkling the earth with heaven's rain. He is compared with the Vedic *Soma* who, like him, was ravished by Indra—and changed into a sparrow-hawk. Ancient astronomers identified him with Aquarius, the Water-carrier.

Ganymede was venerated at Sicyon and at Phlius conjointly with Hebe.

He is depicted as an adolescent in a Phrygian cap and a mantle thrown back over his shoulders, either seated beside Zeus or carried through the air by an eagle.

In spite of the honorary position he occupied on Olympus, Ganymede was not of divine birth, being the son of Tros, King of Phrygia, and of Callirrhoe. At least this was the general opinion, although some said his father was Laomedon, Ilus, Assaracus or even Erichthonius. He was distinguished among mortals for his extraordinary beauty. Zeus was charmed and, wishing to make him his favourite, had him swept up by an eagle from the plains of the Troad and brought to Olympus. It was also said that Zeus himself took the form of an eagle in order to carry off the fair adolescent. The abduction of Ganymede took place, according to various versions, in either Mysia, Harpagia, on Phrygian Ida or on the promontory of Dardanus.

To recompense Tros for the loss of his son Zeus presented him with magnificent steeds, 'swift as the storm'.

On Olympus Ganymede became the cup-bearer

Zeus abducting Ganymede. Early Greek statue. Olympia Museum.

Ganymede being swept up to Olympus by Zeus in the shape of an eagle. Engraving after the painting by Titian.

The three Horae. Bas-relief. Florence.

of the gods and rejoiced the eye of all by his beauty.

The Horae. The Greek word from which the Horae derive their name signifies a period of time which can be applied equally to the year, the seasons, and the hours of the day. These different meanings influenced the successive conceptions of the Horae.

First the Horae were divinities of a meteorological character whose function was limited to showering the earth with life-giving rain. They encouraged the blossoming and ripening of fruits and therefore symbolised spring and summer. Afterwards they presided over the order of nature and the succession of the seasons, with whom in the end they were confused.

The number of the Horae varied. The Athenians venerated two: Thallo, who brought the flowers; and Carpo, who brought the fruits. Hesiod counted three Horae. Eunomia, Dike and Irene. Then their number became four and, according to the classification of Hyginus, as many as ten or eleven.

Their sphere of influence soon became moral as well as physical. Guardians of the order of nature, they also watched over the moral order: Eunomia saw that the laws were observed; Dike attended to justice, Irene to peace. According to Hesiod's expression 'they mellowed the behaviour of men'. Finally they were regarded as the protectors of youth.

The Horae were honoured at Athens, Argos, Olympia and particularly at Corinth.

They are depicted as young maidens, holding in their hands the products of the various seasons: a branch in flower, an ear of corn, a vine-stock.

Even before their number was determined and their names decided, the Horae had their appointed occupations on Olympus. In particular it was their duty to guard the gates of heaven, which they opened or closed to the passage of the Immortals by removing or replacing a thick cloud. This is how they appear in the Homeric poems, where we can also see them harnessing Hera's chariot with the celestial steeds which they fed with ambrosia.

Later their character became definite: it was known that they were three in number, that their names were Eunomia, Dike and Irene, and that they were the daughters of Zeus and Themis. They were charming maidens with lovely hair, golden diadems and a light footstep. On Olympus they loved to dance in company with the Graces, and thus formed part of the retinue of Aphrodite, whom they adorned with their own hands.

When Zeus sent Pandora down to earth to let loose man's afflictions the Horae enhanced her attractions by embellishing her hair with floral garlands.

On many occasions they demonstrated their tenderness towards childhood and youth. It was they who nurtured Hera. It was they again who swaddled Hermes at his birth and wove garlands to shelter him. They received Dionysus when he emerged from the thigh of Zeus. Thallo, the Athenian Hora, was venerated by youthful athletes in the temple of Agraulos.

The adventures which were related of them sometimes appear to arise from confusion with other divinities. For example, it was told that the Hora of springtime had been loved by Zephyrus, to whom she bore a son, Carpos; but the tale seems to apply rather to Chloris, the Flora of the Latins. In the same way Pausanias makes Irene the mother of Plutus because in Athens there was a statue of Irene with Plutus in her arms; nothing, however, authorises such a relationship. Of Carpo, one of the two Athenian Horae, it was said that she fell in love with young Camillus, son of the river-god Maeander, and that in despair she drowned herself in the waters of the river, whereupon Zeus changed her into fruit.

Sidereal and meteorological gods

By his sister Theia (or by Euryphaessa) the Titan Hyperion, son of Uranus and Gaea, had three children: Helios, the sun; Selene, the moon; and Eos, the dawn.

Helios

Although the Greeks considered Apollo to be the god of solar light, the sun itself was personified by a special divinity, Helios. In Greece the cult of Helios was very ancient and was practised throughout the land, at Elis, at Apollonia, on the Acropolis of Corinth, at Argos, at Troezen, on Cape Taenarum, at Athens, in Thrace and, most important of all, in the island of Rhodes which was sacred to him. In Rhodes could be seen the colossal statue of Helios, the renowned work of the sculptor Chares. It was about a hundred feet high, and ships in full sail could pass between the god's legs.

It was related that Helios was drowned in the ocean by his uncles, the Titans, and then raised to the sky, where he became the luminous sun.

Every morning Helios emerged in the east from a swamp formed by the River Ocean in the far-off land of the Ethiopians. The Horae harnessed the winged horses to his golden chariot, which Hephaestus had fashioned. The horses were of dazzling white, their nostrils breathed forth flame and their names were Lampon, Phaethon, Chronos, Aethon, Astrope, Bronte, Pyroeis, Eous and Phlegon. The god then took the reins and climbed the vault of heaven. 'Drawn in his swift chariot, he sheds light on gods and men alike; the formidable flash of his eyes pierces his golden helmet; sparkling rays glint from his breast; his brilliant helmet gives forth a dazzling splendour; his body is draped in shining gauze whipped by the wind.'

At midday Helios reached the highest point of his course and began to descend towards the West, arriving at the end of the day in the land of the

Helios driving through the heavens in his golden chariot drawn by four white horses. Painting by Giulio Romano.

84

Hesperides, where he seemed to plunge into the Ocean. But really he found there a barque or a golden cup, made by Hephaestus, in which his mother, wife and children were awaiting him. He would sail all night and in the morning regain his point of departure.

The abode of Helios was also said to be on the isle of Aeaea where his children Aeëtes and Circe lived. Again it was said that his horses rested on the Islands of the Blessed, at the western extremity of the earth, where they grazed on a magic herb.

Helios possessed other domains on earth. When the gods had divided up the world Helios was absent and was forgotten. He complained about this to Zeus and obtained an island which was just beginning to emerge from the waves. He called it Rhodes after the nymph Rhode, whom he loved.

A dispute arose one day between Helios and Poseidon for the possession of the isthmus of Corinth. The giant Briareus, who was chosen to arbitrate, awarded the isthmus to Poseidon but gave Acrocorinth to Helios, who later relinquished it to Aphrodite.

As well as his horses, Helios owned on the island of Thrinacia seven herds of oxen and seven flocks of ewes with beautiful fleeces, each herd and flock being of fifty head. This number always remained constant, like the three hundred and fifty days and three hundred and fifty nights of the primitive year. Two daughters of the god, Phaetusa and Lampetia, guarded these animals. When Odysseus and his companions landed on the isle of Thrinacia the men, in spite of their chief's warning, laid hands on the sacred cattle. 'Chasing before them the handsome broad-browed heifers which grazed not far from the azure-prowed vessel, they cut their throats, then cut up the flesh in morsels which they fixed to their skewers.' When Helios was told by Lampetia what had occurred he complained to the gods and threatened to shut himself up in the kingdom of Hades and shed his light on the dead. Zeus calmed him by promising to strike these foolish mortals with a thunderbolt.

As god of light Helios saw everything and knew everything. What Pindar said of Apollo could also be applied to Helios: 'He is the god who plumbs all hearts, the infallible, whom neither mortals nor immortals can deceive either by action or in their most secret thoughts.' Nothing escaped Helios. He informed Demeter of the rape of her daughter and revealed Aphrodite's unfaithfulness to Hephaestus.

Aphrodite avenged herself by inspiring in Helios a burning passion for Leucothea, daughter of Orchamos, King of Babylon, and Eurynome. Having assumed the appearance of the venerable Eurynome, Helios was about to approach the young maiden, who received him without suspicion. But Clytie, Leucothea's sister, who had herself enjoyed the favours of the god, was jealous of Leucothea's happiness. She informed Orchamos, who condemned his daughter to be buried alive. Helios came in haste, but his rays could not 'bring back living warmth into the frozen limbs of his mistress'. Incapable of restoring her to life, he changed her into an incense shrub. As for Clytie, she realised that the god was now indifferent

The fall of Phaethon, by Michelangelo.

to her love and, according to Ovid, died of despair. 'Exposed to the weather's inclemency, night and day she slept naked on the ground; for nine days without food or water she could quench her thirst only with the dew and her own tears. . . Her body at last took root in the soil; a mortal pallor spread over her and her limbs changed into a colourless stalk; her head became a flower bright as the violet, and in spite of the root which held her fast to the ground she turned her face towards Helios, whom she never ceased to worship.' She is the heliotrope.

Helios also loved the nymph Anaxibia, but she fled from him and took refuge in the temple of Artemis Orthia and disappeared. Helios was unable to find her and rose up into the sky; the place took the name of Anatolius, which means ascension.

Helios had numerous wives as well: the Oceanid Perse, by whom he had two sons, Aeëtes and Perses, and two daughters, Circe and Pasiphaë; Neaera, who bore him Phaetusa and Lampetia, the guardians of his flocks; the nymph Rhode, by whom he had seven sons, the Heliads, and one daughter, Electryone. The Heliads were distinguished for their intelligence, and to them was attributed the perfecting of naval architecture as well as the division of the day into hours. One of them, Tenagis, was outstandingly learned and finally aroused the jealousy of his brothers, who murdered him. After the murder they dispersed among the islands in the neighbourhood of Rhodes.

Among the wives of Helios were also Gaea, who gave him a son, Achelous; Iphinoë (or Iphiboë) or Naupiadame, mother of Augeias; finally Clymene, wife of Merops, King of the Ethiopians, by whom he

Selene. Detail from the frieze of the Pergamum altar. Pergamum Museum, Berlin.

Endymion asleep. Antique bas-relief. Capitoline Museum, Rome.

had seven daughters—who were also called the Heliads—and one son, Phaethon.

Phaethon. One day Phaethon had a dispute with Epaphus, son of Zeus and Io, who had thrown doubts on his divine origin. Phaethon was mortified and went to his mother to complain. In order to reassure him, she advised him to go to Helios himself and ask for confirmation of his divine birth. Phaethon obeyed and begged Helios to accord him a favour which would prove to all eyes that he was indeed the son of Helios. The god gave his promise and swore it by the Styx, which made the oath irrevocable. Phaethon then demanded permission to drive the sun's chariot for one day. In vain Helios tried to dissuade the presumptuous youth from this insane project. Phaethon insisted and Helios was bound by his oath; he had, therefore, to entrust the sun's impetuous steeds to Phaethon. The horses, no longer restrained by the firm hand of their usual driver, rushed wildly through space, carrying the unhappy Phaethon, who had lost all control over them, on their mad career. The chariot came too near the earth; the rivers dried up and the soil began to burn. The universe would

have been destroyed by flame had not Zeus struck the rash youth with a thunderbolt and sent him tumbling into the waters of the Eridanus. Phaethon was buried by the nymphs. His sisters, the Heliads, came to weep beside his tomb and were changed into poplar trees. Their tears became the amber which was gathered in abundance on the banks of the Eridanus.

Circe. A daughter of Helios was equally celebrated in the mythological annals of Greece: Circe. Because she lived in the west of the isle of Aeaea some have tried to see in Circe a moon-goddess. But more probably she was a goddess of love—degrading love—comparable to the Babylonian Ishtar who was so roughly treated by Gilgamesh.

Circe was above all known for her evil spells and enchantments. Married to the king of the Sarmatians, she poisoned her husband and went to live in the isle of Aeaea where she built herself a magnificent palace. She cast a spell over all who landed on the island and, by means of magic potions, turned them into animals. Thus she changed Odysseus' companions into swine. Odysseus alone escaped their fate, thanks to a herb,

86

moly, which Hermes had given him. Better still, he forced the sorceress to restore his companions to their human form. Nevertheless he spent a year with Circe, forgetting his wife and his country. Circe was said to have been slain by Telemachus, who had married her daughter, Cassiphone.

Selene

Selene, who was also called Mene, was the sister of Helios, and with her golden crown illuminated the shadowy night. Every evening, beginning her journey when her brother had finished his, the divine Selene of the broad wings, 'after bathing her lovely body in the Ocean, clad herself in splendid robes and rose in the sky on her chariot drawn by shining steeds'. Sometimes we also see her mounted on a horse, a mule or even a bull.

Although she was generally considered to be the daughter of Hyperion and Theia (or Euryphaessa) her father was sometimes said to be Helios or even Zeus.

Her beauty attracted the love of Zeus, who made her mother of three daughters: Pandia, 'remarkable for her beauty among the Immortals'; Erse, the dew; and Nemea. It was claimed that the Nemean Lion was also born to Zeus and Selene, and that it fell from the moon on to the earth.

Selene was loved by Pan, who took the shape of a white ram and drew her into the depths of a wood in Arcadia.

Selene and Endymion. The best-known legend of Selene was that of her love for Endymion. The story was told differently in Elis and in Caria. According to the Elians, Endymion was a king of Elis whose tomb was still shown at Olympia and to whom Selene bore fifty daughters. According to the Carian tradition Endymion was a young prince who, hunting on Mount Latmus one day, lay down to rest in a cool grotto where he fell asleep. Selene saw him and, captivated by his beauty, stole a kiss while he slept. Endymion asked Zeus to grant him immortality and eternal youth; Zeus consented on condition that he remained eternally asleep.

Another tradition explains this eternal sleep as a punishment inflicted by Zeus on Endymion who, on his admission to Olympus, had been rash enough to aspire to Hera's love.

Be this as it may, Selene came faithfully night after night silently to contemplate her sleeping lover. Thus the rays of the amorous moon come to caress the sleep of mortals.

Eos

The third child of the Titans Hyperion and Theia was Eos (Aurora), the rosy-fingered dawn with the snowy eyelids. It was she who brought the first glimmer of day to men. Every morning at dawn she slipped from the couch of her husband, Tithonus, and emerging from the ocean rose into the sky. Sometimes she appeared as a winged goddess tilting an urn from which fell the morning dew. Sometimes she was mounted on the horse Pegasus and bore in her hands

a torch. Most often saffron-robed Eos rode on a purple chariot drawn by two horses.

It was only later that Eos was distinguished from Hemera, goddess of the day; originally she was represented as accompanying her brother Helios during his whole journey.

Eos at first united with the Titan Astraeus, to whom she bore the winds, Boreas, Zephyrus, Eurus, Notus and various astral bodies.

Eos was young and lovely and made to awaken desire. She was loved by Ares, which earned her the enmity of Aphrodite. To avenge herself, Aphrodite inspired Eos with love for numerous mortals.

She conceived a passion for the giant Orion, whom she carried off and kept with her, to the great annoyance of the gods. Artemis finally killed him by accident in the isle of Ortygia.

Eos and Tithonus. Then Aphrodite filled the heart of Eos with love for Tithonus, one of Laomedon's sons. Wishing to be bound to her new husband for eternity, Eos begged Zeus to confer immortality on him; but, alas, she had forgotten to ask at the same time for perpetual youth! As the years passed the young and handsome lover of former days became an old man with wrinkled brow. In vain Eos fed him on the celestial ambrosia which rendered the flesh incorruptible; old age gave way to decrepitude. The goddess then shut Tithonus up in a chamber where the impotent old man remained in solitude until the day when the gods took pity and changed him into a cicada.

Eos and Cephalus. Meanwhile the inconstant Eos sought consolation among other mortals. There was Cleitus, grandson of the soothsayer Melampus, for whom she obtained the favour of being admitted into Olympus. There was Cephalus, son of Hermes, or of Deion, King of Phocis, whose fate was more tragic. Cephalus had just married Procris, whom he dearly loved, when Eos saw him hunting on Mount Hymettus and carried him off to Syria. Far from responding to the goddess's love, Cephalus thought

Eos pursuing Cephalus. In the top left-hand corner is Selene. Red-figured vase in the British Museum.

87

The death of Procris, observed by Cephalus and his hound, Erechtheus, and a harpy. Red-figured vase in the British Museum.

only of his beloved Procris. Not unnaturally irritated, Eos filled him with doubts about his wife's fidelity and advised him to test her. Cephalus then approached Procris in disguise and, offering her rich jewels, tried to seduce her. Procris repelled him at first, but finally the temptation was too strong for her. Cephalus revealed his identity and drove her away. The unhappy Procris retired to Euboea and put herself under the protection of Artemis. Artemis—or some say it was Minos—gave her a dog who never lost the scent and a javelin which never missed its mark, and sent her back in disguise to Cephalus. This time, offered the dog and the javelin, Cephalus was himself tempted and, in fact, made the same mistake his wife had previously made. The couple then became reconciled. But Procris still feared that her husband might be unfaithful to her and followed him when he went hunting, spying on him without his suspecting it. One day when Procris was hidden in a thicket Cephalus heard a rustling sound. Thinking it was some wild beast, he threw the javelin which never missed its mark. Procris was slain and Cephalus was summoned before the Areopagus, which banished him from Athens. He went to Thebes, where he visited Amphitryon, and then retired to an island which was named Cephallenia after him. According to another version of the story Cephalus was inconsolable at the death of Procris and threw himself from the promontory of Leucas into the sea.

The Offspring of Eos. By her marriage with Tithonus, Eos had two sons: Memnon and Emathion. Emathion reigned over Arabia and was killed by Hercules. Memnon was King of Ethiopia and went to Troy with an army of Ethiopians and Susians to assist Priam. He was 'the most handsome warrior who had appeared before Troy'. Having killed Antilochus, son of Nestor, he was himself killed by Achilles. Eos obtained immortality for him; none the

less she never ceased to weep each morning for her dearly beloved son, and it was her tears which formed the dew. It seems likely that this hero represents some former Asiatic divinity. Memnon, indeed, was reputed to have founded Susa—where his tomb was— and to have built the walls of Babylon. He was also venerated in Egypt, and the colossal resounding statue at Thebes was called the statue of Memnon.

Among the other sons of Eos must be mentioned Phaethon, son of Tithonus (or of Cephalus) who was carried off by Aphrodite to be the guardian of her temple. He is thus connected with the planet Venus, whose double aspect of morning star and evening star is represented by the other two sons of Eos, Phosphorus and Hesperus.

Phosphorus was the son of Astraeus; he could be seen with a torch in his hand in the guise of a winged spirit flying through the air before his mother's chariot.

Hesperus, 'the most splendid star that shines in the firmament', was sometimes said to be the son of Atlas. Hesperus' own children were: Daedalion, who in despair at the death of his daughter Chione threw himself from the heights of Parnassus and was changed by Apollo into a sparrow-hawk; and Ceyx, who married Alcyone. Ceyx and Alcyone were both turned into birds for having dared to compare themselves to Zeus and Hera. Another version is that when Ceyx perished in a shipwreck Alcyone in despair threw herself into the sea and Thetis changed the couple into halcyons or kingfishers.

The Hesperides. Hesperus was also said to be father of the Hesperides; other versions, however, made them the daughters of Night and Erebus, or of Phorcys and Ceto, or of Zeus and Themis. The Hesperides were three or four in number: Aegle, Erytheis, Hespera, Hestia or Arethusa. Their abode

Eos weeping over the body of her son Memnon, whose armour hangs from a nearby tree. He was killed during the Trojan War by Achilles. Attic amphora. Etruscan Museum, Rome.

The Hesperides guarding the golden apples, by Burne-Jones.

Orion crossing the sea. Bronze Etruscan mirror case. British Museum.

was beyond the River Ocean, at the extreme western limits of the world, where they personified the clouds gilded by the setting sun. They lived in a wondrous garden and guarded the golden apples which grew there. Since, however, the Greeks had two identical words for 'apple' and for 'flock of sheep', it has been wondered if the Hesperides were not rather guardians of the celestial flocks which in Indo-European mythology were symbolised by clouds.

Orion, the Pleiades, the Hyades

The constellations of Orion, the Pleiades and the Hyades occupied a particular place in Greek mythology.

Orion. Orion was a giant of Boeotia famous for his beauty. He was variously described as the son of Mother Earth, of Poseidon and Euryale, and of Hyrieus, King of Hyria in Boeotia. One day when Zeus, Hermes and Poseidon were travelling together on earth they were handsomely received by Hyrieus. In gratitude for his hospitality they promised to grant whatever he asked for. Hyrieus asked for a son. The three gods then took the hide of a heifer, urinated on it and buried it. Nine months later Orion emerged from the ground. This singular mode of procreation seems to arise from a play on words, Orion and Urine being similar also in Greek. Orion was of such gigantic stature that he could walk on the bottom of the sea without wetting his head. He was endowed with prodigious strength and was a passionate hunter.

He followed his favourite sport accompanied by his dog Sirius. He had married Side who, because she boasted that she was more beautiful than Hera, was cast by that goddess into Tartarus. Afterwards Orion fell in love with Merope, daughter of Oenopion, ruler of Chios. He rid the island of all its savage beasts in vain: he was rejected by Oenopion. Orion therefore took Merope by violence. Her father then implored the aid of Dionysus, who plunged Orion into deep slumber; while Orion slept, Oenopion put out his eyes. The giant, however, discovered from an oracle that he could regain his sight if he travelled towards the sun. He went to Lemnos, where Hephaestus gave him his son Cedalion for a guide. When his sight was restored Orion sailed on to Crete, where he went hunting with Artemis. We have seen that he was carried off by Eos. The killing of Orion was attributed to Artemis, though there are various versions of how it occurred. Some said she struck him down on the island of Ortygia after Eos had carried him off, others that she shot him by accident at Apollo's instigation, or that she caused his death by a scorpion's sting after he had attempted to rape her, or, again, because he boasted of having destroyed all the wild beasts in Crete. Asclepius attempted to resuscitate Orion, but Zeus struck him with a thunderbolt. Orion descended into the realm of Hades where, armed with a brazen club, his shade continued to hunt the wild beasts. But according to the more popular tradition Orion was transported to the sky where, in golden armour and with sword in hand, he shines on winter nights. His brilliance, however, fades when the constellation Scorpio appears.

Pleiades and Hyades. The Pleiades were daughters

of Atlas and Pleione or Aethra. There were seven of them: Maia, Taygete, Electra, Alcyone, Celoeno, Sterope and Merope. The first three were loved by Zeus. Poseidon obtained the favours of Alcyone and Celoeno. Ares was Sterope's lover. Only Merope had to be content with the love of a mere mortal, Sisyphus —and she therefore shines less brightly in the sky than her sisters, for they had all been changed into stars: they were being pursued across the mountains of Boeotia by the hunter Orion and were about to fall into his clutches when they cried to Zeus for help; he turned them into doves, then placed them in the sky. It was also related that the Pleiades, inconsolable at the death of their sisters, the Hyades, killed themselves in despair and were then changed by Zeus into stars. They appeared in the sky in the middle of May and thus announced the return of the good weather.

The appearance of the Hyades on the contrary was the signal for the rainy season: their very name meant the Rainy Ones. Like the Pleiades, they were daughters of Atlas and Aethra or Pleione. They vary in number according to different authors from two to seven. Nor are their names fixed. The ones most frequently listed are Ambrosia, Eudora and Coronis. It was related that they had brought up Zeus in Dodona, and later Dionysus in Nysa. In recognition of these services they were placed among the heavenly bodies, where they formed a group of stars in the constellation Taurus. Their metamorphosis was also explained as a recompense for the unhappiness they suffered at the death of their brother Hyas, who was killed while hunting by a serpent or a wild boar

Gods of the winds

The empire of the winds was shared between the four sons of Eos, the dawn, and Astraeus, the starry sky. They were called: Boreas, the North Wind; Zephyrus, the West Wind; Eurus, the East Wind; and Notus, the South Wind.

Boreas dwelt in the mountains of Thrace. It was there that Iris came in search of him to fan the funeral pyre of Patroclus. It was said that Boreas carried off Oreithyia, daughter of Erechtheus, from the banks of the Ilissus, and by her had several children, notably Chione, who was loved by Poseidon; Cleopatra, who married Phineus; and the twins Zetes and Calais, also called the Boreades, who took part in the expedition of the Argonauts, fought victoriously against the Harpies, and were slain by the arrows of Hercules in the island of Zenos. They were changed into favourable winds which blew from the north-east and were given the name *Prodromes*, 'forerunners', because they preceded the rise of the Dog Star.

Boreas assumed the form of a stallion to mate with the mares of Erichthonius, and from this union were born twelve young mares so light of step that 'they ran across fields of standing corn without bruising an ear of grain and over the crests of the waves without wetting their feet'.

In memory of the abduction of Oreithyia the Athenians raised a temple to Boreas on the banks of

Zephyrus pursuing Hyacinthus. Hyacinthus was loved by Apollo, Boreas and Zephyrus, but the last two in jealousy caused a discus thrown by Apollo to kill him. Red-figured vase in the British Museum.

Zephyrus and Aphrodite, detail from the 'Birth of Aphrodite' by Botticelli. Zephyrus played an important role in the birth of Aphrodite by bearing her along the coast of Cythera to the shores of Cyprus, where she rose out of the sea. Botticelli's Zephyrus has become a personification of amorous desire. Uffizi, Florence.

Boreas pursuing Odysseus. From a burlesque vase. Ashmolean Museum, Oxford.

the Ilissus. They especially venerated Boreas because he had dispersed the fleet of the invader Xerxes. Boreas was represented as a winged man of mature age with hair floating in the wind.

The normal companion of Boreas was Zephyrus, who was not, originally, the soft and beneficial wind at whose breath the spring flowers open. Like his brother he was a savage and baleful wind who took pleasure in brewing storms and tossing the waves of the sea. With Boreas he lived in the caves of mountainous Thrace. From his union with the Harpy Podarge were born the two horses Xanthus and Balius, who drew the chariot of Achilles.

Later Zephyrus' violent disposition softened. He became a sweet-scented wind which gently fanned the blessed regions of Elysium. For a wife he was given the gracious Chloris by whom he had a son, Carpus—or 'fruit'. As for Notus and Eurus, their individualities were never clearly defined.

Aeolus.   Another tradition, which has its source in the *Odyssey*, places the abode of the winds in the Aeolian Islands, where they were kept under the guardianship of Aeolus. Aeolus was the son of Poseidon and Arne, and a brother of Boeotus. After an adventurous youth he settled in the Lipari Islands and married Gyane, the daughter of King Liparus. Because of his piety and justice Aeolus became a friend of the gods. It was said that he invented ships' sails. Zeus appointed him guardian of the winds which he could, at will, excite or soothe. When Odysseus landed on his island Aeolus welcomed him hospitably and on his departure gave him a wine-skin in which were tied up those winds which would impede his voyage. Overcome by curiosity the companions of Odysseus untied the wine-skin and let the deadly contrary winds escape.

At first Aeolus was simply the guardian of the winds, but later he became their father and, in Roman mythology, the god of wind. He was supposed to dwell on the island of Lipara, where he kept the winds chained up in deep caverns.

The Chimera and the Harpies.   In opposition to these regular winds there were various monsters who personified the storm-winds who, 'pouncing suddenly on the darkened waves, unleashed the raging tempests to destroy men'. Their father was Typhon, son of Typhoeus, spirit of the hurricane, and their mother was Echidna, the upper part of whose body was that of a young nymph but whose lower part was that of a horrifying serpent covered with scales. Among these monsters it will be sufficient to mention the Chimera and the Harpies. The Chimera had the head of a lion, the body of a goat and the tail of a dragon. She vomited forth horrible flames. It is agreed that she was a personification of the storm-cloud.

The Harpies—who were also said to be daughters of Thaumas and Electra—were tempest-goddesses, 'the ravagers'. Homer names only one of them, Podarge. Hesiod mentions two, Aello and Ocypete, winged creatures as swift as birds and the winds. Later the Harpy type became definite: they were monsters with the face of an old hag, the ears of a bear, and the body of a bird with long hooked claws. It was their habit to snatch and devour food from tables, or else to soil the table, spreading filth and stench and causing famine. Thus when the soothsayer Phineus was condemned by Zeus to eternal old age and everlasting hunger, the Harpies came to steal the food which was laid before him, soiling with their excrement what they did not carry away. They were attacked by the Argonauts and particularly by the Boreades Zetes and Calais, who pursued them through the air and vanquished them. At the request of Iris, however, the Boreades spared the Harpies their lives. According to other traditions one of the Harpies drowned herself in the Tigris, a river in the Peloponnese; the other fled to the Echinade Islands where she turned round and fell to the shore. Thus the islands took the name of the Strophades, from the Greek 'to turn'.

Gods of the waters

Pontus.   The oldest divinity of the waters was Pontus, whom Gaea brought forth at the beginning of time. Pontus is no more than the personified sea. He

The Chimera, personification of the storm-cloud, with her lion's head, goat's body and dragon's tail. Interior of a black-figured cup.

A Harpy carrying off a female figure. Relief from the so-called Harpy Tomb. End of the sixth century B.C. British Museum.

was without physiognomy or character, and all that remained of him was his name, which poets later used to designate the sea.

Oceanus. The primitive Greeks, like the Chaldeans, imagined an immense river which formed a watery girdle around the universe. It lay beyond the sea and embraced the sea, without, however, mingling with its waters. It was the River Ocean, or Oceanus, who, having himself neither source nor outlet, gave birth to 'all the rivers, the entire sea, to all waters which gushed from the earth, to all deep wells'. From him arose all the stars—with the exception of the Great Bear—only to plunge back again. On the shores of Oceanus were the fabulous lands of the virtuous Ethiopians, the fog-bound Cimmerians, the minute Pygmies.

Son of Uranus and Gaea, the Titan Oceanus was one of those elemental forces which had contributed to the formation of the world. In him Homer salutes the essence of all things, even of the gods, and regards him as a divinity whose power was inferior to none but Zeus'.

Oceanus married his sister Tethys and by her had the three thousand Oceanids and the three thousand rivers. According to one tradition Oceanus and Tethys cared for the infant Hera, whom they sheltered in their palace in the west of the world.

The Olympians, however, finally established their empire over the waters, and over the rest of the universe, and the watery element was inherited by Poseidon, who from then on became the uncontested lord of the sea and the rivers, while the aged Oceanus was confined to his distant place of retirement.

Divinities of the sea

The importance assumed by Poseidon in Greek religious belief caused the other and more ancient marine deities to play secondary roles, and their cult retained no more than a popular character.

Nereus. Nereus was the son of Pontus and Gaea. He was born in the earliest times of the world, and the accumulation of centuries had made of him a venerable greybeard. He was often called 'The Old Man of the Sea'. He was kindly and helpful, 'having known only thoughts of justice and kindness'. He left the dwelling he occupied with his wife Doris in the depths of the Aegean Sea only in order to come to the assistance of sailors and give them useful advice. Like other marine deities, however, he spoke only when he had to. Hercules resorted to force in order to learn from him how to reach the land of the Hesperides. Nereus also possessed the gift of prophecy; Paris one day beheld him emerging from the waves and heard him announcing the coming destruction of Troy.

Fifty daughters were born to Nereus and Doris; these were the Nereids, fair virgins with golden hair who lived with their father in his underwater dwelling, but who might sometimes be seen when the sea was calm frolicking with the Tritons on the crest of the waves.

Of most of the Nereids we know only the names; some of them, however, played a part in the legends of Greece.

Arethusa was seen one day by the hunter Alpheius, who immediately fell in love with her. He pursued

Nereus riding a sea-horse. From a Greek cup in the British Museum.

her, and to escape him Arethusa took refuge on the island of Ortygia, where she was changed into a spring. Alpheius, who remained in the neighbourhood of Olympia, was himself changed into a river and his waters, crossing the sea without mingling with it, then joined the waters of the spring Arethusa.

Galatea, another Nereid, was courted by the Cyclops Polyphemus, but she preferred a young herdsman of Sicily named Acis. Polyphemus surprised the two lovers one day while they were conversing in the hollow of a grotto and crushed Acis under an enormous boulder. Galatea, however, succeeded in having Acis changed into a river.

Psamathe had by Aeacus a son Phocus, who reigned over the island of Aegina and who was assassinated by Peleus and Telamon. To avenge the murder of her son Psamathe sent a monstrous wolf who devastated Peleus' flocks.

The most celebrated of the Nereids was Thetis. For her beauty she was sought in marriage by both Zeus and Poseidon. But Themis declared that Thetis would give birth to a son more powerful than his father, and both gods prudently renounced their project. Zeus decided to marry Thetis to a mortal, and chose Peleus, King of Thessaly. Thetis did not accept this alliance without protest, for, being immortal, she considered it beneath her dignity. She attempted to escape from Peleus by taking on various shapes: she changed herself into a fish and then into an animal; into a fluid wave, then into burning flame. Thanks to the advice of the centaur Chiron, Peleus finally succeeded in seizing her and their marriage was celebrated with great pomp in the presence of the gods, who showered fine gifts on the couple. Thetis and Peleus had a son, Achilles. Some said that Achilles

was their seventh child and that Thetis had thrown the first six into the fire to destroy the evidence of an unworthy union. This story sorts rather badly with the tenderness which Thetis always showed towards Achilles. When she learned the fatal destiny which awaited her son she tried to prevent it by rendering Achilles invulnerable. In order to do this, she exposed him to fire every night and dressed his wounds with ambrosia. But Peleus caught her unawares one night and, terrified, snatched the child away. According to a better accredited version, as soon as Achilles was born Thetis plunged him into the Styx, thus making all his body invulnerable, except the heel by which she held him.

Thetis plays a part in many legends. As already mentioned, when Zeus was nearly overcome by Hera, Apollo, Poseidon and Athene, Thetis came to his assistance by bringing the great Briareus to defend him. Thetis and her sister Eurynome sheltered Hephaestus after his fall from Olympus. She also sheltered Dionysus when he fled from Lycurgus.

She was honoured in various parts of Greece, in Thessaly, in Messenia and at Sparta.

Proteus. Proteus was another 'Old Man of the Sea'. He was the son of Oceanus and Tethys, and his duty was to guard Poseidon's herd of seals. At noon each day he would emerge from the waves and come ashore to rest in the shelter of a rock. Around him slept the tight-packed herd of seals, sons of the fair Halosydne. It was the propitious moment to obtain from wise Proteus a revelation of what fate held in store; for he saw into the future and he spoke the truth. But, since he never spoke oracularly unless forced to do so, it was first necessary to catch hold of him—no simple matter, for Proteus could change

93

Above, Nereus and his daughters, the Nereids. Detail from a cup in the Louvre.
Below, Thetis and Nereids conveying armour over the sea to Achilles at Troy. Thetis is seated on a hippocamp; the Nereid on a dolphin. Between them is Eros. From a vase in the British Museum.

shape at will and in order to escape from whoever held him would in succession turn himself into a lion, a dragon, a panther, into water, fire, a tree . . . The important thing was to show no fear of these metamorphoses, for then Proteus would admit himself, vanquished and talk. In this manner Menelaus, following the advice of Idothea, Proteus' daughter, learned from him how to return to his own country. Proteus was represented with the features of an old man, and he lived on the island of Pharos on the Egyptian coast.

This habitat was probably attributed to Proteus because of confusion with a fabled King of Egypt who was also named Proteus. It was said that this king welcomed Paris and Helen when they fled from Sparta, but that he kept Helen with him in order to return her to her legitimate husband. It was also said that he went from Egypt to Thrace, where he married. Later, angered by the cruelty of his two sons, Tmolus and Telegonus, he decided to return to Egypt, and Poseidon hollowed out for him under the sea a road which led him back to Pharos.

Phorcys. The character of Phorcys is more vague. Homer calls him 'the old man who rules the waves'. He says that his daughter was the nymph Thoösa, who bore the monstrous Polyphemus, fathered by Poseidon. According to Hesiod, Phorcys was the son of Pontus and Gaea. He married his sister Ceto and fathered the Graeae, the Gorgons, the dragon Ladon and, perhaps, the Hesperides. It was also said that Scylla was born of his love for Hecate. To judge by his wild progeny Phorcys must in the eyes of the Greeks have personified the perfidious and evil sea. His name seems to indicate the whitish foam which crowns the crest of the waves.

Glaucus. The name Glaucus evokes a picture of the dark greenish-blue which the sea assumes when the winds begin to rise. There were various legends about Glaucus. One related that he was a humble fisherman from Anthedon. One day when he returned from fishing he put down his fish among some herbs which grew beside the shore. He saw them immediately leap up and fling themselves back into the sea. He tasted the herbs himself and was changed into a Triton. He jumped into the sea and was welcomed by the marine deities as one of their own number. Another legend recounts that while pursuing a hare Glaucus saw the creature swallow a blade of this herb and at once recover its agility. In curiosity Glaucus also tasted the mysterious herb and thus acquired immortality. He took to the sea either, because Zeus had secretly instilled in him the impulse to do so, or because he was vexed at being unable to make his fellow men acknowledge his immortality.

Glaucus normally dwelt in Delos. Apollo conferred on him the gift of prophecy, which he transmitted to his daughter, the Sibyl Deiphobe. Once a year Glaucus left his abode in Delos and made a tour of the islands of the Aegean Sea. He would appear to sailors, with his thin body covered with seaweed and seashells, and predict sinister occurrences.

He was a lugubrious divinity and even his love-affairs were unhappy. Except for Syme, whose love he won and whom he carried to a small island near Rhodes, all to whom he paid court repulsed him. He discovered Ariadne on the island of Naxos and attempted to console her, but Dionysus arrived, bound him up with vine-shoots, and consoled Ariadne himself. It was also said that Glaucus turned Scylla into a monster out of resentment; but Scylla's metamorphosis was also attributed to the jealousy of Amphitrite.

Opposite, Achilles and his friend Patroclus, who was killed in the Trojan War. Relief from the Archaeological Museum, Florence.
Page 96, head of Theseus. Detail of a fresco from the basilica, Herculaneum.

94

A Nereid riding on a sea horse, or hippocamp. Red-figured cup in the British Museum.

Triton abducting a nymph. Antique sculpture. Vatican Museum, Rome.

Melicertes Palaemon, another personage of human origin who was raised to the rank of marine divinity was sometimes confused with Glaucus.

Melicertes was the son of Athamas and Semele's sister Ino who had incurred the wrath of Hera for having fed and sheltered young Dionysus after his mother's death. Hera, in vengeance, unbalanced Athamas' mind, and Athamas slew one of his own sons, Learchus. To save the other son, Melicertes, from his father's madness, Ino seized the child and jumped with it into the sea. She was welcomed by the Nereids and became, under the name Leucothea, a divinity who protected mariners. As for Melicertes, his body was carried by a dolphin to the coast of Corinth. Sisyphus found it and erected a tomb for him on the shore. Under the name Palaemon, Melicertes was from then on venerated as a god. On the instructions of the Nereids the Isthmian Games were instituted in his honour. He is usually represented as a child carried by dolphins.

Triton. Around the chariot of Amphitrite, who was escorted by the gracious Nereids, frisked strange creatures called Tritons, half men, half fish, whose bodies were covered with scales, whose teeth were sharp and whose fingers were armed with claws. Their breasts and bellies were supplied with fins, and instead of legs they had the forked tail of a marine monster. This lascivious troop played among the

Opposite, Theseus killing the Minotaur, a monster half human half bull, to whom young Athenians were sacrificed as an annual tribute to Crete. Vase in the British Museum.

Page 97, Hercules fighting with the Centaur Nessus, who attempted to rape the hero's wife Deianeira, while carrying her across a river. Sixteenth-century terracotta attributed to Caccini. Victoria and Albert Museum, London.

waves, noisily blowing on conch shells. Some of their number, who were furnished with a pair of horse's legs as well, were known as Centaur-Tritons.

Although they lived in the sea the Tritons sometimes ventured on to land. At Tanagra, people remembered a Triton who had laid waste the country and ravished the women. To capture him they placed a vase filled with wine on the beach. The Triton drank it, and during his drunken slumber a fisherman cut off his head. They placed a statue of a headless Triton in the temple of Dionysus at Tanagra to commemorate the event.

These marine genii took their name from a primitive god, son of Poseidon and Amphitrite, whose name was Triton. He also was half man, half fish, and lived with his father in the depths of the sea, although his favourite abode was near the coast of Libya. It even seems that in origin Triton was a purely Libyan divinity, unless the Minoan colonists had brought with them to Africa the former god of the River Triton, which flowed into Lake Copais in Boeotia.

As Poseidon's son, Triton shared some of his father's powers: like him he could stir up or quieten the waves. He could be seen riding the waves on a chariot drawn by steeds whose hooves were the claws of crayfish.

On two occasions he did Zeus a good turn. During the war with the Giants, Triton contributed to the victory of the Olympians by frightening the giants with the terrible sounds he made with his conch. Later, it was Triton whom Zeus made responsible for seeing that the waters withdrew after the deluge.

Benevolent and obliging, Triton saved the Argonauts when a tempest drove their ship on to the Libyan coast. He gave them advice and made it possible for them to continue their voyage.

Triton shared the gift of prophecy with the other marine gods, Nereus and Proteus, of whom he may have been originally only a local form. It seems, however, that he more especially personified the roar of the sea or its wild movement, as his attribute, the conch, tends to indicate.

Sea Monsters. The Sirens. The name Siren derives from a Greek root meaning 'to bind or attach' and clearly alludes to the role the Sirens played in mythology. They are, however, most probably divinities who symbolised the souls of the dead. They would thus be funerary genii, avid for blood and hostile to the living. With bird's body and woman's head, they recall the human-headed Egyptian hawk, who also incarnated the souls of the dead. The Sirens were invoked at the moment of death, and their images are frequently found on tombs. Legend, however, has retained nothing of this conception of them, and depicts the Sirens only as malevolent monsters of the sea.

At first they were represented with the head and bust of a woman and the body of a bird, and only later depicted as women whose bodies terminated in fish tails. Their attribute was a musical instrument—a lyre or a double flute. They had a temple at Sorrento.

When Odysseus was about to leave Circe and take to his swift ships again, she warned him of the dangers of the voyage and in particular said:

'First thou shalt arrive where the enchantress Sirens dwell, they who seduce men. The imprudent man who draws near them never returns, for the Sirens, lying in the flower-strewn fields, will charm him with sweet song; but around them the bodies of their victims lie in heaps.'

And so it was that Odysseus came near a rocky islet where he perceived strange creatures, half-women, half-birds, who, seeing his ship, began to sing. These were the Sirens, and they sang:

'Draw near, illustrious Odysseus, glory of the Achaeans; stop thy ship and come to us. None has yet passed by this isle without having listened to the enchantment of our voices and heard us sing of the mighty deeds done by the Greeks beneath the walls of Troy. For we know all that happens on the fruitful earth.'

The sweetness of their voices was such that Odysseus could not have resisted their invitation had he not followed Circe's advice and taken the precaution of having himself lashed to the mast of his ship. As for his companions, he had taken the precaution of stopping up their ears with wax.

Thus they escaped the fearful danger. But the human bones scattered over the green fields of the Siren Island bore mute witness to the imprudence of former sailers and to the ferocity of these insidious-voiced creatures.

They had not always been like this. In primitive times the Sirens, who were daughters of the River Achelous, had been river deities. Different authors make them two, three, four, or even eight in number. They had names which emphasised the charm of their voices: Aglaophonos or Aglaophone (of the brilliant voice); Thelxepeia (of the words which enchant); Peisinoë (the persuasive); Molpe (song).

There were various explanations of their strange shape. According to some they were with Persephone when she was ravished by Hades, and it was at their request that Zeus gave them wings so that they could fly in pursuit of the ravisher. According to others they owed their birds' bodies to the wrath of Aphrodite, who punished them in this way for having been impervious to love.

The Sirens were excessively proud of their voices and their musical talent and were said to have dared one day to challenge the Muses. But the Muses vanquished them and pulled out their wing feathers. The Sirens then left the springs and dales and went to hide their shame among the jagged rocks along the coasts of southern Italy. They lived on Cape Pelorus, Capri, the island of Anthemusa, and the Siren Isles. From the shores they attracted sailors by their songs and devoured the unhappy wretches who had been unable to resist their seduction.

In the end, however, they found their master. When the ship of the Argonauts sailed past their island they tried as usual to exert their power. But only Butes, son of Zelion, jumped overboard to join the treacherous goddesses. The others were prevented by Orpheus, who was with them. He tuned his lyre and began to sing; and his persuasive voice overcame the allure of the Sirens.

Vanquished, the Sirens from that moment lost all power to do harm and were changed into rocks. In vexation one of them, Parthenope, threw herself into the sea. Her body was tossed on to the shore by

Odysseus and the Sirens. Bell krater from Paestum. About 330 B.C. *Former State Museum, Berlin.*

Scylla. She has snaky locks, wings in her hair, over her forehead are two bull's heads and under her chin are twisted marine animals. Bronze. British Museum.

the waves, and a tomb was erected for her on the very spot where later the city of Naples rose.

Charybdis and Scylla. This same Sicilian sea where the Sirens dwelt also harboured two other redoubtable monsters, Charybdis and Scylla.

Of Charybdis we know little more than what Homer tells us. 'With a terrible roar divine Charybdis swallows the waves of the bitter sea and three times each day she throws them up again.' She lived under a rock crowned by a green fig tree. She was called the daughter of Poseidon and the Earth, and it was because she had stolen the oxen of Hercules that Zeus struck her with a thunderbolt and changed her into a whirlpool whose vortex swallowed up ships.

The legend of Scylla was more elaborate. She was the daughter of Phorcys and Crataeis, or of Typhon and Echidna, or of Poseidon. According to others, her mother was Lamia, that queen of Libya who was loved by Zeus and saw her children perish as a result of Hera's jealousy. Misery drove her out of her mind, and she devoured babies whom she tore from their mothers' arms. Scylla was at first a nymph of rare beauty. Whether it was because she repelled the advances of Glaucus and Glaucus punished her for her disdain, or whether, on the contrary, she had given herself to Poseidon and thus excited Amphitrite's jealousy, Scylla was changed by Circe into a monster. While she was bathing in a pool into which Circe had thrown certain magic herbs, six necks suddenly sprang from her shoulders, necks of monstrous length, surmounted by six frightful heads, each with a triple row of teeth. She lurked in a dark cavern hollowed in the middle of a reef from which emerged only her heads, which snapped up passing dolphins, the dogs of the sea, and 'those of the enormous monsters nurtured by the noisy Amphitrite whom she was able to seize'. When a ship passed within her reach each of her heads would carry off a man from the bench of rowers, and no vessel could boast of escaping Scylla without loss.

When Hercules brought Geryon's herd through the straits of Sicily, Scylla seized and devoured one of the oxen. Hercules killed her, but she was resuscitated by her father Phorcys, and mariners passing the straits of Sicily continued to dread these twin perils.

Freshwater divinities

The Rivers. There were three thousand rivers according to Hesiod; they were sons of Oceanus and Tethys, and as they shared in the divine nature of their parents they were worshipped by mortals. Young folk consecrated their hair to them; rams were offered in sacrifice to them; and live horses and bulls were cast into their waters.

The rivers were represented as vigorous men with long beards; their strength was symbolised by the pair of horns which adorned their brow.

The most celebrated and venerated of rivers was the Achelous, which was also the largest watercourse in Greece. Achelous fought against Hercules for the hand of Deianeira. Vanquished, he changed himself into a serpent, then into a wild bull. Hercules, however, overthrew him and tore off one of his horns, with which the nymphs made the Horn of Plenty. Ashamed of his defeat, Achelous threw himself into the river which thenceforth bore his name. Achelous was revered throughout Greece and even in Sicily—six rivers were named after him—and oaths were sworn in his name. It was for having omitted to do him honour during a sacrifice that the daughters of the soothsayer Echinus were changed into islands and became the Echinades.

Almost as famous was the Asopus, a name also found in Thessaly and the Peloponnese. Asopus was a river-god of Boeotia. By his wife Merope he had two sons, Pelasgus and Ismenius, and twelve daughters, among them Sinope, who was carried off by Apollo; Corcyra and Salamis, who were loved by Poseidon; and Aegina, who was ravished by Zeus. Asopus went in search of Aegina and learned from Sisyphus—in exchange for a spring which he made gush forth on Acrocorinth—the name of his daughter's ravisher. He attempted to obtain justice, but Zeus struck him with a thunderbolt and forced him to return to his river bed.

Inachus, river-god of Argolis, also had one of his daughters, Io, seduced by Zeus. During the dispute between Hera and Poseidon for possession of Argolis, Inachus was chosen to arbitrate. He pronounced in favour of Hera, and Poseidon, in annoyance, dried up his waters.

Cephissus was a river-god of Phocis and Boeotia. He appears in mythology only as the father of Narcissus, whose mother was the Oceanid Liriope. There was a sanctuary consecrated to him at Argos.

Other river-gods included Peneius in Thessaly; in Arcadia, Ladon, who was the father of Syrinx and Daphne; in the Peloponnese, Alpheius, who was said to have fallen in love with Artemis. To elude him Artemis took refuge in Elis, and when she reached Letrini made herself unrecognisable by daubing herself with mud. It was also related that Alpheius was

Hercules fighting with Achelous for the hand of Deianeira. The horn which Hercules is tearing off was to become the Horn of Plenty. Red-figured vase in the British Museum.

a hunter who fell in love with the nymph Arethusa and pursued her to the island of Ortygia, where she changed into a spring. Alpheius, in his turn, was changed into a river, but he still obstinately pursued Arethusa. He crossed the sea without mingling with its waters and in Ortygia rejoined his beloved. When bulls were sacrificed in Olympia, past which the Alpheius flowed, it appeared that the waters of the fountain of Arethusa were also tinged with blood. The Eurotas was said to have been a king of Laconia. Among his daughters was Sparta, who was married to Lacedaemon. Eurotas was responsible for draining the marshes which covered Laconia, and his name was given to the canal he dug to carry away the waters. Others said he threw himself into the river which bears his name in despair at having lost a battle.

In Phrygia the two principal river-gods were the Scamander (or Xanthus) and the Maeander. It was Hercules, seized by thirst, who had scooped out the earth and caused the Scamander to gush forth. Scamander took part in the Trojan war and Homer describes his battle with Achilles. He caught up the hero in his nets and it required the intervention of Hephaestus to appease the river-god. As for the Maeander, it owed its name to Maeander, King of Pessinonte, who in the course of a war made a vow that if he were victorious he would sacrifice the first person who came to congratulate him. The first person to do so was his son. Maeander fulfilled his vow, but threw himself in despair into the river which took his name.

Water Nymphs. Just as every river had its own divine personality, so every stream, brook, spring and pool harboured in its waters a divinity who was known as a nymph.

Water nymphs were classified according to the place they inhabited. Potamids were nymphs of rivers and streams; Naiads were nymphs of brooks; Crenae or Pegae were nymphs of springs; Limnads were nymphs of stagnant waters.

Although they occupied an inferior rank in the divine hierarchy they were occasionally admitted to Olympus, and mortals worshipped them.

They had many functions. They had the gift of prophecy and could deliver oracles. They were benevolent deities and cured the sick; they watched over flowers, fields and flocks.

Sometimes they lived in the depths of the waters, sometimes in grottoes near the springs over which they presided. There they would busy themselves weaving and spinning. Sometimes they would mingle with the retinue of certain divinities.

In spite of their divine character they were not immortal. According to Plutarch, the average life span of a nymph did not exceed nine thousand six hundred and twenty years. But it was their privilege always to remain young, beautiful, for their nourishment was ambrosia.

Although they were generally benevolent, they could become dangerous to those mortals whom they marked with their favours. Like the Rusalki of the Slavs, they sometimes dragged such mortals down into the depths of the waters. This, as we have seen, was the fate of Hermaphroditus, victim of the nymph Salmacis. A similar fate overtook young Hylas, the handsome companion of Hercules. When the ship of the Argonauts reached the coasts of the Troad, Hylas, who was a member of the expedition, was sent ashore by his companions in search of water. As it happened he discovered a fountain, but the nymphs of the place were so charmed by his beauty that they carried him to the depths of their watery abode, and in spite of the cries of Hercules which made the shores reverberate with the name Hylas, the young man was never seen again.

Among the nymphs whose name is known to legend may be mentioned Aganippe, nymph of the spring of that name which flowed at the foot of Mount Helicon and whose waters inspired those who drank of them; Cassotis and Castalia, nymphs of prophetic springs on Parnassus; Hago, who presided over a fountain on Mount Lycaeus. During periods of drought the priest of Lycaean Zeus would touch the surface of the fountain with an oak branch. At once a mist would arise which would thicken into a cloud and soon pour forth the wished-for rain. Another nymph was Pirene, whose tears at the death of her son formed a fountain which could be seen near Corinth. Cyane, a Sicilian nymph, was with Persephone when she was carried off by Hades and, heartbroken, turned herself into a fountain. According to another tradition this fountain sprang from the hole Hades made when he plunged into the earth. Every year the people of Syracuse would come there and throw in a bull. Argyra, nymph of a fountain in Arcadia, loved the shepherd Selemnos. When she deserted him Selemnos fell into such despair that Aphrodite took pity on him and changed him into a river, granting him oblivion to cure the sickness of his heart. Thus whoever bathed in the River Selemnos found oblivion from the sorrows of love.

Calypso was the daughter of Atlas and Tethys and, according to ancient tradition, reigned over the island of Ortygia in the Ionian Sea. When a tempest threw Odysseus on her shores she welcomed him hospitably and kept him with her for seven years. To retain him for ever she offered him immortality, but Zeus ordered her to release him. As indicated by her name— derived from a root which means 'to hide', Calypso personified the depths of the waters.

Divinities of the earth

Gaea, Rhea and Cybele

A personification of the earth, Gaea was, as we have already seen, the primitive goddess of the Greeks.

A seventeenth-century interpretation of a Greek river-god. Engraving by Jan Smelinck, Rotterdam.

Though her cult persisted throughout the ages her individuality became submerged in that of other similar divinities. The Pelasgian Gaea was early supplanted by Rhea, whose origin was probably Cretan and who was herself simply the earth deified. Her very name seems to derive from an archaic word meaning earth.

The legend of Rhea was formed by more or less repeating that of Gaea. The couple Rhea-Cronus corresponds exactly to the couple Gaea-Uranus. Both goddesses have the same maternal anxieties and both husbands come to the same unhappy end. In the same way that the primitive Greeks made Gaea the Great Mother and author of all beings, so the supremacy of Rhea was affirmed by the fact that she was made mother of the great gods ruling on Olympus.

In spite of her foreign origin, Rhea soon took on a physiognomy which was plainly Greek. Several regions of Greece claimed the honour of having been the scene of the diverse episodes of her legend. For instance, it was near Chaeronea, on the cliff of Petrachus, that Rhea presented the stone to Cronus; the same scene was also said to have taken place at Methydium in Arcadia. Thebans pointed out the place where Rhea brought Zeus into the world, while the Arcadians said he was born on Mount Lycaeus. The god had grown up either in Olympia of Elis, or on Mount Ithome in Messenia. Finally, Rhea was supposed to reside on Mount Thaumasium in Arcadia.

The Hellenic character of Rhea was, however, altered by the influence of the great Phrygian goddess Cybele, whose cult was early introduced into Greece; but in the end the two goddesses were merged.

Etymologically Cybelle was the goddess of caverns. She personified the earth in its primitive and savage state and was worshipped on the tops of mountains: on Ida in Phrygia, on Berecyntus, Sipyle, and Dindymus. She exercised dominion over wild beasts who customarily formed part of her retinue.

Greek representations of Cybele retained an Asiatic character. The goddess with her turreted crown— the normal attribute of Asian mother-goddesses—is seated on a throne flanked by two lions, or else is placed in a chariot drawn by lions. Sometimes she holds a whip decorated with knuckle-bones. This attribute, emblem of power, was the instrument with which the Galli, priests of Cybele, flagellated themselves.

The Galli were an odd fraternity, who celebrated the cult of their goddess with convulsive dances to the sound of flutes, drums and cymbals, while clashing their shields with their swords. In their orgiastic fury they would sometimes voluntarily mutilate themselves. They were known in Greece under the name of the Corybantes and were said to be the issue of a certain Corybas, son of Cybele. Later they were identified with the Cretan Curetes.

Attis, a god of lesser rank, was associated with the great Phrygian goddess; her role in relation to Cybele was analogous to that of Tammuz to the Babylonian Ishtar, or Adonis to the Phoenician Astarte; like them he was a vegetation god. The Phrygians honoured him under the name *Papas*, the father.

103

As the cult of Cybele spread through Greece the figure of Attis became modified. He was presented as a young and handsome shepherd from Celaenae with whom Cybele fell in love. She chose him as her priest and imposed upon him a vow of chastity. When Attis broke his vow and married the daughter of the River Sangarius, Cybele struck him with frenzied delirium in the course of which he mutilated himself. When he recovered from his madness he was on the point of killing himself when Cybele changed him into a fir tree. According to another tradition—obviously inspired by the myth of Adonis—Attis perished as a victim of the jealousy of Zeus, who sent a wild boar against him. The tomb of Attis was at Pessinus, and each year at the beginning of spring his festival was celebrated for five days. The first was a day of mourning when in the midst of lamentation a sacred fir wound with woollen bands was carried through the streets. On the second day the Galli worked themselves into a fever to the sound of savage music. The third day was marked by bloody mutilations. On the fourth day joyful dancing commemorated the resurrection of Attis. The fifth and last day was devoted to rest.

Cybele entered a union with the King of Phrygia, Gordius, who had devised the famous Gordian knot. By him she had a son, Midas, who succeeded to his father's throne. He was a wise and pious king who established the cult of the Great Zeus of Ida and instituted the mysteries of Cybele. His kindness to Silenus who, when drunk one day on the banks of the Sangarius, had been tied up by peasants, earned Midas the gratitude of Dionysus. The god asked him to make a wish and Midas asked that everything he touched should be turned into gold. He soon regretted his rashness, for even the food he ate immediately turned into gold. Dionysus took pity on him and sent him to purify himself in the River Pactolus, which thenceforth flowed with gold dust.

Midas was less fortunate with Apollo. Asked to

Demeter, with her hair knotted in a ribbon and carrying a jar round which twines a snake, attribute of Demeter. Relief from the Pergamum altar. Pergamum Museum, Berlin.

arbitrate between Apollo and Marsyas as to which played the lyre or the flute better, Midas voted against Apollo, who, as a reward, gave him a pair of ass's ears. Midas was able to hide these ears under his Phrygian cap and his disgrace was known only to his barber. The secret weighed heavily on the poor barber, who dug a hole in the ground and confided it to the earth. Now reeds grew in this spot, and whenever the wind stirred among them they could be heard to repeat: 'King Midas has ass's ears.' In despair Midas killed himself by drinking, they say, the blood of a bull.

Demeter

Character and Functions. Gaea and her substitutes, Rhea and Cybele, personified the earth as such, while Demeter represented the fertile and cultivated soil. Of the two elements which compose her name—a variant or a more ancient form of a word meaning 'earth-mother'—the maternal part finally assumed the greater importance among the Greeks.

The primitive character of Demeter was preserved in certain regions of Greece, notably in Arcadia, where the goddess was represented with a horse's head, surrounded by serpents and ferocious beasts, bearing in one hand a dolphin and in the other a dove. But elsewhere, and particularly in Attica, Demeter appeared above all as a goddess of the fruits and riches of the fields. She was primarily the corn-goddess: wheat and barley were sacred to her. She presided over the harvest and all the agricultural labours which attend it.

Goddess of the earth, Demeter's sphere of influence also reached the Underworld; but her character of Underworld divinity soon devolved on a special goddess—Kore or Persephone—who was made the daughter of Demeter.

Apollo, King Midas and Pan. Parma.

Demeter always remained in contact with mortals on whom she heaped the benefits of civilisation. Thus she was called *Thesmophoros*, 'who gives laws', though this title may have been given to her in her capacity of goddess of marriage.

Cult and Representations. Demeter was worshipped in Attica, Arcadia and Argolis, at Delos, in Crete, in Asia Minor and in Sicily. Her cult was surrounded by mystery and accompanied by orgies. Her temples, called *Megara*, were often found in forests.

It is above all Demeter's maternal aspect that art has accentuated in the various portrayals of the goddess. She sometimes appears seated, sometimes walking, dressed in a long robe and often wearing a veil which covers the back of her head. Sometimes she is crowned with ears of corn or a ribbon, and holds in her hand either a sceptre, ears of corn, or a torch.

Demeter's Suitors. Demeter was a daughter of Cronus and Rhea and thus belonged to the group of great Olympians. She had an austere beauty, its severity scarcely relieved by her hair, which was as fair as ripened grain.

Poseidon desired her, but Demeter refused herself to him. To escape him she fled to Arcadia where, assuming the shape of a mare, she mingled with the herds of King Oncus. Poseidon, however, succeeded in finding her, changed himself into a stallion and made her the mother of the horse Arion, who was endowed with the gift of speech and whose right feet were those of a man. By Poseidon Demeter also had a daughter, whose name has remained concealed and who was known only as the mistress—Despoena.

Demeter was infuriated at the outrage to which Poseidon had submitted her and left Olympus. She took on the aspect of a Fury—thus in Arcadia she was entitled Erinnys—and hid her shame in a cavern. In order to bring her back to Olympus Zeus himself had to intervene. She resumed her place among the Immortals after purifying herself in the waters of the Ladon.

Demeter was also desired by Zeus, whom she resisted in a similar fashion. Zeus, however, deceived her by turning himself into a bull and made her mother of Kore.

But the heart of Demeter was not always untouched by sentiment. It was said that she loved Iasion, 'lay with him in a thrice-ploughed field' and had by him a son, Plutus. According to some Zeus was jealous of Iasion and struck him with a thunderbolt; according to others, he lived for a long time with Demeter and introduced her cult into Sicily.

Demeter and Kore. Demeter, however, was chiefly celebrated for her maternal tribulations. She loved her daughter Kore tenderly. One day Kore was gathering flowers in the fields of Nysa with her companions when she suddenly noticed a narcissus of striking beauty. She ran to pick it, but as she bent down to do so the earth gaped open and Hades appeared. He seized her and dragged her with him down into the depths of the earth. According to another tradition, the abduction of Kore took place

Veiled Demeter. Greek sculpture. Louvre.

Above, Demeter, seated and holding her attributes of sceptre and ears of corn, with Kore, who holds two torches. Votive relief of the fifth century B.C. Eleusis Museum.
Below, Kore. Statue of 480 B.C. Eleusis Museum.

on the heights near the town of Enna in Sicily. And in the neighbourhood of Syracuse they showed the place where Hades plunged back into the earth, hollowing out a vast cavity in the process, since filled by waters from the spring of Cyane. Colonus in Attica, Hermione in Argolis, Pheneus in Arcadia and even Crete, likewise claimed for their territory the honour of this divine abduction.

Demeter meanwhile had heard her child's despairing cry for help. 'Then,' says the poet of the Homeric hymn, 'bitter sorrow seized her heart... Over her shoulders she threw a sombre veil and flew like a bird over land and sea, seeking here, seeking there...' For nine days the venerable goddess ranged the world, bearing flaming torches in her hands. At last, on Hecate's advice, she went to consult the divine Helios, who revealed to her the name of her daughter's ravisher. 'No other god is guilty,' he said to her, 'but Zeus himself, who awarded thy daughter to his brother Hades so that he might call her his flowering bride.' This revelation overwhelmed Demeter. In rage and despair she withdrew from Olympus and in the guise of an old woman sought refuge among the cities of men. For long she wandered aimlessly. One day she arrived in Eleusis and sat down to rest near the palace of the wise Celeus, who reigned in that country. The king's daughters saw her and questioned her kindly. Demeter told them that she had been carried off by Cretan pirates who had brought her to these parts, where she was a stranger. She was in search of refuge and would be glad to work as a servant or nurse.

It happened that Metaneira, the wife of Celeus, had just been delivered of a son, Demophoön. Metaneira, therefore, welcomed the goddess under her roof; but when Demeter crossed the threshold her head brushed the rafters and from her emanated a divine radiance. Metaneira was filled with respect and offered her her own seat. But Demeter remained standing and silent, her eyes fixed on the ground, refusing food and drink; for she was consumed with longing for her flower-girdled daughter. Finally young Iambe who, though she was the daughter of Pan and Echo, served as a slave in Celeus' palace— and to whom was attributed the invention of Iambic verse—succeeded in cheering up Demeter with her buffoonery. She persuaded Demeter to drink a little *kykeon*, a beverage made of water, flour and mint.

Later legend substituted Baubo for Iambe. Baubo was upset when Demeter refused the drink she offered her and made an obscene gesture at which the goddess, in spite of herself, laughed.

Demeter was put in charge of bringing up the infant Demophoön. She gave him nothing to eat, but instead breathed softly on him, anointed him with ambrosia and at night hid him in the fire, a burning coal, in order to destroy all that was mortal in him. Thus, to the amazement of his parents, the child grew like a god. Intrigued by this prodigy Metaneira spied on the nurse and caught her just as she was placing the little boy in the middle of the flames. Metaneira screamed with terror. Incensed, the goddess withdrew Demophoön from the fire and put him on the ground. 'Had it not been for your imprudence,' she said to his mother, 'I should have put this child for ever beyond the reach of old age and death; but now it is no longer possible for me to shelter him from death.' Then she assumed her divine form. She revealed her name and ordered that a temple be erected for her in Eleusis where the initiated should celebrate her mysteries.

Before departing, Demeter wished to show her gratitude to her hosts; she gave Triptolemus, Celeus' oldest son, the first grain of corn, and taught him the art of harnessing oxen to the plough and how to sow the soil with grain from which would spring fair harvests. She gave him as well a winged chariot harnessed with dragons, and bade him travel the world spreading the benefits of agriculture among all men. Thus Triptolemus ranged all Greece, taught Arcas, King of Arcadia, how to make bread, and founded many towns in Arcadia. He also visited Thrace, Sicily and Scythia, where King Lyncus tried to murder him while he was asleep and was changed by Demeter into a lynx. He visited Mysia, where the King of the Getae, Carnabon, tried in vain to harm him, and finally returned to Eleusis. There Celeus plotted to have him slain, but was thwarted by Demeter. Celeus then resigned the throne to Triptolemus.

Demeter's stay at Eleusis was the chief episode in the course of her wanderings on earth, but she also stayed with Pelasgus in Argos. She visited Phytalus to whom she gave the olive tree. She was received in Attica by Misme, whose son Ascalabos made Demeter the butt of his jokes and was punished by being turned into a lizard.

Still inconsolable at the loss of her daughter, Demeter retired to her temple at Eleusis. There 'she prepared for mankind a cruel and terrible year: the earth refused to give forth any crop. Then the entire human race would have perished of cruel, biting hunger if Zeus had not been concerned.' He hastened to send his messenger Iris to Demeter, but without success. Then all the gods came one by one to plead with the implacable goddess. She stated firmly that she would not permit the earth to bear fruit unless she saw her daughter again. There was no solution except to give in. Zeus commanded Hermes to descend into the kingdom of Hades and obtain Hades' promise to return young Kore—who since her arrival in the Underworld had taken the name Persephone—to her mother. Hades complied with the will of Zeus, but before sending his wife up to Earth tempted her to eat a few pomegranate seeds. Now this fruit was a symbol of marriage and the effect of eating it was to render the union of man and wife indissoluble.

When Kore returned to the world of light her mother hastened to her and embraced her with transports of joy. 'My daughter,' she cried, 'surely thou hast eaten nothing during imprisonment in the dark regions of Hades! For if thou hast not eaten thou shalt live with me on Olympus. But if thou hast, then thou must return to the depths of the earth!' Kore admitted that she had tasted of the fatal pomegranate. It seemed that Demeter was again to lose her daughter.

As a compromise Zeus decided that Persephone should live with her husband for one-third of the year and pass the other two-thirds with her mother. The august Rhea herself brought this proposal to Demeter who agreed to it. She set aside her anger and bade the soil again be fertile. The vast earth was soon covered with leaves and flowers. Before she returned to Olympus, Demeter taught the kings of the earth her divine science and initiated them into her sacred mysteries.

This legend explained why each year when the cold season arrived the earth took on an aspect of sadness and mourning: no more verdure, nor flowers in the fields, nor leaves on the trees. Hidden in the bowels of the ground the seeds slept their winter sleep. It was the moment when Persephone went to join her husband among the deep shadows. But when sweet-scented

The rape of Kore. Classical sculpture from a sarcophagus. Uffizi Gallery, Florence.

Demeter and Kore offering a libation to Triptolemus before he sets out to spread the benefits of agriculture to mankind. Red-figured vase in the British Museum.

spring came, the earth put on its mantle of a thousand flowers to greet the return of Kore, who rose in radiance, 'a wondrous sight for gods and men'.

The Eleusinian Mysteries. This double event—the disappearance and return of Kore—was the occasion of great festivals in Greece. In the *Thesmophoria*, which were celebrated in Attica in the month of October, the departure of Kore for the sombre dwelling was commemorated. These festivals and ceremonies were exclusively reserved for married women and lasted three days.

The return of Kore was celebrated in the Lesser Eleusinia, which took place in the month of February.

As for the Greater Eleusinia, which took place every five years in September, it seems that they had no direct connection with the story of Kore. It was a solemn festival—the greatest festival of Greece—in honour of Demeter, and its principal object was the celebration of the mysteries of the goddess. The scene of the Greater Eleusinia was Athens and Eleusis.

On the first day the *ephebi* (youths) of Athens would go to Eleusis to fetch the sacred objects *(hiera)* kept in the temple of Demeter, and bring them back with great pomp to Athens, where they were placed in the Eleusinion, at the foot of the Acropolis. The following day the faithful *(mystae)* who were judged to be worthy of participating in the mysteries would assemble in Athens at the call of the hierophant. Afterwards they would go to purify themselves in the sea, taking with them pigs which were bathed and then sacrificed. Finally the solemn procession towards Eleusis took place and the *hiera* were returned with the same ceremonial as before. At the head of the

procession was carried the statue of Iacchus, a mystic name for Dionysus.

In Eleusis the mysteries themselves were then celebrated. Only the initiated could participate and they were forbidden to divulge what occurred. Initiation comprised two stages; the second could be undertaken only after a year's probation.

As far as one can conjecture, the *mystae*, after drinking the *kykeon* and eating the sacred cakes, entered the *Telesterion*, where they attended a liturgical drama concerning the abduction of Kore. The *epoptae*—or those belonging to the highest grade—

The return of Persephone from Hades. Painting of the second century A.D. *British Museum.*

108

attended another liturgical drama whose subject was the union of Demeter and Zeus, and whose protagonists were the priestess of Demeter and the hierophant.

It is not easy to understand the exact meaning of these mysteries. They were, however, probably more than a simple commemoration of the legend of Demeter and must also have had to do with the problem of future life, the revelation of which the initiated awaited from the goddess.

Dionisus

Character and Functions. Dionysus is etymologically the 'Zeus of Nysa' and seems, by several similarities of legend and function, to be the Greek form of the Vedic god Soma. The cradle of his cult was Thrace. It was brought to Boeotia by Thracian tribes, who established themselves in that country, and was afterwards introduced to the island of Naxos by Boeotian colonists. The cult of Dionysus spread throughout the islands, then returned to continental Greece, first to Attica, and later to the Peloponnese.

The figure of the primitive Dionysus is complicated by traits borrowed from other and foreign gods, notably the Cretan god Zagreus, the Phrygian god Sabazius, and the Lydian god Bassareus. Thus his sphere of influence widened as his character became enriched with fresh contributions. In origin Dionysus was simply the god of wine; afterwards he became god of vegetation and warm moisture; then he appeared as the god of pleasures and the god of civilisation; and finally, according to Orphic conceptions, as a kind of supreme god.

Cult and Representations. Dionysus was honoured throughout Greece; but the character of the festivals which were dedicated to him varied.

One of the most ancient festivals was that of the *Agrionia*, first celebrated in Boeotia, especially at Orchomenus, where the Bacchantes immolated a young boy. Human sacrifice was also practised at Chios and at Lesbos; it was later replaced by flagella-

tion. In Attica, they celebrated rural Dionysia: in December the *Lenaea*, festival of the wine press, when the god was offered the new wine; at the end of February the *Anthesteria*, floral festivals which lasted three days, during which wine of the last vintage was tasted. In the sanctuary of Lenoeon there was a procession followed by a sacrifice offered by the wife of the archon-king, and finally boiled seed was offered to Dionysus and Hermes. The most brilliant festivals were the Greater Dionysia, or urban Dionysia, at the beginning of March. It was during these festivals that dramatic performances were given. In addition to these dignified ceremonies all Greece celebrated festivals of orgiastic character as well.

The appearance of Dionysus altered at the same time as his legend. He was first depicted as a bearded man of mature age, with brow generally crowned with ivy. Later he appears as a beardless youth of rather effeminate aspect. Sometimes the delicate nudity of his adolescent body is half-covered by the *nebris*, the skin of a panther or fawn; sometimes he wears a long robe such as women wore. His head, with its long curly hair, is crowned with vine leaves and bunches of grapes. In one hand he holds the *thyrsus*, and in the other, grapes or a wine cup.

The Birth and Childhood of Dionysus. When the earth has been made fertile by life-giving rains it must, in order that its products may reach maturity, endure the bite of the sun which burns and dries it up. Only then do its fruits develop and the golden grapes appear on the knotty vine. This seems to be the meaning of the myth of Semele, who was normally considered to be the mother of Dionysus.

Semele, daughter of Cadmus, King of Thebes, was seen by Zeus and yielded to him. Zeus would come to her father's palace to visit her. One day, at the suggestion of the treacherous Hera, who had assumed the guise of her nurse, Semele begged Zeus to show himself to her in his Olympian majesty. She was unable to endure the dazzling brilliance of her divine lover and was consumed by the flames which emanated from Zeus' person. The child she carried in her

The Birth of Dionysus. The infant springs from Zeus' thigh into the arms of Hermes. Classical bas-relief. Vatican Museum, Rome.

womb would also have perished had not a thick shoot of ivy suddenly wound around the columns of the palace and made a green screen between the unborn babe and the celestial fire. Zeus gathered up the infant and, as it was not yet ready to be born, enclosed it in his own thigh. When the time was come he drew it forth again, with the aid of Ilithyia, and it is to this double birth that Dionysus owed the title *Dithyrambos*.

Zeus entrusted his son to Ino, sister of Semele, who lived at Orchomenus with her husband Athamas.

Such was the commonest version of the story. It was also related that Cadmus, learning of the guilty liaison of his daughter Semele, had her shut up in a chest and thrown into the sea. The chest was carried by the waves as far as the shores of Prasiae in the Peloponnese; when it was opened Semele was dead, but the child was still alive. He was cared for by Ino.

Hera's jealous vengeance was unappeased and she struck Ino and Athamas with madness. Zeus succeeded in saving his child for the second time by changing him into a kid, whom he ordered Hermes to deliver into the hands of the nymphs of Nysa.

Where was Nysa? Was it a mountain in Thrace? One seeks its precise situation in vain; for every region where the cult of Dionysus was established boasted of having a Nysa.

Dionysus passed his childhood on this fabled mountain, cared for by the nymphs, whose zeal was later recompensed; for they were changed into a constellation under the name of the Hyades. The Muses also contributed to the education of Dionysus, as did the Satyrs, the Sileni and the Maenads.

Dionysus on his travels. Interior of a red-figured cup by Exekias. Middle of the sixth century B.C. *Munich.*

With his head crowned by ivy and laurel, the young god wandered the mountains and forests with the nymphs, making the glades echo with his joyful shouts. Meanwhile old Silenus taught his young mind the meaning of virtue and inspired him with the love of glory. When he had grown up Dionysus discovered the fruit of the vine and the art of making wine from it. Doubtless he drank of the wine without moderation at first, for the story was that Hera had stricken him with madness. But the disease was short-lived. To cure himself Dionysus went to Dodona to consult the oracle. On the way he came to a marsh which he crossed on the back of an ass. To reward the animal he bestowed on it the gift of speech. When he was cured Dionysus undertook long journeys across the world in order to spread the inestimable gift of wine among mortals. Marvellous adventures marked his passage through the countries he visited.

The Travels of Dionysus. Coming from the mountains of Thrace Dionysus crossed Boeotia and entered Attica. In Attica he was welcomed by the king, Icarius, to whom he presented a vine-stock. Icarius was rash enough to give his shepherds wine to drink; as they grew intoxicated they thought they were being poisoned and slew him. The daughter of Icarius, Erigone, set out to look for her father and, thanks to her dog Maera, at last discovered his tomb. In despair she hanged herself from a nearby tree. In punishment for this death Dionysus struck the women of Attica with raving madness. Icarius was carried to the heavens with his daughter and her faithful dog. They were changed into constellations and became the Waggoner, Virgo and the Lesser Dog Star.

In Aetolia Dionysus was received by Oeneus, King of Calydon, and fell in love with Althaea, his host's wife. Oeneus pretended not to notice and the god rewarded his discretion by giving him a vine-stock. From the fleeting union of Dionysus and Althaea was born Deianeira.

After continental Greece Dionysus visited the islands of the Archipelago. It was in the course of this voyage that the god, walking one day by the seashore, was abducted by Tyrrhenian pirates and carried aboard their ship. They took him for the son of a king and expected a rich ransom. They tried to tie him up with heavy cords, but in vain. The knots loosened of their own accord and the bonds fell to the deck. The pilot, terrified, had a presentiment that their captive was divine and attempted to make his companions release him. The pirates refused. Then occurred a series of marvels. Around the dark ship flowed wine, fragrant and delicious. A vine attached its branches to the sail, while around the mast ivy wound its dark green leaves. The god himself became a lion of fearful aspect. In horror the sailors leapt into the sea and were immediately changed into dolphins. Only the pilot was spared by Dionysus.

One day on the island of Naxos Dionysus perceived a young woman lying asleep on the shore. It was the daughter of Minos, Ariadne, whom Theseus had brought with him from Crete and just abandoned. When she awoke Ariadne realised that Theseus had

left her and gave way to uncontrollable tears. The arrival of Dionysus consoled her and shortly afterwards they were solemnly married. The gods came to the wedding and showered gifts on the couple. Dionysus and Ariadne had three sons: Oenopion, Euanthes and Staphylus. The Homeric tradition has a different version of the Ariadne episode. Ariadne was supposed to have been killed by Artemis and it was only after her death that Dionysus married her. In Naxos they showed the tomb of Ariadne and in her honour two festivals were celebrated: one mournful, bewailing her death; the other joyful, commemorating her marriage to Dionysus.

The travels and adventures of Dionysus were not limited to the Greek world. Accompanied by his retinue of Satyrs and Maenads he went to Phrygia, where Cybele initiated him into her mysteries. At Ephesus in Cappadocia he repulsed the Amazons. In Syria he fought against Damascus, who destroyed the vines which the god had planted and was punished by being skinned alive. Then he went to the Lebanon to pay a visit to Aphrodite and Adonis, whose daughter, Beroë, he loved. After reigning for some time over Caucasian Iberia, Dionysus continued his journey towards the East, crossing the Tigris on a tiger sent by Zeus, joined the two banks of the Euphrates by a cable made of vine-shoots and ivy-tendrils, and reached India, where he spread civilisation. We also find him in Egypt, where he was received by King Proteus; in Libya where he helped Ammon to reconquer his throne, from which he had been deposed by Cronus and the Titans.

Left, Dionysus. An example of later representations of effeminate type. The god's head is crowned with vine leaves and bunches of grapes. Classical sculpture. Villa Albani, Rome.
Above, Dionysus and Ariadne at a Dionysian thiasus or festival. They are surrounded by Satyrs and Maenads. Vase in the British Museum.

111

The triumph of Dionysus and Ariadne, by Cima da Conegliano. Poldi Pezzoli Gallery, Milan.

After these expeditions Dionysus returned to Greece. He was no longer the rather rustic god recently down from the mountains of Boeotia. His contact with Asia had made him soft and effeminate: he now appeared in the guise of a graceful adolescent, dressed in a long robe in the Lydian fashion. His cult became complicated by orgiastic rites borrowed from Phrygia. Thus he was received in Greece with distrust, sometimes even with hostility.

When he returned to Thrace, notably, the king of that country, Lycurgus, declared against him. Dionysus was obliged to flee and seek refuge with Thetis, in the depths of the sea. Meanwhile, Lycurgus imprisoned the Bacchantes who followed the god, and Dionysus struck the country with sterility, depriving Lycurgus of his reason. In his madness Lycurgus killed his own son, Dryas, whom he mistook for a vine-stock. The desolation of Thrace did not cease until the oracle ordered that Lycurgus be conducted to Mount Pangaeum, where he was trampled to death under the hooves of wild horses.

Dionysus was no better received by Pentheus, King of Thebes, who threw the god into prison. Dionysus escaped without trouble and struck Agave, the mother of Pentheus, as well as the other women of Thebes, with madness. They were transformed into Maenads and rushed to Mount Cithaeron where they held Dionysian orgies. Pentheus had the imprudence to follow them and was torn to pieces by his own mother. This drama forms the subject of Euripides' *Bacchae*.

A similar tragedy overtook the inhabitants of Argos, who had also refused to recognise the divinity of Dionysus: the women, driven out of their minds, tore up and devoured their own children.

Among the chastisements which Dionysus inflicted, one of the most famous concerned the daughters of Minyas, King of Orchomenus. They were three sisters: Alcithoë, Leucippe and Arsippe. Since they refused to take part in the festivals of Dio-

nysus, he visited them in the guise of a young maiden and tried to persuade them by gentleness. Being unsuccessful, he turned himself successively into a bull, a lion and a panther. Terrified by these miracles the daughters of Minyas lost their reason and, one of them, Leucippe, tore her son Hippasus to pieces with her own hands. Finally they underwent metamorphosis: the first became a mouse, the second a screech-owl, the third an owl.

Thenceforth no one any longer dreamed of denying the divinity of Dionysus or of rejecting his cult.

The god crowned his exploits by descending into the Infernal Regions in search of his mother, Semele. He renamed her Thyone and brought her with him to Olympus among the Immortals.

On Olympus Dionysus took part in the struggle against the Giants; the braying of the ass on which he rode terrified the Giants, and Dionysus killed Eurytus or Rhatos with his *thyrsus* or staff.

Foreign Divinities Assimilated by Dionysus. The multiplicity of the legends of Dionysus is explained not only by his great popularity but also because, as we have already said, the personality of Dionysus absorbed that of several foreign gods, notably the Phrygian Sabazius, the Lydian Bassareus and the Cretan Zagreus.

Sabazius, who was venerated as the supreme god in the Thracian Hellespont, was a solar divinity of Phrygian origin. Traditions concerning him were very diverse. Sometimes he was the son of Cronus, sometimes of Cybele, whose companion he became. His wife was either the moon-goddess Bendis, or else Cotys (or Cottyto), an earth-goddess analogous to the Phrygian Cybele. Sabazius was represented with horns and his emblem was the serpent. The *Sabazia*, nocturnal festivals of orgiastic character, were celebrated in his honour.

When Sabazius was later assimilated by Dionysus their legends became amalgamated. Some said that

Sabazius had kept Dionysus enclosed in his thigh before entrusting him to the nymph Hippa; others claimed that on the contrary Sabazius was the son of Dionysus. Finally, it was as a result of such confusions that Dionysus was supposed to have come from the Thracian Hellespont.

Sometimes the Bacchantes were called *Bassarids* and Dionysus himself had the epithet *Bassareus*, when he was represented wearing a long robe in the Oriental fashion. The lexicographer Hesychius considered this to be a reference to the fox-skins which the Bacchantes wore; but it seems more likely that it was an allusion to an Oriental divinity absorbed by Dionysus. Indeed a god similar to the Phrygian Sabazius was venerated in Lydia. The place of his cult was Mount Tmolus where, according to Orphic-Thracian legend, Sabazius delivered the infant Dionysus to Hippa. Tmolus actually became one of the favourite haunts of Dionysus. It has been conjectured that the name of the Lydian god was Bassareus. He was doubtless a conquering god and to him may be attributed the origin of Dionysus' distant conquests. Assimilation of Bassareus could also explain the visit of Dionysus to

Above, Dionysus. His head is crowned with ivy leaves, he wears a panther's skin around his shoulders, and he carries a drinking cup. Detail from an amphora of about 500 B.C. Munich.

Below, Dionysus holding his thyrsus surrounded by dancing Maenads and Satyrs. Attic vase. Louvre.

Aphrodite and Adonis, and perhaps also the legend of Ampelus, a youth of rare beauty whom Dionysus cherished with particular affection. One day when he was attempting to master a wild bull Ampelus was tossed and killed by the animal. Dionysus was heartbroken and obtained the permission of the gods to change Ampelus into a vine.

The identification of Dionysus with the Cretan god Zagreus, who was very probably in origin the equivalent of the Hellenic Zeus, introduced—under the influence of Orphic mysticism—a new element into the legend of the god, that of the Passion of Dionysus.

Dionysus Zagreus was said to be the son of Zeus and Demeter — or Zeus and Kore. The other gods were jealous of him and resolved to slay him. He was torn into pieces by the Titans, who threw the remains of his body into a cauldron. Pallas Athene, however, was able to rescue the god's heart. She took it at once to Zeus, who struck the Titans with thunderbolts and from the still beating heart created Dionysus. As for Zagreus, whose remains had been buried at the foot of Parnassus, he became an underworld divinity who welcomed the souls of the dead to Hades and helped with their purification.

These trials and the resurrection were given a mystic significance by the initiates of Orphism, and the character of Dionysus underwent profound modification. He was no longer the rustic god of wine and jollity, who originally came down from the mountains of Thrace; he was no longer even the god of orgiastic delirium, who came from the Orient. Henceforth Dionysus—in Plutarch's words 'the god who is destroyed, who disappears, who relinquishes life and then is born again'—became the symbol of everlasting life.

Thus it is not surprising to see Dionysus associated with Demeter and Kore in the Eleusinian mysteries. For he, too, represented one of the great life-bringing forces of the world.

The retinue of Dionysus — rural divinities

From early times in Greece the wine festivals were occasions for joyful processions in which priests and men and women who followed the cult of Dionysus took part. These devotees were called Bacchants and Bacchantes or Maenads. It was the habit to provide the god with a cortège or thiasus composed of secondary divinities more or less closely bound up with his cult: Satyrs, Sileni, Pans, Priapi, Centaurs, Nymphs.
Satyrs and Sileni. The Satyrs represented the elementary spirits of the forests and the mountains. They were a kind of wood-genii whose sudden appearance would terrify shepherds and travellers. With their low forehead, snub nose, pointed ears, hairy body ending in a goat's tail, and cloven hooves, there was something about them of both monkey and he-goat. Such at least was their primitive aspect; later, traces of the beast which at first dominated survived only in their pointed ears and the small horns on their brow, while their features took on an

expression of youth and gentleness. Their character also altered. According to Hesiod the Satyrs were originally a lazy and useless race who loved only pleasure and good cheer. Sensual and lascivious, they delighted in chasing the nymphs through the forests. Later, although they preserved their playful nature, they acquired more grace and specialised in the pleasures of music and dancing. They were thought to be brothers of the nymphs and the Curetes. They were faithful companions of the god and played the principal role in his orgiastic festivals.

One of the most picturesque figures in the retinue of Dionysus was Silenus, a fat old man, who followed the god. He was bald, snub-nosed, always drunk and sometimes supported by Satyrs, sometimes swaying precariously on an ass. Nevertheless this cheerful drunkard was full of wisdom. He had been the tutor of Dionysus and had helped to form his character. His knowledge was immense: he knew both the past and the future, and could reveal the destiny of anyone who succeeded in tying him up during the heavy slumber which followed his drinking-bouts. Plato felt no irreverence in comparing his master Socrates with Silenus. Silenus was generally held to be the son of Hermes and the Earth. Others say that he was born of the blood of the mutilated Uranus.

In reality the name Silenus is a generic term which applies to a category of rural divinities, rather similar to the Satyrs and often confused with them. The Sileni were native not to Greece, but to Phrygia, and personified the spirits of springs and rivers.

Unlike the Satyrs who derive chiefly from the he-goat, the Sileni derive from the horse whose tail, hooves, and even ears they possess. Marsyas, who is generally made a Satyr, was in reality a Silenus and, at the same time, a river-god of Phrygia. That was why the Phrygian Midas—whose legend is closely connected with that of the Sileni—voted for Marsyas in the famous music contest with Apollo.

Pan, Aristaeus, Priapus. Another divinity later incorporated in the retinue of Dionysus, and often confused with the Satyrs because of his physical resemblance to them, was the god Pan, whose cult was for long centred in Arcadia. Hence he was made the son of Hermes, the great Arcadian god. His mother was either the daughter of King Dryops, whose flocks Hermes had tended, or Penelope, whom Hermes had approached in the form of a he-goat. Pan himself came into the world with the legs, horns and beard of a goat.

Various etymologies have been suggested for the

Opposite, Dionysus revelling together with satyrs and maenads. Vase in the British Museum.

Page 116, Atalanta, renowned for her fleetness of foot and the notable part she played in the Calydonian Boar-hunt. Roman mosaic of the fourth century A. D.
Medea demonstrating to Pelias and his daughters how she can rejuvenate a ram; Medea thus persuaded Pelias to agree that she should do the same for him, but in fact killed him by boiling him alive. Vase in the British Museum.

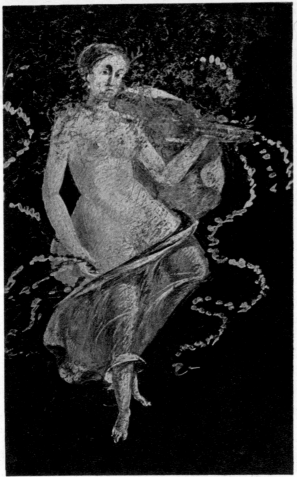

Above, Head of a Satyr from Pompeii. National Museum, Naples.

Below, Bacchante. Fresco from Pompeii.

114

Sileni playing the cithara. From a Greek vase-painting.

name Pan. The Homeric hymn connects it with the adjective which means 'all', with the explanation that the sight of Pan on Olympus amused *all* the Immortals. The same etymology was invoked by the mythologists of the school of Alexandria, who considered Pan to be the symbol of the Universe. It seems more likely that the name comes from the root which means 'to eat' which gave Latin the verb *pascere*, 'to graze or pasture'. Pan, indeed, was above all a shepherd-god, god of woods and pastures, protector of shepherds and flocks. He lived on the slopes of Mount Maenalus or Mount Lycaeus, in grottoes where the Arcadian shepherds came to worship him. He made their goats and ewes multiply —whence his aspect of a phallic divinity—and caused wild beasts to be killed by hunters; when the hunt was unsuccessful they would whip his image by way of reprisal. Pan himself delighted in roving the forests, frisking with the nymphs, whom he sometimes terrified with his appearance. One day he was chasing the nymph Syrinx and had nearly caught her when she cried aloud on her father, the river-god Ladon, to change her into a reed. Her prayer was granted. Pan consoled himself for his disappointment by cutting some reeds with which he made a flute of a new sort, giving it the name Syrinx, or Pan-pipes. He was more successful with the nymph Pitys who preferred him to Boreas. Boreas, the bitter

Opposite, Silenus, one of the rural divinities associated with Dionysus. He was always drunk, but full of wisdom. Fresco from the Villa of Mysteries, Pompeii.

Page 117, Oedipus solving the enigma posed by the Sphinx, a fabulous monster who had the face of a woman, the body of a lion and the wings of a bird, and who devoured those who could not answer her riddles. Painting by Ingres. Louvre.

North Wind, was enraged and flung himself on Pitys, throwing her against a rock where her limbs were crushed. In pity Gaea transformed her into a pine. It was told that Pan succeeded in seducing the moon-goddess Selene; he disguised himself in the fleece of a dazzling white ewe and drew her into the forest with him, or he himself took the shape of a white ram.

For long Pan was confined to the mountains of Arcadia, where he amused himself by giving the lonely traveller sudden frights, called for this reason panics. He penetrated into Attica only at the time of the Persian wars. Shortly before the battle of Marathon he appeared to the ambassadors whom the Athenians had sent to Sparta, and promised to put the Persians to flight if the Athenians consented to worship him in Athens. In gratitude they erected a sanctuary for him on the Acropolis and from there the cult of Pan spread throughout Greece.

Every region in Greece had its own Pan. That of Thessaly was called Aristaeus. Without doubt this Aristaeus was a great primitive deity of Thessaly, for his name means 'the very good', which was also the epithet of Zeus in Arcadia. Moreover Pindar says that 'after his birth Aristaeus was carried by Hermes to Gaea and the Horae, who fed him on nectar and ambrosia and transformed him into Zeus, the immortal god, and into Apollo, the pure, the guardian of flocks and the hunt and pasturage'. According to legend, Aristaeus was the son of Uranus and Gaea or of Apollo and Cyrene. He was brought up by the Centaur Chiron and instructed in the arts of medicine and soothsaying. He was considered the protector of flocks and agriculture, particularly of the vine and olive. It was he who taught men bee-keeping.

His civilising influence was felt throughout Greece. In Boeotia he married the daughter of Cadmus, Autonoë, and had by her a son, Actaeon. During his stay in Thrace he fell in love with Eurydice, the wife

119

of Orpheus. It was in fleeing from Aristaeus that she was mortally bitten by a serpent. The end of Aristaeus was mysterious; he vanished from the earth on Mount Haemus.

The Pan of Mysia, in Asia Minor, was Priapus. He was particularly venerated at Lampsacus. His origin is rather vague. His mother was said to be Aphrodite or Chione, and his father Dionysus, Adonis, Hermes or Pan.

It was told that Hera, jealous of Aphrodite, caused Priapus to be born with the deformity to which he owes his name. His mother abandoned him and he was sheltered by shepherds. Priapus presided over the fecundity of fields and flocks, over the raising of bees, the culture of the vine and over fishing. He protected orchards and gardens where his phallic image was placed. He was evidently introduced into the retinue of Dionysus by way of Asia.

The Centaurs. In addition to the Satyrs and the Sileni another kind of monstrous creature formed part of the cortège of Dionysus: the Centaurs. A Centaur's torso and head were those of a man; the rest of his body was that of a horse. Centaurs had not always been like this: the first representations show them as giants with hairy bodies; then they were depicted as men with the hindquarters of a horse. The definitive appearance goes no farther back than the period of Phidias.

Natives of Thessaly, the Centaurs were descendants of Ixion, son of Ares. Ixion was engaged to marry Dia, daughter of Eioneus. There was a dispute between Ixion and his future father-in-law, and Ixion threw

Centaur teaching a young hero to play the lyre. Fresco from Herculaneum. National Museum, Naples.

120

him into a burning pit. This crime earned universal reprobation and Ixion was forced to seek refuge with Zeus, who offered him hospitality. But Ixion had the audacity to covet Zeus' own wife, Hera. In order to test how far his impudence would go, Zeus formed a cloud into the likeness of Hera and gave it to Ixion. From this strange union was born a monster, Centaurus, who, himself uniting with the mares of Pelion, fathered the race of the Centaurs.

Some have interpreted all this as a Hellenic equivalent of the Vedic Gandharvas. But it is more likely that the Centaurs—whose name etymologically means 'those who round up bulls'—were a band of cowherds, living in Thessaly, who, like American cowboys, rounded up their cattle on horseback. Their behaviour was rough and barbarous, whence the savagery always attributed to the Centaurs—cruel, gross creatures, given to lechery and drunkenness.

Some of their number were, however, famed for their wisdom. Such was Pholus, who entertained Hercules. Such, especially, was Chiron, who was educated by Artemis and Apollo themselves, and who in his turn was the teacher of many heroes. He died from a wound made by Hercules with a poisoned arrow. The wound was incurable and Chiron exchanged his immortality for the mortality of Prometheus. Zeus placed him among the stars, where he became part of the constellation Sagittarius.

The chief episode in the legend of the Centaurs was their battle with the Lapiths at the marriage of Peirithous. The Lapiths were also a fabulous people from Thessaly. Their king, Peirithous, was marrying Hippodameia and had invited the Centaur Eurytion to the festivities. Excited by the wine, Eurytion attempted to abduct the bride, but was prevented from doing so by Theseus. Eurytion returned to the attack with a troop of Centaurs armed with slabs of stone and the trunks of pine trees. A general battle took place from which the Lapiths at last emerged victorious, thanks to the courage of Theseus and Peirithous. The Centaurs were driven to the frontiers of Epirus and took refuge on Mount Pindus.

The Nymphs. Among these graceless and brutal divinities the nymphs were conspicuous for the charm of their youth and beauty. The nymphs of Dionysus' retinue were in all points similar to their sisters who peopled the rivers and springs. Like the nymphs found in the retinue of Artemis and Apollo they were tutelary deities of the forests and mountains. They were named according to the places they inhabited. The Oreads were nymphs of the mountains and the grottoes. The Napaeae, the Auloniads, the Hylaeorae and the Alsaeids haunted the woods and valleys. Only the Dryads, forest nymphs who protected trees, never mingled with divine processions. Crowned with oak-leaves, sometimes armed with an axe to punish outrages against the trees which they guarded, they would dance around the oaks which were sacred to them. Certain of their number, the Hamadryads, were still more closely united with trees, and were said to form an integral part of them. .

Among the nymphs who followed Hera there was an Oread named Echo who, every time that Zeus paid

Above, Pan teaching his half-brother Daphnis to play the pan-pipes. Sculpture by Heliodorus. National Museum, Naples.
Below, The battle of the Centaurs and Lapiths. A Centaur seizes Hippodameia and is about to be struck by Theseus. From a Greek vase in the British Museum.
Right, The nymph Leucothea (Ino) giving the infant Dionysus a drink from the Horn of Plenty. Classical bas-relief. Lateran Museum, Rome.

Narcissus looking at his reflection. Wall-painting from Pompeii.

court to some nymph, would distract Hera's attention with her chattering and singing. When Hera discovered this she deprived Echo of the gift of speech, condemning her to repeat only the last syllable of words spoken in her presence. Now Echo fell in love with a young Thespian named Narcissus. Unable to declare her love, she was spurned by him and went to hide her grief in solitary caverns. She died of a broken heart, her bones turned into stone, and all that was left of her was the echo of her voice.

As for Narcissus, the gods punished him for having spurned Echo by making him fall in love with his own image. The soothsayer Teiresias had predicted that Narcissus would live only until the moment he saw himself. One day when he was leaning over the limpid waters of a fountain Narcissus caught sight of his own reflection in the water. He conceived such a passion for this phantom that nothing could tear him away from it, and he died there of languor. He was changed into the flower which bears his name and which grows at the edge of springs.

Another victim of the nymphs was the handsome Sicilian herdsman Daphnis. Daphnis was the son of Hermes and a nymph. Abandoned by his mother, he was taken in by shepherds living at the foot of Mount Etna and shared their daily life. He was loved by a nymph, Echenaïs, Xenaea or Lyce, who made him swear eternal fidelity to her under pain of going blind. Infatuated by the princess Chimera, Daphnis broke his vow and lost his sight. He tried to console himself with poetry and music; he was called the inventor of pastoral poetry. He killed himself one day by jumping from the top of a cliff.

Divinities concerned with the life of man

Zeus, sovereign lord of mortals, did not rule directly over their fate. He delegated this task to secondary divinities who accompanied men throughout their physical and moral life.

Divinities of birth and health

Ilithyia. In primitive times there were two Ilithyias, daughters of Hera, who presided over birth and brought to women in labour both pain—the keen arrows of the Ilithyias—and deliverance. No child could be born unless they were present, no mother could find relief without them. Thus when Apollo was born the jealous Hera detained Ilithyia on Olympus for nine days and nine nights when she had been on the point of going to the aid of Leto. Hera repeated this manoeuvre when Alcmene was about to give birth to Hercules.

The two Ilithyias finally merged into a single person, the goddess of childbirth. She was, in fact, a very ancient divinity believed to have originated in Crete. She is most often depicted kneeling, a position which was believed to aid delivery, and carrying a torch, symbol of light, while with her other hand she makes a gesture of encouragement.

Certain goddesses known to be particularly concerned with women were sometimes given the epithet Ilithyia: Hera at Argos, for instance, and Artemis at Delos. It is even possible that Ilithyia is simply a double of Hera.

Asclepius. We have seen, in discussing Apollo, the tragic circumstances of the birth of Asclepius, son of Apollo and Coronis. Apollo snatched him from the burning pyre on which his mother's body had just been consumed and carried him to Mount Pelion, where he was entrusted to the care of the Centaur Chirob. Chiron taught him to hunt and instructed him in the science of medicine. The medical career of Asclepius then began. With his miraculous cures he soon earned immense renown. He even succeeded in restoring the dead to life, thanks either to the Gorgon's blood which Athene had given him or to the properties of a plant which a serpent had told him about. Hades felt that he was being wronged. He went to Zeus to complain, and Zeus agreed that mortals must follow their destiny. Thus Asclepius was guilty of thwarting the order of nature and Zeus struck him dead with a thunderbolt.

Apollo avenged the death of his son by exterminating the Cyclopes, who had forged the thunderbolt. Apollo was banished from Olympus for a considerable time as a punishment for this massacre.

At Epidaurus another version of the birth of Asclepius was current. They said that Coronis gave birth to her son Asclepius while her father, Phlegyas, was on an expedition to the Peloponnese. She abandoned the newborn child on Mount Titthion where a goat fed it and a dog guarded it. One day

Aresthanas, a shepherd, discovered it and was struck by the supernatural light which played over the child.

Be that as it may, the god of health was always considered to be the offspring of light or fire. He restored to the sick the warmth they had lost, and was therefore greatly venerated in Greece. He was surrounded by auxiliary divinities. Epione, his wife, bore the two Asclepiads, Podaleirius and Machaon. Both took part in the Trojan war, at the head of the Thessalians of Tricca. They were as skilled in medicine as their father, especially Machaon, who cured Menelaus of an arrow wound and also cured Philoctetes. He himself was killed at Troy and Nestor brought his body back to Greece. Podaleirius survived

Asclepius, god of health, with his attribute, the serpent, which sometimes represents the god himself. Florence.

the expedition and on his return was cast by a tempest on to the shores of Caria and settled there.

Asclepius also had daughters: Iaso, Panacea, Aegle and above all Hygieia, who was closely associated with the cult of her father as goddess of health. Finally we must mention the guardian spirit of convalescence. Telesphorus, who was represented wearing a hooded cape, the costume of those who had just recovered from illness.

Asclepius was sometimes represented as a serpent, but more frequently as a man of middle age with an expression of benevolence, and his cult was at the same time a religion and a system of therapeutics. His sanctuaries, such as those at Tricca, Epidaurus, Cos and Pergamum, were built outside the towns on particularly healthy sites. The priests in charge of them at first held a monopoly of medical knowledge, which they handed down from father to son. It was only later that they admitted outsiders as neophytes.

In the *Asclepeia* special rites were observed. After much purificatory preparation, baths, fasting, sacrifices, the patient was permitted to spend the night in the temple of Asclepius, where he slept either on the skin of the sacrificed animal or on a couch placed near the statue of the god. This was the period of incubation. During the night Asclepius would appear to the patient in a dream and give him advice. In the morning the priests would interpret the dream and explain the god's precepts. Patients would thank Asclepius by tossing gold into the sacred fountain and by hanging ex-votos on the walls of the temple.

Divinities concerned with morality

The Moerae or Fates. The Moerae, whom the Romans called the Parcae, were for Homer the individual and inescapable destiny followed by every mortal being. Only in Hesiod's *Theogony* are they treated as goddesses. They were three in number, daughters of Night, and they were called Clotho, Lachesis and Atropos. Clotho, the spinner, personified the thread of life. Lachesis was chance, the element of luck that a man had the right to expect. Atropos was inescapable fate, against which there was no appeal. The whole of man's life was shadowed by the Moerae. They arrived at his birth with Ilithyia. When he was married the three Moerae had to be invoked so that the union should be happy. And when the end approached the Moerae hastened to cut the thread of his life. Hesiod placed them with the Keres, thus giving them the role of divinities of violent death.

The Moerae were subject to the authority of Zeus, who commanded them to see that the natural order of things was respected. They sat in the assemblies of the gods and possessed the gift of prophecy.

Nemesis. Like the Fates, Nemesis personified at first a moral idea, that of the unalterable equilibrium of the human condition. Man could displease the gods in two manners, either by offending the moral law—in which case he incurred their wrath—or by attaining too much happiness or riches—in which case he excited their jealousy. In either of these cases the imprudent mortal was pursued by Nemesis, or the divine anger. If he had offended only by an excess of good fortune he might hope to propitiate the goddess by sacrificing a part of his happiness.

Polycrates, tyrant of Samos, was terrified of the unheard-of luck which followed him, and wished to forestall the jealousy of the gods by throwing into the sea a priceless ring of which he was especially fond. But when the ring was returned to him by a fisherman who had found it in the belly of a fish, Polycrates realised that Nemesis had refused to accept his personal sacrifice and that unhappiness was in store for him. And, indeed, it overtook him shortly afterwards.

Nemesis later became a goddess with more definitely defined personality, and various genealogies were ascribed to her. According to some she was the daughter of Oceanus. According to others she was born of Night and Erebus, in which case she was a deadly power. But when Dike was made her mother she became an equitable divinity. She was, however, always responsible for seeing that order was maintained. One of her titles was Adrasteia—the Inevitable. She is sometimes depicted with a finger to her lips—suggesting that silence is advisable in order not to attract the divine anger. The principal sanctuary of Nemesis was at Rhamnus, a small town in Attica. There was a statue of the goddess there which Phidias carved from the marble which the Persians, rashly counting on victory in advance, had brought with them before the battle of Marathon, expecting to erect a monument with it.

Tyche, Ate, Litae. To complete the list of divinities whose functions were moral, we must also mention Tyche, goddess of fortune. Hesiod calls her the daughter of Oceanus and Tethys. She was represented in various ways by different cities each of which had its own Tyche. Adorned with the mural crown, she wears the attributes of abundance.

Ate, daughter of Eris or of Zeus, was on the other hand a malevolent divinity who prompted men to irresponsible acts. She led both men and gods into error and false ways. It was she who, when Hercules was born, suggested to Zeus the imprudent vow which caused the hero such hardship subsequently. For this the master of the gods punished the wicked goddess by banishing her permanently from Olympus and 'from the heights of heaven flung her into the midst of man's affairs'.

In order to repair the damage done by the treacherous Ate, Zeus sent the Litae after her. The Litae were Prayers and also daughters of Zeus. Wrinkled and lame, they limped after their sister Ate, attempting to mitigate the evils which she caused, and whoever welcomed the Litae with respect was showered with blessings.

The Underworld and its divinities

In Greek mythology the Infernal Regions were the mournful abode where, separated from their bodies, the souls of those who had finished their earthly existence took refuge.

Situation and Topography of the Underworld. There were two successive conceptions of where the afterworld was situated. 'The Afterworld,' says Circe to Odysseus, 'lies at the extremity of the earth, beyond the vast Ocean.' The earth was thought of as a flat surface limited by an immense encircling River Ocean. This river had to be crossed in order to reach the desolate and uncultivated shore of the Infernal Regions. There few things grew, the soil was barren and no living being could survive, for the sun's rays could not penetrate so far. Black poplars were found there, and willows which never bore fruit. The ground supported asphodel, a funerary plant of ruins and cemeteries.

This was the tradition of the epic poems. It was altered with the progress of geography when navigators discovered that very far to the west—where the infernal regions were supposed to be—there existed lands which were in fact inhabited. Popular belief then placed the Kingdom of Shadows elsewhere: from then on it was situated in the centre of the earth. It continued to remain a place of shadows and mystery, of Erebus. Its approaches were no longer the Ocean. The Underworld communicated with the earth by direct channels. These were caverns whose depths were unplumbed, like that of Acherusia in Epirus, or Heraclea Pontica. Near Cape Taenarum

Hygeia. Classical bas-relief. British Museum.

Nemesis. Classical statue. Vatican Museum, Rome

The Moerae. Engraving by Hans Baldung Grien, 1513.

there was one of these entrance gates and also at Colonus in a place dedicated to the Eumenides.

In the same way certain rivers whose course was partly underground were thought to lead to the Infernal Regions. Such was the Acheron in Thesprotia, into which flowed the Cocytus. It must, moreover, be remarked that the names of these rivers were given to them because they were believed to flow into the Underworld. Acheron derives from the word which means 'affliction'. It was the river of sadness and Cocytus was the river of lamentation.

Though the ancients carefully described the exterior appearance and approaches of the Underworld, they were vaguer about its interior. On this aspect of the Infernal Regions we have little information. According to what we have, the actual Underworld was preceded by a vestibule called the Grove of Persephone. Here the black poplars and sterile willows were again found. It had to be crossed before reaching the gate of the Kingdom of Hades. At the gate was posted Cerberus, the monstrous watch-dog with fifty heads and a voice of bronze. He was born of the love of the giant Typhoeus for Echidna. Cerberus was variously represented. Sometimes he had only three heads, sometimes he bristled with serpents and his mouth dribbled black venom. He was always to be feared. When a shade entered the Underworld, the terrible beast would appear friendly, wagging its tail and ears. But no one passing him could ever come out of the Underworld again. Cerberus, however, could be appeased by tossing to him cakes of flour and honey. Hermes could calm him with his caduceus and Orpheus charmed him with his lyre. Only Hercules dared measure his strength with Cerberus and, vanquishing

him, carried him for a while up to earth. Cerberus infected certain herbs with his venom and these were afterwards gathered by magicians who used them in the preparation of various baleful philtres.

Within the Underworld flowed subterranean rivers: Acheron with its affluent the Cocytus swelled by the Phlegethon, Lethe and, finally, the Styx. Acheron was the son of Gaea. He had quenched the thirst of the Titans during their war with Zeus and been thrown into the Underworld, where he was changed into a river. To cross Acheron it was necessary to apply to old Charon, the official ferryman of the Underworld. He was a hard old man, difficult to deal with. Unless the shade of the deceased newcomer presented him with an obol (a silver coin) before embarking, Charon could mercilessly drive away an intruder so ignorant of local usage. The shade was then condemned to wander the deserted shore and never find refuge. The Greeks therefore carefully put an obol into the mouths of the dead.

The Styx surrounded the Underworld with its nine loops. The Styx was personified as a nymph, daughter of Oceanus and Tethys. She was loved, it was said, by the Titan Pallas and by him had Zelos (Jealousy), Nike (Victory), Kratos (Force), and Bia (Violence). As a reward for the help she rendered the Olympians during the revolt of the Titans it was decided that the Immortals should swear by her name, and such vows were irrevocable.

Those who drank of the waters of Lethe forgot the past. Lethe flowed, according to some, at the extremity of the Elysian Fields; according to others at the edge of Tartarus. The Elysian Fields and Tartarus were the two great regions of the Underworld.

Above, the Underworld. In the centre, Hades and Perse-phone; below them, Cerberus. Vase from Tarentum. Fourth century B.C. *Munich Museum.*

Centre, Sisyphus, Ixion and Tantalus being tortured in the Underworld. Engraving published in 1790.

Below, the Eumenides sleeping while Apollo purifies Orestes with a young pig, after his acquittal by the court of the Areopagus. Fifth-century Greek krater. Louvre.

The sovereign of the Underworld

Hades. It seems that the name of the ruler of the Underworld derives from the privative prefix '*a*' and the verb 'to see'. The name Hades thus meant 'Invisible' and evoked an idea of mystery. He was also called Pluto, from the word for 'riches'. It was he who received buried treasure. Afterwards he was considered the god of agricultural wealth; from the centre of the earth he exerted his influence on cultivation and crops.

Hades—also called Aidoneus—was the son of Rhea and the ferocious Cronus, who devoured him as he devoured his brothers and sisters. Fortunately Hades was delivered by his brother Zeus, from whom he received as his share of the inheritance the Kingdom of the Underworld.

Over this domain Hades ruled as absolute master. He seemed happy there and was seen to leave his kingdom on only two occasions: once to abduct Persephone and the other time to go in search of Paean in order to be cured of a wound inflicted by Hercules, who had struck his shoulder with a sharp-pointed arrow. On the other hand, if an impulse to emerge from the Underworld seized him, no one could see him; for his helmet made him invisible.

Hades was not a particularly inconstant husband. Persephone had only twice to complain of his infidelity. First he became interested in Minthe, a nymph of the Cocytus. Persephone—or perhaps it was Demeter—pursued the unfortunate nymph and trod her ferociously underfoot. Hades transformed her into a plant which first grew in Triphylia; this was mint, which was afterwards sacred to Hades.

Hades also brought a daughter of Oceanus to his kingdom, one Leuce, who died a natural death and became a white poplar, the tree of the Elysian Fields. When Hercules came up from the Underworld he was crowned with its foliage.

Hades was very little venerated, though as Pluto he received much more homage. This was because Hades was essentially a god of terror, mystery and the inexorable. Pluto, on the contrary, was regarded as a benevolent deity and his cult was sometimes associated with that of Demeter.

To pray to him—Homer says—one struck the ground with bare hands or with rods. One sacrificed to him a black ewe or a black ram. Plants sacred to the god of the Underworld were the cypress and the narcissus.

Persephone. The name of the wife of Hades occurs in several forms: Persephone, Persephoneia, Phersephone, Persephassa, Phersephatta. It is difficult to discover the etymology of all these variations. It is believed that the last half of the word Persephone comes from a word meaning 'to show' and evokes an idea of light. Whether the first half derives from a word meaning 'to destroy'—in which case Persephone would be 'she who destroys the light'—or from an adverbial root signifying 'dazzling brilliance' as in the name Perseus, it is difficult to decide.

The problem is complicated by the fact that Persephone is not a purely infernal divinity. Before marrying Hades she lived on earth with her mother Demeter, who had conceived her by Zeus. Her name had then been Kore.

It is probable that originally mother and daughter were merged in one and the same divinity. Demeter, as we have seen, had in her province not only the surface of the earth, but also its interior. Subsequently the personality of Demeter split and her subterranean functions devolved on a distinct goddess who was, however, an offspring of the primitive goddess. This is the meaning of the Kore-Persephone myth.

The dramatic circumstances of Kore's abduction will be recalled: how Hades surprised her while she was gathering flowers in a field, carried her away in his chariot and plunged with her into the depths of the earth; how Demeter, unable to regain full possession of her daughter, accepted the gods' proposal that Persephone should pass at least part of the year with her.

Persephone's legend is limited to this single episode, though the initiates of Orphism tried to enrich it by making the goddess the mother of Dionysus-Zagreus. Confined, like Hades, to her shadowy empire, Persephone was exempt from the passions which swayed other divinities. At most she was said to have felt a certain tenderness for the beautiful Adonis.

As goddess of the Underworld Persephone's attributes were the bat, the narcissus and the pomegranate. She was honoured in Arcadia under the names Persephone Soteira and Despoena. She was also venerated at Sardes and in Sicily. But usually her cult was joined to Demeter's and the rites of both were almost always similar.

Hecate. Hecate is best treated as a divinity of the Underworld, though she was in origin a moon-goddess. She was a native of ancient Thrace and in some ways she resembled Artemis, with whom she was sometimes merged. Her name seems to be the feminine form of a title of Apollo's—the far-darter. Thus Hesiod makes her the daughter of the Titan

Nike of Brescia, the winged goddess of victory, daughter of Tethys.

Charon in his boat receiving a shade which Hermes Psychopompus has brought to him. Attic white lekythos. 425 - 400 B.C. Athens Museum.

Perses and the Titaness Asteria, both symbols of shining light. Hecate's lunar character always remained: she and Helios together witnessed the abduction of Kore by Hades.

Hecate was powerful both in the sky and on earth: she gave men riches, victory and wisdom; she watched over the prosperity of flocks and presided over navigation. During the war with the Giants she was the ally of Zeus; she therefore continued to be honoured on Olympus.

A later tradition says that Hecate was the daughter of Zeus and Hera. It was said that she incurred her mother's wrath by stealing her rouge to give to Europa. She fled to the earth and hid in the house of a woman who had just given birth to a child, contact with whom rendered Hecate impure. To remove the stain the Cabeiri plunged her into the Acheron, and that was how Hecate became a divinity of the Underworld. In the infernal regions Hecate's authority was considerable: she was called Prytania of the Dead or the Invincible Queen. She presided over purifications and expiations. She was the goddess of enchantments and magic charms as well. She sent demons to the earth to torment men. She herself would appear at night accompanied by her retinue of infernal dogs. The places that she haunted most frequently were crossroads, spots near tombs or the scenes of crimes. Thus at crossroads her image could be found, either columns or statues of the goddess with three faces, called triple Hecates; on the eve of the full moon, offerings would be left before these images to propitiate the redoubtable goddess.

The auxiliaries of Hades

Thanatos and Hypnos. Thanatos (Death) naturally supplied Hades with his subjects. He was the son of Night. Euripides shows him dressed in a black robe, holding in his hand the fatal sword, as he walks among men. But normally Death did not appear in this sinister aspect; Thanatos was more usually represented as a winged spirit. He then completely resembled his brother Hypnos (Sleep), who lived with him in the Underworld. Hypnos put men to sleep by touching them with his magic wand or by fanning them with his dark wings. He had power also over the gods, and Homer tells us how at Hera's

Above, Hades and Persephone in the Underworld. Interior of a red-figured cup in the British Museum.
Below, Hypnos and Thanatos carrying off the body of Sarpedon. After a vase by Pamphaios. British Museum.

request he took the form of a night bird and sent Zeus to sleep on Mount Ida. The son of Hypnos was Morpheus, god of dreams.

The Keres. The Keres executed the will of the Moerae or Fates and were no doubt originally confused with them. When the implacable deities had fixed the fatal hour, it was the Keres who appeared. They would then seize the unhappy mortal, deliver the decisive blow, and carry him down to the land of shadows. In the midst of battle especially they could be seen to hover, with a sparkling eye, grimacing mouth, and sharp teeth whose whiteness contrasted with the sombre hue of their visage. They wore red robes and cried out dismally as they finished off the wounded. They would dig in their sharp claws, then greedily drink the streaming blood. Not without reason were they called the dogs of Hades.

The Erinnyes. The Erinnyes were also sometimes called the 'dogs of Hades'. They, too, were infernal deities whose special mission was to punish parricides and those who had violated their oaths. Their genealogy was rather vague: according to Hesiod they were born to Gaea fertilised by the blood of Uranus. Aeschylus calls them 'the children of Eternal Night' and Sophocles 'Daughters of the Earth and the Shadow'. It seems that they were first venerated in Arcadia, where a Demeter Erinnyes, from whom they were perhaps derived, was worshipped. Their number for long remained undetermined, but was later fixed at three, and they were given the individual names of Tisiphone, Megara and Alecto.

When a crime was committed in a family—above all when a son's hands were stained with the blood of his parents—the black goddesses would immediately appear, their hair bristling with serpents, armed with torches and whips. They would sit at the threshold of the guilty one's house and it was useless to attempt escape. Even in the Underworld they pursued their vengeance and tormented the guilty in Tartarus.

The cult of the Erinnyes was spread throughout all Greece, and above all in Athens, where they had a temple near the Areopagus. Here they were honoured under the name of the Eumenides—the Benevolent Ones—in memory of the mildness they had shown towards Orestes, who, after the murder of his mother, had come to seek refuge in Athens.

Life in the Underworld. Souls of the dead, when they had left the earth, retained only a pale reflection of their former personality. Physically they were diaphanous and insubstantial. Morally they were also shadows: their courage and intelligence had disappeared. Only a few privileged persons lived in the Underworld as they had lived on earth, following the same occupations. Orion continued to hunt, Minos judged souls, Hercules was always ready to overthrow some monster or other.

In brief the Underworld, in this primitive conception of it, was a sort of dismal house of retirement. Only the outstandingly guilty suffered eternal torture.

Little by little, however, the Underworld came to be thought of, not as a limbo, but as a place of justice where each received exactly what he deserved.

Souls on their arrival appeared before a tribunal

composed of Hades and his three assessors: Aeacus, Minos and Rhadamanthys.

The last two were sons of Zeus and Europa and had been kings, Minos of Crete and Rhadamanthys of the Cyclades. Aeacus was the son of Zeus and Aegina, and during his life had been distinguished for his piety and love of justice. The gods themselves had chosen him as an arbiter. After his death he was appointed in the Underworld especially to judge Europeans, while Rhadamanthys tried Asiatics. It was Aeacus who held the keys of the Underworld.

After they had been examined and judgment pronounced, the souls of the dead were either cast into Tartarus or conducted to the Elysian Fields or to the Islands of the Blessed.

Tartarus with its gates of bronze was the sombre gaol of those who had committed crimes against the gods. It was surrounded by a triple wall and bathed by the waters of the Phlegethon. The avenue which led to Tartarus was closed by a diamond gate. Here the most notorious prisoners were the Titans and the giant Tityus, on whom two vultures fed because he had attempted to violate Leto. Tantalus could also be seen, eternally tortured by hunger and thirst; Sisyphus, who without respite rolled his rock up a steep

One of the Erinnyes or Furies. Etruscan bronze figure found near Mount Vesuvius. British Museum.

hill; Ixion, bound to his flaming wheel spinning in the air; and the Danaids, condemned eternally to fill a bottomless barrel.

In Elysium, on the contrary, snow and rain and tempests were unknown. Soft breezes for ever refreshed this abode of happiness, which was at first reserved for the children of the gods, but later opened to the favourites of the Olympians and the souls of the just.

The heroes

The Greeks' Idea of the Hero. The Greek Hero was not always a supernatural being related to the gods. Homer made him a man of strength and courage or one who was especially venerated for his wisdom, like Laertes, Aegyptus and Demodocus. The hero could also be simply a prince of an illustrious family, like Odysseus and Menelaus. It is only incidentally that the heroes of Homer's poems are related to gods.

Hesiod, on the other hand, generalised the idea of the superman and recounted his origin. According to him, heroes were the offspring of the fourth generation of mythical men: that is to say the generation which took part in the battles of Troy and Thebes. In those times, indeed, gods and mortals often mingled.

Cult of the Heroes. The cult which the Greeks devoted to their heroes closely resembled the veneration with which they honoured their own ancestors. The hero, they believed, was in fact their most illustrious ancestor. Heroes and ancestors alike were offered sacrifice at the end of the day: the sacrificial victim was turned towards the West and at the foot of the altar a trench was dug to receive the victim's head. But the chief role of the hero was to act as intermediary between men and the gods. While men after death became insubstantial shadows, heroes retained their original qualities and could intercede for

Hades abducting Persephone. Statue by Bernini. Borghese Museum, Rome.

mortals. In brief, the heroes, who were originally idealised men, became demi-gods and in the hierarchy occupied a position midway between men and the Olympians.

Hercules

We are not very certain about the etymology of the word Heracles (the Latinised form being Hercules, which is used here throughout). Various hypotheses have been advanced to explain it. The ancients claimed that Heracles was thus named because he owed his glory to Hera. The name has also been translated as 'glory of the air'. But none of the theories put forward is more convincing than the others.

The Functions of Hercules. Hercules was thought of as the personification of physical strength. In his aspect of athlete-hero the foundation of the Olympic Games was ascribed to him. Pindar says that he arranged all the rules and details. But the chief function of Hercules was to play the part of a protector. When men were in danger Heracles *Alexikakos* was their chief resort. In consequence he was even ascribed medical powers: he was invoked in case of epidemics, while certain medicinal springs at Himera and Thermopylae were sacred to him. Finally, sometimes as Heracles Musagetes he played the cithara. In sum, he presided over all aspects of Hellenic education and, after being the god of physical prowess, he was the god who sang of victory and accompanied himself on the lyre. More than any other he was the friend and counsellor of men.

Representation and Cult. The glorious hero, the invincible athlete, is depicted as a man of mature strength endowed with great muscular power, whose head is rather small in relation to his body. Generally Hercules stands, leaning on his heavy club. In his statues and busts we observe a rather sad and severe expression, as though Hercules, the eternal conqueror,

Hercules, known as the Farnese Hercules, attributed to the sculptor Lysippus. National Museum, Naples.

never knew repose. His appearance suggests that he is waiting for yet another superhuman task to fulfil.

Hercules was venerated like other heroes and with the same rites, but his cult was much more general. All Greece honoured him. His exploits took place all over the Hellenic world. Thebes and Argos were the centres from which his legend spread.

The Birth of Hercules. His Childhood and First Exploits. Hercules descended from Perseus, whose son Alcaeus (the Strong) was the father of Amphitryon, the supposed father of Hercules. On his mother's side, Electryon (the Brilliant), another son of Perseus, was the father of Alcmene (woman of might). Hercules, then, was born under the sign of strength and light; furthermore, his paternity was divine. Zeus, wishing to have a son who should be a powerful protector of both mortals and Immortals, descended one night to the city of Thebes, where he assumed the appearance of Amphitryon and lay with Amphitryon's wife, Alcmene. Shortly afterwards Amphitryon himself returned from a victorious expedition and took his wife in his arms. From the two successive unions Alcmene conceived twins: Hercules and Iphicles.

Their birth was fraught with difficulties. On the

The infant Hercules strangling the serpents. Classical sculpture. Capitoline Museum, Rome.

day Hercules should have been born Zeus swore a solemn and irrevocable oath before the Olympians that the descendant of Perseus who was about to be born should one day rule Greece. At these words Hera, doubly jealous, hurried to Argos, where she caused the wife of one Sthenelus—himself a son of Perseus—to give birth prematurely. The child was Eurystheus. Hastening to Thebes, Hera simultaneously retarded the birth of Hercules. Thus Eurystheus came into the title of ruler of Greece and Zeus, bound by his solemn oath, was obliged to recognise him. And that was why Hercules all his life found the hardest tasks imposed on him by the rival whom Hera had set up against him. Nor was her vengeance yet satisfied. One night while all in the palace of Amphitryon were asleep, two serpents attacked the infant Hercules. While Iphicles screamed pitifully, Hercules firmly grasped the two monsters, one in each hand, and wrung their necks. To encourage such promise Hercules was then handed over to illustrious tutors. Rhadamanthys taught him wisdom and virtue while Linus taught him music. Linus was, however, killed by the young hero in a fit of temper. Amphitryon then entrusted his divine offspring to some shepherds who lived in the mountains. There Hercules gave himself over to physical exercise and developed his strength. At the age of eighteen he killed a ferocious lion which came to devour Amphitryon's herds. While waiting for the beast, the hero hid in the house of King Thespius and, legend has it, made use of the occasion to lie in a single night with host's fifty daughters.

Hercules shortly afterwards defended his native city against Orchomenus. He met the herald of Orchomenus, who had come to Thebes to collect the tribute, and cut off his nose and ears, thus starting the war. Amphitryon, fighting beside his two sons, was killed. But Hercules, aided by Athene, defeated Erginus, King of Orchomenus. Creon became king of that country and gave his daughter Megara to Hercules as a wife. Their marriage was unhappy. Hera sent Lyssa, the Fury of madness, to Hercules. The hero was seized with the deadly malady, mistook his own children for those of Eurystheus, and massacred them and their mother. After this fearful crime Hercules had to flee the country. He went to Argolis, where he spent twelve years under the orders of Eurystheus, who imposed upon him the most arduous labours. For thus the oracle of Delphi had commanded when Hercules, wishing to remove the stain of his crime, consulted it.

The twelve labours

The Nemean Lion. The first monster that Hercules had to exterminate was the Nemean Lion, the skin of which Eurystheus ordered him to bring back. Hercules attempted in vain to pierce the beast with his arrows, then engaged it hand to hand, and finally strangled it in his powerful grip. He removed the skin and from it made a garment which rendered him invulnerable. He then returned to Tiryns with his trophy.

The Lernaean Hydra. This hydra, born of Typhon and Echidna, was an enormous serpent with nine heads. Its den was a marsh near Lerna in the Peloponnese. It would issue forth to ravage the herds and crops; its breath was so poisonous that whoever breathed it fell dead.

Accompanied by Iolaus, son of Iphicles, Hercules arrived at Lerna, found the monster near the spring of Amymone and by means of flaming arrows forced it to emerge from the marshes. Wielding his mighty club, he then tried to overwhelm it. But in vain; for every time he struck off one of the hydra's nine heads two grew in its place. Then Iolaus set the neighbouring forest on fire and with the help of red-hot brands

Hercules slaying the hydra of Lerna. Engraving after a sixteenth-century painting by de Vrient.

Hercules bringing the Erymanthean boar back to Eurystheus, who is so frightened that he has hidden himself in a wine jar. Vase in the British Museum.

Hercules and the Stymphalian birds. As his fourth labour Hercules slew these birds with their iron beaks, claws and wings. Greek vase in the British Museum.

burnt the serpent's heads. Hercules cut off the final head and buried it. Then he soaked his arrows in the hydra's blood, thus making them poisonous and deadly.

The Wild Boar of Erymanthus. This savage beast came down from Mount Erymanthus, on the borders of Arcadia and Achaia, and devastated the territory of Psophis. Hercules succeeded in capturing it and carried it to Tiryns. Eurystheus was so terrified at the sight of the monster that he ran away and hid himself in a bronze jar.

On his way to Mount Erymanthus Hercules had received the hospitality of the Centaur Pholus, who in his honour broached a barrel of delicious wine which had been a present from Dionysus. The other Centaurs were attracted by the bouquet of the wine and came running to the house of Pholus, armed with stones and uprooted fir trees, to demand their share of it. Hercules drove them off with his arrows. The Centaurs were decimated, and took refuge near Cape Malea.

The Stymphalian Birds. The marshes of Stymphalus in Arcadia were peopled by monstrous birds whose wings, beaks and claws were of iron. They fed on human flesh and were so numerous that when they took wing the light of the sun was blotted out. Hercules frightened them with brazen cymbals and slew them with arrows.

The Ceryneian Hind. Eurystheus then ordered Hercules to bring him back alive the hind of Mount Ceryneia, whose hooves were of bronze and her horns of gold. Hercules chased her for an entire year before he at last caught her on the banks of the Ladon.

The Stables of Augeias. Augeias, King of Elis, owned innumerable herds of cattle, among which were twelve white bulls sacred to Helios. One of them, whose name was Phaethon, was privileged to shine like a star. Unhappily these magnificent animals lived

in foul stables, heaped high with dung of many years' accumulation. Hercules undertook to clean them out in one day on condition that the king gave him a tenth part of the herd. In order to do this he breached the walls of the building and, altering the course of the rivers Alpheus and Peneius, made them rush through the cowsheds. When the job was done, Augeias, under the pretext that Hercules was merely executing the orders of Eurystheus, refused to fulfil his part of the bargain. Later the hero was to punish this dishonesty.

The Cretan Bull Poseidon had given Minos a bull, believing that Minos would offer it in sacrifice to him. As the king did nothing of the sort, Poseidon drove the animal mad. The country was terrorised and Minos appealed to Hercules, who at the time happened to be in Crete. The hero managed to capture the animal and carried it on his back across the sea to Argolis.

The Mares of Diomedes. Diomedes, son of Ares and King of the Bistones, owned mares which he fed on human flesh. Hercules, accompanied by a few volunteers, approached Thrace and captured these terrible mares, having first killed their guardians. The alert was given, the Bistones rushed upon him and the battle began. Hercules at last vanquished his assailants and Diomedes was given to his own mares to eat.

The rescue of Alcestis is usually said to have taken place at this same time. Admetus, King of Pherae, had obtained from the Fates, through the mediation of Apollo, an assurance that he would not die if someone consented to die in his stead. When the fatal moment arrived his wife, Alcestis, took his place. They were about to bury the unhappy woman when Hercules passed by and engaged in dreadful struggle with Thanatos—Death himself. Hercules succeeded in wrenching Alcestis from Death's grasp and returned her to her husband.

The Girdle of Hippolyte. Hippolyte, whom some call Melanippe, was the Queen of the Amazons in Cappadocia. As a mark of her sovereignty she had a magnificent girdle given to her by Ares. Admete, daughter of Eurystheus, greatly coveted this marvellous adornment, and Hercules was therefore given orders to go and fetch it. Accompanied by several celebrated heroes—Theseus, Telamon, Peleus—he embarked. His first port of call was Paros, where he fought with the sons of Minos. Next he reached Mariandyne in Mysia, where he helped King Lycus to conquer the Bebryces. In gratitude Lycus built the town of Heracles Pontica.

When at last he reached the country of the Amazons Hercules at first encountered no obstacle: Hippolyte agreed to give him the girdle. But Hera was enraged and, disguising herself as an Amazon, spread abroad the story that Hercules planned to abduct the queen. The Amazons seized their weapons. Hercules, believing they had betrayed him, slaughtered the Amazons, together with their queen. He took the girdle and then proceeded towards Troy.

The Cattle of Geryon. Geryon was a triple-bodied monster who reigned over the western coast of Iberia or, according to others, over Epirus. He owned a herd of red oxen which were guarded by the herdsman Eurytion and the dog Orthrus. On the orders of Eurystheus, Hercules took possession of the oxen after killing Eurytion, Orthrus and finally Geryon. On his return journey he had various adventures. He slew the sons of Poseidon, who attempted to steal the oxen, and he had to go to Eryx, King of the Elymans, in Sicily, to recapture an ox which had escaped and been put in the stables of Eryx. Eryx refused to return the beast unless Hercules beat him in a series of boxing and wrestling bouts. Hercules finally overthrew and killed him. In the hills of Thrace Hera sent a gadfly which drove the animals mad; they dispersed through the mountains and Hercules had great trouble in herding them together again. When he had done so he brought the cattle to Eurystheus, who sacrificed them to Hera.

It was in the course of this expedition that Hercules went into Gaul, where he abolished human sacrifice. He fought the Ligurians with the aid of stones which Zeus caused to rain down from the sky and which covered the plain of the Crau. The River Strymon refused to let him cross and he filled up its bed with stones.

The Golden Apples of the Hesperides. Eurystheus next commanded Hercules to bring to him the golden apples which the Hesperides, daughters of Atlas and Hesperus, guarded in their fabulous garden at the western extremities of the world. Hercules first travelled towards the north where, on the banks of the Eridanus, the nymphs of the river advised him to consult Nereus about the route. Hercules succeeded in capturing the prophetic god, who told him how to reach the garden of the Hesperides. Crossing Libya, Hercules measured his strength with Antaeus, a monstrous bandit who forced all travellers to wrestle with him. Antaeus was the son of Gaea, Mother Earth, and had the power of regaining his strength simply by

Hercules breaking off the golden horns of the Ceryneian hind. He is watched by Athene and Artemis. Greek vase in the British Museum.

touching earth with his feet. Hercules in the end choked him to death by holding him high in the air in his arms. Hercules was next attacked while asleep by the Pygmies. He sewed them up in his lion skin. Then he arrived in Egypt, where Busiris, the king, sacrificed a foreigner every year in order to put an end to a terrible famine. Hercules was chosen as victim, put in chains and conducted to the temple. But he threw off his chains suddenly and slew Busiris and his son Amphidamas (Iphidamas). He then resumed his journey. He crossed Ethiopia, where he killed Emathion, son of Tithonus, and replaced him with Memnon. He crossed the sea in a golden barque which the Sun had given him. In the Caucasus he slew with his arrows the eagle which gnawed the liver of Prometheus and finally reached the garden of the Hesperides. He killed the dragon Ladon which guarded the entrance, seized the apples, and delivered them to Eurystheus. Eurystheus made him a gift of them, and Hercules in his turn presented them to Athene, who returned them to the Hesperides.

It was also related that Hercules was aided by Atlas on this enterprise. He persuaded Atlas to pick the apples while he, Hercules, meanwhile supported the world on his shoulders. When Atlas returned with the apples he was reluctant to reassume his traditional burden and would have refused to do so had not Hercules outwitted him.

Hercules' Journey to the Underworld. In despair of ever getting the better of Hercules, Eurystheus commanded him as a final labour to fetch Cerberus, guardian of the infernal gates. Hercules first had himself initiated into the infernal mysteries at Eleusis and then, guided by Hermes, he took the subterranean passage which descended at Cape Taenarum. Everything fled before him except Meleager and the Gorgon. Farther on Theseus and Peirithous, who had imprudently ventured into the Underworld, implored his assistance. Hercules saved Theseus, but was prevented from rescuing Peirithous by a sudden earthquake. He relieved Ascalaphus of the boulder which was crushing him, overthrew Menoetes, or Menoetius, the herdsman of Hades, wounded Hades himself and finally obtained the permission of Hades to carry off Cerberus, providing that he could conquer the monster without other weapons than his bare hands. Hercules leapt on Cerberus and at last mastered him by strangling him. Then he dragged the brute by the scruff of its neck back to earth, in order to show him to Eurystheus, and afterwards sent him back to Hades again.

Other Exploits of Hercules. When at last he was freed from servitude, far from resting on his laurels, Hercules set forth on new adventures. When King Eurytus promised the hand of his daughter Iole to any man who could vanquish him in an archery contest, Hercules arrived and triumphed. The king refused to keep his word. Shortly afterwards the king's son, Iphitus, asked Hercules to help him search for some stolen horses, and Hercules, distraught with fury, killed him. For this crime Hercules went to Delphi to be purified. The Pythia refused to answer him and Hercules made off with her tripod. A bitter quarrel with Apollo ensued in which Zeus himself had to intervene. At last the oracle condemned Hercules to a year's slavery, and obliged him to hand over his year's wages to Eurytus. It was Omphale, Queen of Lydia, who bought the hero for three talents when he was offered for sale as a nameless slave. In spite of the tradition which showed Hercules during this period softened by pleasures and dressed in a long oriental robe while he spun wool at the feet of this mistress, he did not remain inactive. He captured the Cercopes, evil and malicious demons who were, perhaps, only a horde of brigands camped near Ephesus. He killed the king of Aulis, Syleus, who forced strangers to work in his vineyards and then cut their

Hercules capturing the mad bull of Poseidon. Engraving after a sixteenth-century painting by de Vrient.

throats. He rid the banks of the Sagaris of a gigantic serpent which was ravaging the countryside, and finally threw the cruel Lityerses into the Maeander. Lityerses had been in the habit of forcing strangers to help with his harvest and then cutting off their heads with a scythe. Omphale was overcome with admiration and restored the hero's freedom.

Hercules then offered to rescue Hesione, daughter of Laomedon, King of Ilium. This unfortunate princess had been chained to a rock as an expiatory victim against an epidemic. When a dragon came to devour her Hercules prevented the tragedy, but Laomedon refused to give him the reward which had been agreed upon. The hero returned to Ilium with six ships, besieged the town, took it by assault, killed Laomedon and his sons, and gave Hesione in marriage to his friend Telamon. On his return journey he was thrown on to the shores of the island of Cos by a storm raised by Hera. The inhabitants received him badly and he avenged himself by sacking the island and slaying its king, Eurypylus. Next, he took part at Phlegra in the battle between the gods and the giants.

Hercules had not forgotten the dishonesty of Augeias in the matter of the Augeian Stables. He marched against him and devastated his domain. On this occasion he had to fight the Molionids, sons of Poseidon. It was said that they had been hatched from a silver egg and had but one body with two heads, four arms and four legs.

Hercules also restored Tyndareus to his throne after he had been usurped by Hippocoön and his sons. Passing through Tegea in Arcadia Hercules seduced Auge, daughter of Aleus and a priestess of Athene. She bore him a son, Telephus, whom she hid in the temple of the goddess. Athene, angered by this profanation, sent a plague to the country. Aleus discovered his daughter's shame and drove her away. She took refuge with King Teuthras in Mysia and exposed her child on Mount Parthenius. When Telephus grew to manhood he went in search of his mother. He found her in Mysia and, not recognising her, was on the point of marrying her when Hercules intervened and prevented the incest.

The last adventure of Hercules took place in Aetolia and in the land of Trachis. He obtained the hand of Deianeira, daughter of Oeneus, King of the Aetolians, after having triumphed over another suitor, the river-god Achelous. But shortly afterwards the accidental murder of young Eunomus, who served at his father-in-law's table, obliged Hercules to fly from the country, together with his wife. When he arrived at the River Evenus Hercules gave Deianeira to the Centaur Nessus to carry across to the opposite bank. But halfway across Nessus attempted to rape Deianeira. Hercules saw this and at once struck him with an arrow. As Nessus died he gave his blood to Deianeira, telling her that it would preserve the love and fidelity of her husband.

Unfortunately Hercules then conceived the fateful idea of going back to punish Eurytus. He slew Eurytus and his sons, and brought away Iole, whom he had never ceased to love. On his return he stopped at Cenaeum in Euboea to offer a sacrifice to Zeus.

Above, Hermes Psychopompus (conductor of souls) leading the shade of the nymph Eurydice to her husband Orpheus. Attic bas-relief. Villa Albani, Rome.

Page 135, the Argonauts setting out under the leadership of Jason on their expedition to capture the golden fleece. Detail from a fifteenth-century interpretation by the painter Lorenzo Costa. Padua Museum.

Before doing so he sent his companion Lichas to Deianeira in Trachis to fetch a white tunic. Deianeira was worried at the thought that Iole was with her husband and, remembering the words of Nessus, soaked the tunic in the Centaur's blood before sending it to Hercules, hoping thus to regain his love. Scarcely had Hercules put on the tunic when he felt himself devoured by inner fire. Maddened with pain, he seized Lichas by the feet and flung him into the sea; then, tearing up pine -trees by their roots, he made himself a funeral pyre, mounted it and ordered his companions to set it alight. All refused. Finally Poeas, father of Philoctetes, lighted the pines and Hercules rewarded him by giving him his bow and arrows.

The flames crackled and rose around the hero. At the moment they reached his body a cloud descended from the skies and in an apotheosis of thunder and lightning the son of Zeus disappeared from the eyes of men. He was admitted to Olympus, where he was reconciled with Hera. He was married to her daughter Hebe and from then on lived the blissful and magnificent life of the Immortals.

The Progeny of Hercules. Legend ascribes nearly eighty sons to Hercules; their fortunes varied. Certain of them, called the Heraclids, distinguished themselves by conquering the Peloponnese.

After their father's death the sons of Hercules, fearing Eurystheus' persecution, left Mycenae and for a long time searched in vain for refuge. Finally Demophon, son of Theseus, received them in Athens. This was sufficient pretext for war between Eurystheus and the inhabitants of Attica. Iolaus, a former companion of Hercules, killed Eurystheus. The Heraclids thought they could return to the Peloponnese. But their return was premature and caused an outbreak of plague; again they went into exile.

Afterwards they attempted five consecutive invasions. Only the last one was successful. Its leaders were Temenus, Cresphontes and Aristodemus, greatgrandsons of the hero. Allied with them were Dymas and Pamphylus, sons of the king of the Dorians. They chose the sea route and embarked at Naupactus to sail through the straits of Corinth. Before they left they had the misfortune to kill a prophet of Apollo. In anger the god destroyed their fleet and struck the expedition with famine. When the oracle of Delphi was consulted, it told the allies that they required a guide with three eyes. In the end they discovered a one-eyed man whose name was Oxylus, who rode towards them on a horse and thus, with his mount, fulfilled the conditions the oracle had demanded. Oxylus then became leader of the expedition, which was successful.

Theseus and the heroes of Attica

The Birth and Youth of Theseus. Theseus, like Hercules, was a great destroyer of monsters; and like Hercules he perished tragically. His birth also was similar to that of the Theban hero. His mother was Aethra, daughter of Pittheus, King of Troezen. She was loved at the same time by Aegeus, King of Athens, and by Poseidon. Theseus, who was con-

Above, Hercules accompanied by Hermes leads Cerberus out of the Underworld. Black-figured vase, from the Journal of Hellenic Studies.
Below, Hercules killing Nessus, who is holding Deianeira. Red-figured vase in the British Museum.

ceived of this double union, thus had two fathers, a mortal and a god. Aegeus was obliged to return to Athens before the child was born, and he hid his sword and his sandals under a heavy rock. When Theseus had grown strong enough to lift the rock and find these paternal souvenirs, he was to come to Athens and rejoin his father. So Theseus spent his childhood with his mother. When he was sixteen years old Aethra revealed the secret of his birth and showed him the famous rock. Theseus had already shown promise of bravery. As a child he had attacked, under the mistaken impression that it was alive, the terrifying body of the Nemean Lion which Hercules, visiting Pittheus, had placed on a table. Theseus now

Hercules holding up the vanquished Cercopes. Metope from Selinus. National Museum, Palermo.

in search of a wild bull which was devastating Attica. He succeeded in capturing it near Marathon, brought it back to Athens and sacrificed it to Apollo Delphinios.

Theseus and the Minotaur. In the midst of all this ambassadors arrived from Crete coming for the third time to collect the annual tribute—seven virgins and seven young men—which had been imposed on Athens since the murder of Androgeus. When they arrived in Crete, these unfortunate young people were thrown as food to a monster called the Minotaur. Theseus embarked with the victims with the intention of destroying the monster. He told his father that if he were victorious the ship when it returned would carry a white sail; if he were vanquished the black sail would be retained. When he arrived in Crete, Theseus said that he was the son of Poseidon. To test this boast, Minos tossed a golden ring into the sea and requested the hero to bring it back to him. Theseus dived in and returned not only with the ring but with a crown which Amphitrite had given him. Ariadne, the daughter of Minos, fell in love with Theseus and furnished him with a ball of string by means of which he could guide himself through the

lifted the mighty rock, took possession of his fathers' sword and sandals and set forth for Athens.

His First Exploits. His first adventures occurred on his journey to Athens. Near Epidaurus, he killed a dangerous bandit, Periphetes, son of Hephaestus, and took from him his terrible club. In the forests of the isthmus he inflicted on Sinis, son of Poseidon, the same torture which Sinis imposed on others: namely, tearing them asunder by tying them to sprung pine trees. He killed the wild sow of Crommyon, called Phaea. On the slopes of Megaris he dashed Sciron against a boulder. Sciron had forced travellers to wash his feet, and when they stooped to do so he would kick them over the cliff into the sea, where they were devoured by a monstrous turtle. At Eleusis he vanquished Cercyon the Arcadian and, a little farther on, put an end to the criminal career of the giant Polypemon, known as Procrustes, who forced his victims to lie on a bed too short for them and then cut off whatever overlapped. Alternatively he would stretch them if the bed proved too long. Theseus made him undergo the same treatment. When he had purified himself after all these killings on the banks of the Cephissus, Theseus at last reached Athens.

He had donned a white robe and carefully arranged his beautiful fair hair. The workmen building the temple of Apollo Delphinios mocked at his innocent air and foppish appearance. Without deigning to reply Theseus picked up a heavy ox-cart and tossed it clean over the temple. Then he arrived at his father's palace. Aegeus had meanwhile married Medea who was instinctively jealous of the stranger and therefore during the ensuing feast attempted to poison him. When Theseus drew his sword, his father recognised it and him. Aegeus then drove Medea and her children away and shared his throne with his son. From then on Theseus fought to strengthen his father's authority. First he exterminated the Pallantids, who were nephews of Aegeus and had schemed to overthrow their uncle. Then he went

Theseus killing the Minotaur. Classical sculpture. Villa Albani, Rome.

Theseus recognised by his father. Bas-relief. Villa Albani, Rome.

Theseus carrying off Helen. His friend Patroclus is on the left. From a red-figured Greek vase.

Labyrinth in which the Minotaur was kept and, after killing him, return. When Theseus had slain the beast he left Crete and took Ariadne and her sister Phaedra with him; but he abandoned Ariadne on the island of Naxos. We have already seen how she was consoled by Dionysus.

In the joy of victory Theseus forgot to change the black sail which his ship was carrying. Aegeus saw it from the shore and, believing that his son was dead, threw himself into the sea. The ship which had been used on this expedition was piously preserved by the Athenians and carefully kept in a state of repair. It was named the *Paralia* and every year took gifts from Attica to Delos.

The Last Exploits of Theseus. At the death of his father Theseus became king of Attica and endowed his people with wise institutions. He united them in a single group, built a communal prytaneum in Athens, divided the citizens into three classes, erected temples, and instituted the Panatheneae. At the same time he continued his wandering life of adventure.

He accompanied Hercules on his expedition against the Amazons, took part in hunting the wild boar of Calydon, and sailed with the Argonauts. He was usually accompanied by his faithful friend Peirithous, who at first had been his enemy. With Peirithous he also attacked the Amazons and abducted one of them, Antiope—the cause of an Amazonian invasion of Attica. Antiope bore him a son, Hippolytus, but he repudiated her and instead married Phaedra. Again with Peirithous he went to Sparta and carried off young Helen. The two friends drew lots for her and she fell to Theseus. To console himself Peirithous decided to abduct Persephone, and the two heroes set forth for the Underworld. They succeeded in getting in, but they could not get out again and it required Hercules to rescue Theseus. When he returned to Athens the king found his house in an uproar. The Dioscuri, as Helen's brothers were called, had come to take their sister back; and Phaedra had conceived an incestuous passion for her stepson Hippolytus, who, being

consecrated to Artemis, had made a vow of chastity and refused her. In mortification Phaedra told Theseus that his son had made an attempt on her honour and, too credulous, Theseus banished Hippolytus and called down Poseidon's wrath on the youth. The god summoned up a marine monster who terrified the youth's chariot horses, and Hippolytus was crushed to death. At Troezen his tomb could be seen near the tomb of Phaedra. In the temple which was consecrated to him maidens would hang up a lock of their hair on the eve of their wedding.

Stricken by these tragedies, Theseus left Athens and retired to Skyros, to the palace of King Lycomedes. But Lycomedes was jealous of his guest's great fame and treacherously threw him into the sea. The remains of Theseus were interred at Skyros and later found by Cimon, who brought them back to Athens and placed them in the sacred enclosure of the Theseum.

Other heroes of Attica

Cecrops. Cecrops, who was called Autochthonus or 'born of the earth', was regarded as the founder of Athens. It was during his reign that the dispute between Athene and Poseidon for the possession of Attica took place.

Erichthonius. Erichthonius was the son of Hephaestus who had fathered him by Gaea, the Earth, after being repulsed by Athene. In spite of this, Athene took charge of the infant, enclosing him in a chest which she entrusted to Pandrosos, the eldest daughter of Cecrops, and forbidding her to open it. But the sisters of Pandrosos could not control their curiosity. When they saw that a serpent was entwined round the newborn child they were seized with terror. In their wild flight they fell from the top of the Acropolis and were killed.

Erichthonius was king of Athens; he introduced the worship of Athene and the use of silver. He made war on Eumolpus and the Eleusinians. This Eumolpus, son of Poseidon, had come from Thrace to Eleusis and there instituted the mysteries of Demeter. It was told how Eumolpus was slain by Erichthonius and how, in expiation of the murder, Poseidon demanded the death of one of the King of Athens' daughters. There were four of them, and they decided to die together. Erichthonius was struck dead Zeus.

Descendants of Erichthonius. One of his daughters, Oreithyia, was seen one day by Boreas while she was playing on the shore; he carried her off and married her. Another daughter, Creusa, was loved by Apollo and by him had a son, Ion, whose adventure has been related in the chapter on Apollo.

Pandion, son of Erichthonius, succeeded him to the throne of Athens. He had three daughters: Procris, Philomela and Procne. All three had tragic fates. Procris was married to Cephalus and we have already seen how the jealousy of Eos brought them to disaster.

Philomela and Procne. When Pandion made war on Labdacus, King of Thebes, he was assisted by Tereus, King of Thrace, to whom he had given his daughter, Procne, in marriage. Procne bore Tereus a son, Itys. But when Tereus laid eyes on Philomela his sister-in-law, he fell in love with her, raped her, and, for fear that she would reveal the crime, cut out her tongue. Nevertheless the wretched Philomela was able to tell her sister what had occurred by embroidering the shocking story on a peplos. Procne, out of her mind with rage, killed Itys and served him to Tereus for dinner. Then she and Philomela fled, while the tyrant Tereus pursued them with drawn sword. A benevolent deity intervened and turned

Tereus into a hoopoe, Procne into a swallow and Philomela into a nightingale. As for Itys, he was resuscitated and changed into a goldfinch.

Bellerophon and the heroes of Corinth

Sisyphus. If Bellerophon was Corinth's most valiant hero, his grandfather, Sisyphus, was its most cunning. Sisyphus was the son of Aeolus and founded Ephyra, the ancient name of Corinth. As far back as Homeric times he was reputed to be craftiest of men. Sometimes he was even alleged to be the father of Odysseus, so great was their resemblance in this respect. It was Sisyphus who told the river-god Asopus that his daughter Aegina had been abducted by Zeus. Zeus in fury sent Thanatos for him, but the cunning Sisyphus succeeded in trapping the god of death and Ares had to come to set him free. This time Sisyphus had to submit to his destiny. But before dying he advised his wife not to pay him funeral honours. He had scarcely arrived in the Underworld when he went to Hades to complain of his wife's negligence and to ask for permission to go back to earth for a moment in order to punish her. Permission was granted and Sisyphus, back on earth again, refused to return to the Underworld. Hermes had to deal personally with this recalcitrant shade. Sisyphus was punished for his deceitfulness by being eternally condemned to roll up the slope of a mountain an enormous boulder which, each time it nearly reached the summit, rolled down again.

Bellerophon. Sisyphus had a son, Glaucus, who

Hippolytus in his quadriga. Detail from a Greek vase in the British Museum.

The meeting of Ariadne and Theseus. Interior of a red-figured cup in the British Museum.

offended Aphrodite and, in the course of funeral games, was trampled and killed by his horses, whom the goddess had driven mad. Afterwards the ghost of Glaucus continued to frighten horses. The son of Glaucus, Hipponous, was more celebrated under the name of Bellerophon, which was given to him after he had murdered a Corinthian named Bellerus. In expiation of the murder Bellerophon went to the palace of Proetus, King of Tiryns. The king's wife, Stheneboea, at once fell in love with the young hero. Bellerophon scorned her and she told her husband that he had attempted to seduce her. Proetus did not dare to kill a man who was his guest and, instead, sent him to his father-in-law, Iobates, with a sealed message containing his death sentence. Iobates imposed various tasks on Bellerophon, trusting that in the attempt to accomplish them he would perish. First, he ordered Bellerophon to fight the Chimaera. Now Bellerophon had a marvellous winged horse called Pegasus, born of the Gorgon's blood, which he had succeeded in taming thanks to a golden bridle that Athene gave him. Mounted on Pegasus, Bellerophon flew over the Chimaera and stuffed the monster's jaws with lead. The lead melted in the flames which the Chimaera vomited forth, and killed it.

Bellerophon next triumphed over the savage tribes of the Solymia and the Amazons. On his return he successfully overcame an ambuscade which Iobates had laid for him. Iobates was so filled with admiration that he gave the hero his daughter in marriage. The end of Bellerophon's life, however, was tragic. His two children, Laodameia and Isandrus, were slain; the first by Artemis, the second by Ares. According to Pindar, Bellerophon himself attempted to reach Olympus on his flying steed, but was flung to earth by Zeus and lamed by his fall. Odious to all the Immortals, Homer says, Bellerophon wandered the earth, his heart consumed with misery, alone.

Perseus and the heroes of Argolis

When Io, daughter of the river-god Inachus, arrived in Egypt after all her tribulations she bore a son, Epaphus. The great-grandsons of Epaphus were Aegyptus and Danaus. Both married, and Aegyptus had fifty sons while Danaus had fifty daughters. A quarrel broke out between the two brothers and on Athene's advice Danaus embarked with his fifty daughters and sailed towards Greece. He landed on the Peloponnesian coast and was received at Argos by Gelanor, the king, whose crown he later seized.

Some time later the sons of Aegyptus came to find their uncle, Danaus, and as a token of reconciliation asked him for the hand of his daughters. Danaus consented, but his rancour still seethed. On their wedding day he gave each of his daughters a dagger and ordered her to kill her husband during the night. All obeyed with the exception of Hypermnestra, who fled with her husband Lynceus. The Danaids were condemned to everlasting torture in the infernal regions.

Acrisius, who grieved at having no heir, learned from the oracle at Delphi that his daughter Danae would have a son who would kill his grandfather, namely himself. In vain he shut Danae up in a subterranean chamber. We have already seen how Zeus, in the guise of a shower of gold, reached Danae and made her the mother of a son, Perseus. Again in vain. Acrisius put mother and son into a chest which he cast into the sea: they were washed ashore at Seriphos and taken in by Polydectes, king of that country. Some

Perseus rescuing Andromeda. Classical bas-relief. Capitoline Museum, Rome.

years later Polydectes fell in love with Danae, but was embarrassed by the presence of Perseus, who had become a robust young warrior. He therefore pretended that he wished to marry Hippodameia, asking his vassals to bring wedding gifts. Each did his best, and Perseus, anxious to distinguish himself, promised to bring back the Gorgon's head. Polydectes was relieved to think he had seen the last of him.

Perseus then left Seriphos and reached the abode of the Graeae, frightening old shrews who among them had but one tooth and one eye which all three used in turn. Perseus stole their single tooth and only eye, and in this way persuaded them to tell him where the Gorgons lived. He also stole from them a magic wallet and a dark helmet which made its wearer invisible.

Thus equipped Perseus reached the westernmost extremities of the earth where, says Aeschylus, 'dwell monsters abhorred by mortals, whose hair is formed of serpents, and whom none looks upon without perishing'. They were the three sisters Stheno, Euryale and Medusa, daughters of Phorcys and Ceto. Instead of teeth they had the tusks of wild boars, their hands were of bronze, golden wings were fixed to their shoulders, and whoever dared to look them in the face was instantly turned to stone. Only one of them was mortal—Medusa. It was therefore she whom Perseus attacked. Armed with a bronze *harpe* which Hermes had given him, he averted his eyes; letting Athene guide his arm, he then struck. According to another version, he fixed his eyes on Medusa's reflection in the polished surface of his shield. Then he cut off her head with one stroke of the sickle, and from her bleeding neck sprang Pegasus and Chrysaor, father of the infamous Geryon. Perseus put the terrible head into his wallet and fled on Pegasus' back, while the other two Gorgons pursued him in vain.

Perseus reached Ethiopia to find the country in a state of desolation. Cassiopeia, wife of the king,

Cepheus, had offended the Nereids by proclaiming that she was more beautiful than they. In this quarrel Poseidon had taken the part of the Ocean nymphs and sent a marine monster to devour men and beasts. When the oracle of Ammon was consulted he answered that only Andromeda, daughter of King Cepheus, could save the country by offering herself as a victim to the monster. When Perseus arrived on the scene he found the unhappy Andromeda chained to a rock, awaiting death. He fell in love with her at first sight. The sequel may be guessed: he killed the monster, freed Andromeda and married her. He took her back with him to Seriphos, where he found that his mother was being persecuted by Polydectes. He put an end to this and to Polydectes by holding up the head of Medusa. Polydectes saw it and was turned to stone.

Perseus returned the magic wallet and dark helmet to Hermes and presented Athene with the head of the Gorgon, which she placed on her shield. Then, with his mother and his wife, he set forth for Argos. Acrisius, remembering what the oracle had said long ago, fled at the approach of his daughter's son. But fate ordained that one day while Perseus was throwing the discus during funeral games Acrisius was present and the discus struck and killed him. Perseus did not wish to succeed to his grandfather's throne and instead reigned only over Tiryns and Mycenae. He founded the family of the Perseids, of which one day Hercules was to be such a famed representative.

Other Heroes of Argolis

The Pelopids. Although the race of Pelopids took their name from Pelops, they owed their origin to Pelops' father, Tantalus.

Tantalus was king of Phrygia or of Lydia. He was invited to dine with the gods on Olympus and he stole their nectar and ambrosia. He returned their invitation, and when they sat at his table he served to them, in

Perseus, accompanied by Athene and armed with the harpe she had given him, carries off Medusa's head. From a vase by the 'Pan' painter. British Museum.

order to test their divinity, the body of his own son, Pelops. The guests immediately realised this; Demeter alone, more absent-minded or else more hungry than the others, ate flesh from the shoulder. Zeus ordered that the child's remains should be thrown into a magic cauldron and Clotho restored Pelops to life. Only one of his shoulders was missing and had to be replaced in ivory.

For these crimes Tantalus was cast into the Infernal Regions. He stood waist-deep in the middle of a lake in Tartarus surrounded by trees laden with delicious fruit. Thirst and hunger which he could never satisfy tortured him; for when he reached out his hand the fruit evaded him, when he leaned down to drink the water receded.

When he was grown up Pelops left Phrygia and went to Pisa in Elis, where he competed for the hand of Hippodameia. Her father, Oenomaus, had promised to give his daughter to the first suitor who vanquished him in a chariot race. Fifteen suitors had already been defeated and killed. Pelops bribed Myrtilus, Oenomaus' charioteer, to loosen one of his master's chariot wheels, and thus he won the race and the hand of Hippodameia. Afterwards he killed Myrtilus in order to get rid of an embarrassing accomplice. But the father of Myrtilus was Hermes, and Hermes avenged the death of his son by laying a curse on Pelops and all his house.

By Hippodameia Pelops had several children, among them Atreus and Thyestes. By another wife he had a son Chrysippus, whom he particularly loved. At Hippodameia's instigation Atreus and Thestes murdered Chrysippus, and for this crime were forced to go into exile. They reached Mycenae, and at the death of Eurystheus, King of Mycenae, Atreus succeeded to the throne. His brother Thyestes was jealous and seduced the wife of Atreus, Aerope, and in addition stole from him a ram with a golden fleece which had been a present from Hermes. He was driven from Mycenae but left Pleisthenes to avenge him. Now Pleisthenes was Atreus' son, and had been brought up by Thyestes as his own son. Pleisthenes was on the point of striking down Atreus, but Atreus killed him instead, realising too late that it was his son. To avenge himself, Atreus pretended to be reconciled with Thyestes and invited him and his children to return to Mycenae. In the course of a feast he served to Thyestes the bodies of two of his sons. The sun, it was said, hid himself in order not to cast light on a crime so atrocious. Later Atreus was killed by Aegisthus, another son of Thyestes, whom Atreus had brought up with his own children, Agamemnon and Menelaus.

The series of these revolting crimes did not stop at this point. Thyestes, who had succeeded his brother to the throne of Argos, was driven from it by his nephews Agamemnon and Menelaus. On his return from the Trojan War, Agamemnon, in his turn, was murdered by Aegisthus, who was living in adultery with Agamemnon's wife, Clytemnestra. Eight years later Aegisthus and Clytemnestra perished by the hand of Clytemnestra's son, Orestes, who expiated this matricide by a long period of suffering. Only then

Pollux and his mother, Leda. From a vase by Exekias. Etruscan Museum, Rome.

were the Furies satisfied and an end put to the atrocities which had stained the family of Atreus with blood.

The Dioscuri and the heroes of Laconia

The Dioscuri. The founder of the Laconian dynasties was Lelex who, by his union with a Naiad, had a son Eurotas, whose daughter Sparta married Lacedaemon. Lacedaemon reigned over Sparta and gave his name to that city. The most famous of his descendants were Hippocoön, who was killed by Hercules; Icarius, to whom Dionysus 'taught the secret of wine-making and who was killed by drunken shepherds; and finally Tyndareus, husband of Leda and father of Helen, of Clytemnestra, and of the Dioscuri, Castor and Pollux.

It was said that Zeus had played a certain part in this paternity, since he had paid court to Leda in the guise of a swan. Leda had brought forth two eggs, from one of which issued Pollux and Helen, regarded as the children of Zeus, and from the other Castor and Clytemnestra, reputed to be the children of Tyndareus.

In spite of their different paternity Castor and Pollux were both given the name Dioscurus, which meant 'young son of Zeus'. They always lived on terms of close friendship.

Among the exploits of the Dioscuri may be mentioned their expedition against Athens to rescue their sister Helen from Theseus, who had abducted her. They also joined Jason on the Argonauts' expedition, and Zeus showed his benevolence towards them during a storm which battered the ship *Argo* in the sea of Colchis. While Orpheus called upon the gods, two flames descended from the sky and hovered over the heads of the Dioscuri. This was the origin of Saint Elmo's Fire, which still today announces to sailors the end of a storm.

The Dioscuri carrying off the daughters of Leucippus. Detail from a red-figured vase in the British Museum.

Afterwards Castor and Pollux carried off the two daughters of Leucippus and married them. This was the occasion of their quarrel with the Aphareids, Idas and Lynceus, who were also paying court to the young women. This rivalry must have been unfortunate for the Dioscuri, although no one knows exactly how it turned out. According to Pindar the Dioscuri went on an expedition with the Aphareids and cheated them out of their share of the booty. According to other authors the four young men had a dispute over the division of a herd of oxen. Idas quartered an ox and ruled that half the spoil should go to the man who ate his share first, the other half going to the man who finished second. So saying he swallowed his own quarter and his brother's quarter and drove off the whole herd.

The Dioscuri then led an expedition against the Aphareids, and in the course of the battle Pollux killed Lynceus and Castor was mortally wounded by Idas. Pollux wept over the body of his brother; for being himself immortal he could not follow him to the Kingdom of Hades. Zeus was touched by this brotherly devotion and authorised Pollux to share with his brother the privilege of immortality: thus the Dioscuri continued to live each on alternate days. Another tradition says that Zeus placed them among the stars, in the constellation Gemini, the Twins.

Venerated at first in Achaia, the Dioscuri were afterwards honoured throughout Greece as the tutelary divinities of sailors and as protectors of hospitality. Sometimes they can be seen, dressed in white robes and purple mantles, starred bonnets on their heads, arriving in cities to test what sort of welcome the inhabitants will give to strangers.

Helen and the Trojan war

Helen, sister of the Dioscuri, was celebrated for her great beauty. When she had scarcely reached the age of ten Theseus carried her off, but the Dioscuri brought her home again. She was besieged by suitors. Her father Tyndareus made each of them swear that he would in case of need come to the aid of the lucky man who became Helen's husband. He then chose Menelaus. For three years the couple lived happily together. Then Paris, son of the Trojan King Priam, visited the court of Menelaus, fell in love with Helen and carried her off. This was the cause of the Trojan War. All the princes of Greece, faithful to their oaths, took arms under the command of Agamemnon to avenge the outrage done to Menelaus. For ten years the struggle raged before the walls of Troy. Neither the wiliness of Odysseus, the bravery of Diomedes, nor the dash of Achilles could conquer the resistance of the Trojans, led by the valiant Hector. Finally the Greek warriors were able to enter the city by hiding in the hollow flanks of a huge wooden horse, which the Trojans themselves dragged into the city. Troy was taken and set on fire. Old Priam was slain and the rest of his family slaughtered or carried away as slaves. Menelaus regained his wife and was reconciled with her. The story was sometimes told that the real Helen had always remained in Egypt, where her husband later found her, and that Paris had brought only the phantom of Helen back with him to Troy. But this tale was manifestly invented to save poor Menelaus' self-esteem.

The end of Helen was variously reported. After her husband's death she was admitted among the stars with the Dioscuri. Or else she was united to Achilles in the Islands of the Blessed. Or, again, she was driven from Sparta and went to Rhodes, where she was hanged from a tree on the orders of Queen Polyxo. She was venerated on this island of Rhodes under the epithet Dendritis.

Clytemnestra. The second daughter of Tyndareus, Clytemnestra, was first married to Tantalus, and then to Agamemnon. She could never forgive Agamemnon for having sacrificed their daughter Iphigenia to the gods, and on his return from Troy she slew him in his bath, with the complicity of her lover Aegisthus. The two murderers were killed by Orestes, Clytemnestra's son.

Oedipus and the heroes of Boeotia

Cadmus. The principal heroes of Thebes belonged to the family of the Labdacids, whose founder was Cadmus. He was the son of Agenor and Telephassa. Phoenix and Cilix were his brothers and Europa his sister. When Europa was carried off by Zeus, the three brothers set out to find her. Cilix and Phoenix soon tired of the search and settled down in the countries which were to be known as Cilicia and Phoenicia. Cadmus was more persistent and consulted the oracle of Delphi, which advised him to abandon his search and when he came across a cow to let her guide him. Where she stopped, he was to build a city. In Phocis Cadmus found the fateful animal and followed her into Boeotia, where she stopped. There he founded the city of Thebes and constructed the Cadmean Acropolis. He then decided to sacrifice the cow to Athene. In preparation for this ceremony he sent servants to fetch water from the Spring of Ares; but at the spring they encountered a dragon which devoured them. When Cadmus heard this he attacked the monster and killed it. Athene had helped him and she now advised him to draw the teeth of the dragon and sow them in a near-by furrow. The teeth at once began to sprout and from them sprang forth warriors, the Sparti (from the Greek 'to sow'), who immediately began to fight among themselves and kill each other. Only five survived and they became the ancestors of the Thebans.

Meanwhile, in order to expiate the murder of the dragon who was a son of Ares, Cadmus had to spend a few years serving as a slave. After this Athene recompensed him by awarding him the crown of Thebes, while Zeus granted him the hand of the dazzling maiden Harmonia, daughter of Ares and Aphrodite, or possibly of Zeus and Electra.

The couple lived happily together. Their children were Semele, mother of Dionysus; Ino, mother of Melicertes; Autonoë, mother of Actaeon; Agave, mother of Pentheus; and Polydorus, father of Labdacus, who was the ancestor of the Labdacids. Towards the end of their lives Cadmus and Harmonia

went to reign over Illyria, then were changed into dragons and transported to the Islands of the Blessed.

In Greece Cadmus was considered to be a divine legislator and the promoter of Boeotian civilisation: to him were ascribed the discovery of casting metal and the invention or importation of the alphabet.

Amphion and Zethus. Amphion and Zethus were twins, and the legends concerning them belong to the earliest days of Theban royalty. They were sons of Zeus and Antiope. Persecuted by her father, Antiope sought refuge with Epopeus at Sicyon. Epopeus married her, but her brother, Lycus, marched on Sicyon, killed Epopeus and brought Antiope back a captive. On the return journey, in a wayside thicket, Antiope brought her twins into the world. They were abandoned on Mount Cithaeron and taken in by shepherds. Antiope was long held prisoner, but one day her chains fell from her of their own accord. She fled and rejoined her sons, Amphion and Zethus, who then attacked Thebes, where Lycus now reigned. They killed Lycus and also his wife, Dirce, who was tied to the horns of a wild bull. The two brothers then fortified the city. Zethus carried stones while with the magic sounds of his lyre Amphion caused the stones

Above, The wooden horse of Troy. Vase painting. Bibliothèque Nationale.
Below, Orestes and Electra killing Aegisthus in the presence of their mother Clytemnestra.

145

to move of their own accord and gently slide into the desired position in the walls.

Afterwards Zethus married Thebe and Amphion married Niobe, who bore him twelve children. Niobe was proud of her twelve children and rashly dared to scoff at Leto, who had only had two. Apollo and Artemis punished this insult to their mother by shooting down all of Niobe's children. The unhappy mother, prostrate with grief, was changed by Zeus into a rock on the deserted summits of Mount Sipylus.

Oedipus. Laius, son of Labdacus, King of Thebes, had married Jocasta. Having been warned by an oracle that his son would one day kill him, Laius carried the child to which Jocasta had just given birth to Mount Cithaeron. He pierced the infant's feet with a nail and tied them together firmly, hoping thus to be rid of him. But a shepherd found the child and took him to Polybus, King of Corinth, who adopted him and named him Oedipus because of his wounded foot. When Oedipus had grown up he learned his destiny from an oracle, which told him that he would kill his father and marry his mother. Oedipus believed that he could escape this fate by exiling himself for ever from Corinth, never again seeing Polybus and his wife, whom he assumed to be his true parents. This scruple proved his undoing. He went to Boeotia, and on the road quarrelled with an unknown man whom he struck with his staff and killed. The victim was Laius, his own father. Oedipus continued on his journey without suspecting that the first half of the oracle's prediction had been fulfilled. He arrived in Thebes, where he learned that the region was being devastated by a fabulous monster with the face and bust of a woman, the body of a lion and the wings of a bird. Guarding the road to Thebes, the Sphinx—as the monster was called—would stop all travellers and pose enigmas to them; those who were unable to solve her riddles she would devour.

Cadmus killing the dragon. From a Laconian kylix. Louvre.

Creon, who had governed Thebes since the recent death of Laius, promised the crown and the hand of Jocasta to the man who delivered the city from this scourge. Oedipus resolved to attempt the feat. He was successful. The Sphinx asked him: 'Which is the animal that has four feet in the morning, two at midday and three in the evening?' He answered: 'Man, who in infancy crawls on all fours, who walks upright on two feet in maturity, and in his old age supports himself with a stick'. The Sphinx was vanquished and threw herself into the sea.

And thus, still without realising it, Oedipus became the husband of his mother, Jocasta. From their union two sons were born, Eteocles and Polyneices, and two daughters, Antigone and Ismene. Oedipus, in spite of the double crime he had innocently committed, was honoured as a sovereign devoted to his people's welfare, and appeared to prosper. But the Erinnyes were waiting. A terrible epidemic ravaged the land, decimating the population, and at the same time an incredible drought brought with it famine. When consulted, the oracle of Delphi replied that these scourges would not cease until the Thebans had driven the still unknown murderer of Laius out of the country. Oedipus, after having offered ritual maledictions against the assassin, undertook to find out who he was. His inquiries finally led to the discovery that the guilty man was none other than himself, and that Jocasta, whom he had married, was his mother. Jocasta in shame and grief hanged herself and Oedipus put out his own eyes. Then he went into exile, guided by his faithful daughter Antigone. He took refuge in the town of Colonus in Attica and, at last purified of his abominable crimes, disappeared mysteriously from the earth.

As for his sons, victims of the paternal curse, they perished by each other's hand. They had agreed to reign for alternate years. But when the time came Eteocles refused to hand over the crown. Polyneices gathered together an army of Argives and laid siege to Thebes. It was during this siege that the two brothers slew each other in single combat. The senate of Thebes decreed that the body of Polyneices should be left unburied, but Antigone nevertheless rendered her dead brother funeral honours. For this she was condemned to be buried alive. Her sister Ismene shared her fate. And thus the unhappy family came to an end.

The ancestor of the Aetolians was Aetolus, son of Endymion. Because of an accidental murder Aetolus was forced to leave the land of his father and he established himself in the region of Greece which afterwards took his name. Among his descendants was Oeneus, to whom Dionysus made a gift of the first vine-stock. Oeneus had two sons, Meleager and Tydeus.

Meleager and the heroes of Aetolia

Meleager's mother was Althaea, who was the first wife of Oeneus. When he was seven days old the Fates appeared to his mother. Clotho predicted for the child great generosity; Lachesis, extraordinary strength; Atropos declared that he would live only so

Oedipus and the Sphinx. Attic cup of the fifth century B.C. *Vatican Museum, Rome.*

long as a certain brand which was burning on the hearth continued to exist. Althaea hastened to rescue the brand, extinguished it and put it in a place of safety. Meanwhile, as the Fates had foretold, Meleager became a hero full of valour. His father, Oeneus, once forgot to offer to Artemis the first fruits of his harvest and the angry goddess sent a monstrous wild boar to ravage Aetolia. To hunt the monster Meleager invited all the most celebrated heroes of Greece, among them a young Arcadian woman named Atalanta. The hunt was cruel and hard. Many were killed by the wild boar. Atalanta was the first to wound it, with an arrow in the back, and Meleager finished it off with his spear. A dispute arose among the huntsmen over the monster's remains, which Meleager had presented to Atalanta. Meleager's uncles attempted to take it away from her and Meleager killed them. When she learned how her brothers had been slain by her too quick-tempered son, Althaea threw the fatal brand into the fire and Meleager immediately died.

According to the latter version, war meanwhile broke out between the Aetolians and the Curetes, over whom Meleager's uncles had reigned. The hero fought valiantly at first, but when he learned that his mother had cursed him he shut himself up in his house. The Curetes thus gained the advantage and broke into the town, setting fire to the houses. Stubbornly Meleager ignored the entreaties of relations and friends and refused to fight. He gave in at last to the prayers of his wife, Cleopatra, and resuming his place at the head of his troops put the enemy to flight. During the battle he was killed by Apollo.

Atalanta. Atalanta, the unwitting cause of Meleager's troubles, was the daughter of the Arcadian Iasus. Iasus had wanted a son and he abandoned his infant daughter on Mount Parthenius, where she was suckled by a bear and taken in by hunters whose rough life she shared. When grown up Atalanta continued to live in rural solitude, taking pleasure only in hunting and despising the thought of marriage.

She slew the Centaurs Rhaecus and Hylaeus, who had tried to rape her. She took an illustrious part in Meleager's boar hunt, and vanquished Peleus in wrestling at the funeral games held in honour of Pelias. Her father Iasus finally recognised her and decided to have her married. She declared that she would only marry a man who could run more swiftly than herself. More than one suitor had competed and been killed by Atalanta, when a certain Melanion thought of a trick. While he ran he dropped one by one three golden apples which Aphrodite had given him. Atalanta paused to pick them up. She was thus beaten and married Melanion.

Tydeus and Diomedes. Meleager's half-brother, Tydeus, killed his cousins for having plotted against his father. He had to leave Aetolia and went to Argos, where he married the daughter of King Adrastus. He took part in the expedition of the seven chieftains against Thebes and distinguished himself by various exploits, notably by killing fifty Thebans who had laid an ambush for him. He fell, however, under the blows of the Theban Melanippus. Though he was grievously wounded Athene brought him an elixir which would have cured him and made him immortal. She was about to offer it to him when the soothsayer Amphiaraus, who was a personal enemy of Tydeus, presented him with the head of Melanippus. In a transport of rage Tydeus split open his recent enemy's skull and devoured his brain. Outraged by such savagery, Athene left him to his fate and Tydeus died shortly afterwards.

His son Diomedes avenged him by sacking Thebes with the help of the Epigoni. The same Diomedes was renowned for his exploits before Troy: he wounded Aphrodite and even Ares. With Odysseus he seized the Palladium, on which the safety of Troy depended. After the war his return to Greece was marked by many adventures. He was tossed by a storm on to the coast of Lycia and very nearly sacrificed to Ares by King Lycus, but was saved by the king's daughter, Callirrhoë, who loved him and when he departed killed herself in despair. When he returned to Argos he learned that his wife had been unfaithful to him. He left Argos, but later reconquered it. He finished his valorous career in Italy with King Daunus, whose daughter he married.

Peleus, the Argonauts and the heroes of Thessaly

Peleus. Although Peleus was one of the most famous heroes of Thessaly, he was not a native of that country. He was the son of Aeacus, who reigned over the island of Aegina. Peleus fled from Aegina with his brother Telamon after they killed their half-brother Phocus. Telamon established himself in Salamis, where he inherited the crown of Cychreus, the king. Peleus first went to Phthia, where he visited Eurytion. Unwilling to present himself without an escort, he prayed to Zeus, who changed certain ants into men, who were henceforth called Myrmidons. Eurytion welcomed him warmly and gave him a third of his estates, together with the hand of his daughter Anti-

147

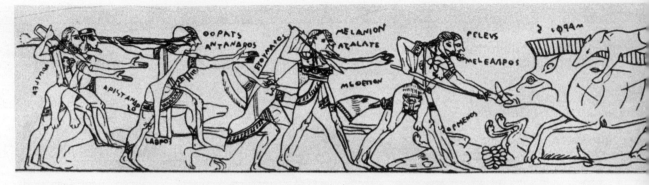

The Calydonian Boar-hunt. From a black-figured painting on the 'Francois' Vase at Florence. Peleus and Meleager face the boar, followed by Atalanta and others.

gone. Unfortunately Peleus and Eurytion took part in Meleager's boar hunt, during which Peleus accidentally killed his father-in-law. He then took refuge in Iolcus with Acastus, who purified him. The wife of Acastus conceived an amorous passion for Peleus, but was repulsed by him. She avenged herself by falsely telling Antigone that Peleus had been unfaithful to her. Antigone hanged herself in grief. Acastus' wife also told her husband the same story. The laws of hospitality forbade Acastus to kill Peleus; instead he took his guest hunting on Mount Pelion, hoping to see him killed. But Peleus vanquished the wildest and most dangerous beasts, thanks to a fabulous dagger which had been made by Hephaestus. While Peleus was asleep Acastus stole this dagger and hid it, thinking in this way to leave him without defence against the ferocious Centaurs, who peopled the mountain. The project nearly succeeded, but by luck Peleus was saved by the Centaur Chiron who returned his dagger. Peleus used it to punish Acastus and his treacherous wife, and himself became king of the land.

Shortly afterwards Peleus married the Nereid Thetis, not without resistance on the part of the bride who, once courted by Poseidon and Zeus himself, considered marriage to a mortal to be an insult to her dignity. Thanks to the advice of Chiron, Peleus overcame the efforts of Thetis to elude him and the marriage was sumptuously celebrated on the crests of Mount Pelion. From their union Achilles was born. We have already seen how Thetis attempted to bestow immortality on her son. Her efforts were interrupted by Peleus, and Thetis in vexation rejoined her sisters, the Nereids. Young Achilles was put in the care of the Centaur Chiron, who fed him on the marrowbones of bears and the entrails of lions.

Achilles. Thus Achilles grew in years and strength. He was nine when the seer Calchas predicted that he alone would conquer Troy. Thetis, who knew that in Troy he would meet his death, tried to avoid the peril by hiding him, disguised as a girl, in the palace of Lycomedes, King of Skyros. But the Greeks, helped by Odysseus, discovered the so-called 'maiden' by an ingenious trick. Odysseus one day came to Lycomedes' palace with gifts for the king's daughters. Among them he slipped a shield and a spear. Then he and his companions gave battle cries and sounded the trumpets. Achilles, thinking they were being attacked, rushed for the weapons. The Greeks then took him

with them, for he could not escape his destiny. We know what valour he displayed beneath the walls of Troy; in single combat he killed the valiant Hector. But he himself perished before Troy was taken, pierced in his vulnerable heel by an arrow, shot either by Apollo or by Paris.

But to return to Peleus: while his son grew up his own adventurous life continued. He took part in the voyage of the Argonauts. He fought with the Lapiths against the Centaurs. He seconded Hercules during his own expedition against Troy. He outlived his son and had a listless old age.

Jason and the Argonauts. The expedition of the Argonauts was celebrated in the annals not only of Thessaly but of all Greece. Its object was the conquest of the Golden Fleece, the origin of which was as follows: Phrixus and Helle, the two children of the Boeotian King Athamas, were hated by their stepmother Ino. Their very lives were threatened and they fled, mounted on a fabulous ram which was a gift of Hermes. This ram was endowed with reason and speech; it had a fleece of gold and could move through the air as well as it could over the earth. In the course of their flight Helle fell into the sea, giving her name to the Hellespont. Phrixus was more fortunate, and reached Colchis on the Black Sea. There he sacrificed the ram to Zeus, and offered its fleece to the king of the country, Aeëtes, who suspended it from a tree and set a dragon who never slept to guard it.

Meanwhile, Pelias was reigning at Iolcus in Thessaly, having usurped the throne of his brother, Aeson. Aeson's son, Jason, had been entrusted to the care of the Centaur Chiron. When he reached man's estate Jason went to his uncle and demanded his share of the kingdom. Pelias was greatly disturbed, for an oracle had once told him to 'beware of the man who wears but one sandal', and Jason had appeared before him with only one foot shod. He therefore told his nephew that he would willingly comply with his demand on condition that Jason first brought him back the Golden Fleece.

With the help of Hera or Athene Jason immediately built a ship with fifty oars, the *Argo*, in which he had set a bough of the prophetic oak of Zeus at Dodona. He gathered together the most famous heroes, among them Amphion, the Dioscuri, Hercules, Orpheus, Peleus, Theseus and Meleager. Then the hardy adventurers set forth in search of the fabled Golden Fleece. Their

voyage was full of incident: they were forced to struggle against the elements as well as against men. Finally they reached the mouth of the Phasis and rowing up the river came to the kingdom of Aeëtes. Aeëtes agreed to give up the Golden Fleece, but imposed his own conditions. Jason had first to harness a plough with two wild bulls whose hooves were of bronze and whose breath was of flame. With them he must plough a field and plant it with dragons' teeth. Luckily for Jason the daughter of Aeëtes, Medea, fell in love with him and, as she was a skilled magician, showed him how to overcome these fearful conditions. Then Aeëtes refused to keep his word; Medea again helped Jason to vanquish the dragon who guarded the Golden Fleece and to seize the precious trophy. Both left the country in haste, pursued by Aeëtes. In order to delay her father's pursuit Medea did not hesitate to scatter the route with the dismembered body of her own brother, whose throat she had cut. After a long and perilous voyage which took them across the Danube, the Ocean, the Libyan deserts, the Red Sea and the Mediterranean, the Argonauts finally returned to Iolcus. During Jason's absence Pelias had put Aeson to death. Others say that Aeson was still alive and was even rejuvenated by one of Medea's magic philtres. In any case, Jason avenged himself on his uncle. Medea persuaded the daughters of Pelias that with her charms she could rejuvenate their father, but that first they must cut him up into pieces and cook him. They carried out these instructions and Medea left matters as they were. After this atrocious murder Medea and Jason withdrew to Corinth. There they lived happily for ten years, whereupon Jason fell in love with Creusa (or Glauce), daughter of King Creon, and abandoned Medea. Medea avenged herself by sending a wedding present to the new bride: a fine robe which consumed her with inextinguishable fire. Medea then cut the throats of the children she had had by Jason and fled to Athens, where she married Aegeus. She had to leave Athens, after she had tried to poison Theseus. She returned to Colchis and was reconciled to her father Aeëtes.

As for Jason, some say that he grew weary of life and killed himself. Others say that while he was resting in the shade of the ship *Argo*, the poop fell on him and accidentally crushed him to death.

Orpheus and the heroes of Thrace

Orpheus, the great hero of Thrace, was very different in character from the other Greek heroes. He was not distinguished for his warlike exploits. He was in origin perhaps a Thracian king, and he owed his fame above all to his amazing musical talent. Son of Apollo, he sang and played the lyre with such art that the savage beasts came running to listen and even trees would follow him. His talent performed miracles during the voyage of the Argonauts. The ship *Argo*, high on the beach, descended to the sea of its own accord at the sound of his singing. His songs arrested the Symplegades, those terrible moving rocks which threatened to crush the ship, and sent them down to the bottom of the sea. By singing he helped to lull to sleep the dragon who guarded the Golden Fleece. And finally his songs conquered the Sirens and permitted the Argonauts to escape their fearful seductions.

Such was the power of his voice and the harmony of his lyre that even the infernal deities submitted to them. He had married the nymph Eurydice, whom he passionately loved. One day when Eurydice was fleeing from Aristaeus she was mortally bitten by a snake hidden in the grass. Orpheus was heartbroken at the death of his wife and resolved to descend into the Underworld to reclaim her. He was able to charm Hades and Persephone, who gave him permission to take Eurydice back to earth on the sole condition that he should not turn to look at her during the journey. The couple had almost reached the gates of Hades when Orpheus impatiently and imprudently turned to look at his wife. At once she was whisked back into the sombre abode of the dead and vanished, this time for ever.

Orpheus was inconsolable and, some said, killed himself. But the more widely held opinion was that he was torn in pieces by Thracian women who were infuriated at this single-minded love for his wife. His head and his lyre were flung into the River Hebrus and carried as far as Lesbos. The head of the divine singer was caught in a fissure of rock, where for long it delivered oracles.

Other Thracian Poets. Thrace took pride in other famous poets and musicians, such as Philammon, also said to be a son of Apollo, and to whom was attributed the institution of choral dance in the temple of Delphi.

Thrace also boasted Eumolpus, son of Poseidon and Chione, who was a daughter of Boreas. Eumolpus was thrown into the sea by his mother, who wished to conceal her shame. He was found by Boreas, who carried him to Ethiopia. From there Eumolpus went to the court of Tegyrius, King of Thrace. He was killed by Erechtheus when he was fighting with the

Eleusinians against Athens. Some say that Eumolpus instituted the Eleusinian mysteries in honour of Demeter who had taught him how to cultivate the vine and trees. He also taught Hercules to sing and play the lyre.

Minos and the heroes of Crete

The ancient legends of Crete were early imported into Greece and were, as we have seen, a basis of Hellenic mythology, taking on new aspects as they became adapted to continental traditions. They centred for the most part on the figure of the fabulous King Minos. It seems, however, that we should distinguish at least two kings called Minos, of which one was the grandson of the other.

Minos then—with Rhadamanthys and Sarpedon—was a son of Zeus and Europa. After her arrival in Crete Europa married the king of the island, Asterius, who adopted her children. Minos succeeded Asterius to the throne of Crete; he distinguished himself by the wisdom of his laws and his sense of justice which, after his death, earned him promotion to the position of judge of the Underworld.

Minos had married Pasiphaë. She had already given him several children when Poseidon, angered by Minos, inspired her with a monstrous passion for a bull. From this union was born the Minotaur, a monster which was half human, half bull.

The Athenians had killed the son of Minos, Androgeus, and in reprisal Minos laid siege to Athens. Previously he had besieged Megara and vanquished the king, Nisus, helped by the treachery of Scylla, Nisus' daughter. Scylla was in love with Minos and had therefore cut a golden lock of hair—on which the safety of the city depended—from her father's head. Minos took advantage of this treacherous act, but punished its author. He had the infatuated Scylla drowned in the Saronic Sea, where she was changed into a lark. Before Athens, however, Minos was less successful. The siege dragged on. Minos implored the aid of Zeus, who visited Athens with a plague. To rid themselves of this plague the Athenians consented to send Minos an annual tribute of seven youths and seven maidens who were to be fed to the Minotaur. We have already seen how with the help of Ariadne Theseus freed his city from this wretched servitude.

The Minotaur, who fed exclusively on human flesh, had been enclosed by Minos in an amazing palace from which no one could find an exit: the Labyrinth. The Labyrinth had been constructed by Daedalus, an Athenian distinguished for his ingenuity and cunning. To Daedalus was ascribed the invention of the axe and the saw. It was he, they said, who first fixed arms and legs to the *xoana*, the shapeless primitive statues of the gods. He killed his nephew who was a rival craftsman and sought asylum with Minos. Daedalus helped Ariadne when she gave Theseus the precious ball of thread which enabled the hero to find his way out of the Labyrinth. For this act of treachery Minos had Daedalus and his son Icarus locked up in the Labyrinth for a while. They flew to freedom with the help of an ingenious pair of wings which Daedalus devised. In the course of their flight Icarus waa imprudent enough to approach too near the sun. The wax by which his wings were attached melted and he plummeted into the sea which henceforth took his name, the Icarian Sea. Daedalus landed in Cumae, and from there went to Sicily, where he gained the favour of King Cocalus. Therefore when Minos came in pursuit of Daedalus and landed on the island, Cocalus not only refused to hand over his guest, but drowned Minos in the bath. Such was the reputed end of this famous monarch, even though his tomb was pointed out in Crete.

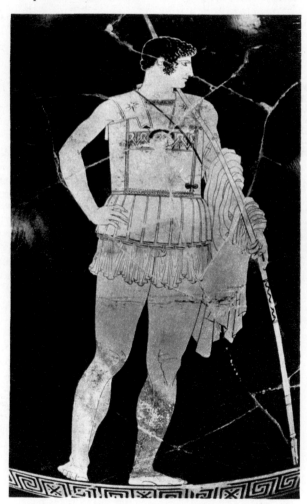

Achilles. Detail from an Attic amphora of the fifth century B.C. Etruscan Museum, Rome.

index

Figures in italics refer to illustrations

152